CONTENTS

THE CAMINO DEL NORTE AND CAMINO PRIMITIVO

About the Authors

Laura Perazzoli lives and works in Portland, Oregon. She completed her first pilgrimage in 2004 on the Camino Francés. After this trip, she was excited to provide others with a similar experience and has since led student pilgrimage trips on the Camino Francés, the Camino del Norte and Primitivo, the Via Francigena and Le Puy route in France. Laura first walked the Camino del Norte and Primitivo in 2009 and has since walked these routes three additional times to ensure up-to-date route information for this guidebook.

Dave Whitson is a high-school History teacher in Portland, Oregon. He made his first pilgrimage in 2002 on the Camino Francés and was inspired to return with a group of his high-school students, which he did in 2004. He has led a total of 15 student pilgrimage trips and completed many others independently. Dave first walked the Camino del Norte and Camino Primitivo in 2008 and has subsequently returned on six other occasions.

THE CAMINO DEL NORTE AND CAMINO PRIMITIVO

TO SANTIAGO DE COMPOSTELA AND FINISTERRE FROM IRÚN OR OVIEDO

by Laura Perazzoli and Dave Whitson

JUNIPER HOUSE, MURLEY MOSS,
OXENHOLME ROAD, KENDAL, CUMBRIA LA9 7RL
www.cicerone.co.uk

© Laura Perazzoli and Dave Whitson 2019
Third edition 2019
ISBN: 978 1 78631 014 9

Replaces *The Northern Caminos* (ISBN: 978 1 85284 794 4), together with companion volume *The Camino Inglés and Ruta do Mar* (ISBN: 978 1 78631 006 4)

Printed in China on behalf of Latitude Press Ltd

A catalogue record for this book is available from the British Library.

Route mapping by Lovell Johns www.lovelljohns.com
All photographs are by the authors unless otherwise stated.
Contains OpenStreetMap.org data © OpenStreetMap contributors, CC-BY-SA. NASA relief data courtesy of ESRI

lovelljohns.com

Updates to this Guide

While every effort is made by our authors to ensure the accuracy of guidebooks as they go to print, changes can occur during the lifetime of an edition. Any updates that we know of for this guide will be on the Cicerone website (www.cicerone.co.uk/1014/updates), so please check before planning your trip. We also advise that you check information about such things as transport, accommodation and shops locally. Even rights of way can be altered over time. We are always grateful for information about any discrepancies between a guidebook and the facts on the ground, sent by email to updates@cicerone.co.uk or by post to Cicerone, Juniper House, Murley Moss, Oxenholme Road, Kendal LA9 7RL.

Register your book: To sign up to receive free updates, special offers and GPX files where available, register your book at www.cicerone.co.uk.

Front cover: Pilgrims cross the medieval bridge through Ponte Maceira (Camino Finisterre, Stage 1)

Symbols used on route maps

～	route
⌐ ⌐ ⌐	alternative route
>	direction of route
Ⓢ Ⓢ	start/alternative start point
Ⓕ Ⓕ	finish/alternative finish point
	woodland
	urban areas
▬▬■▬▬	station/railway
⬆ ⬆	albergue/other accommodation
⬛	campsite
⬛ ⬛	bar/café
Ⓐ	all facilities
⊕	pharmacy
■	building
✚	church or cathedral
⬤	supermarket/grocery store
⬛	bus station/bus stop
⬛	rail station
Ⓗ	hospital
ⓘ	pilgrim info/TIC
⬛	fountain
✈	airport

Relief
in metres

2800–3000	
2600–2800	
2400–2600	
2200–2400	
2000–2200	
1800–2000	
1600–1800	
1400–1600	
1200–1400	
1000–1200	
800–1000	
600–800	
400–600	
200–400	
0–200	

SCALE: 1:100,000

0 kilometres   1   2

0 miles   1

Town map scales vary –
see individual maps

Contour lines are
drawn at 50m intervals
and highlighted at
200m intervals.

GPX files
GPX files for all routes can be downloaded for free at www.cicerone.co.uk/1014/GPX

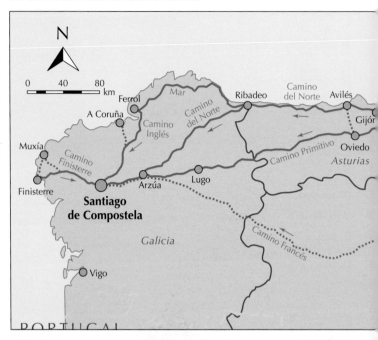

Zarautz and the region's longest beach (Camino del Norte, Stage 2)

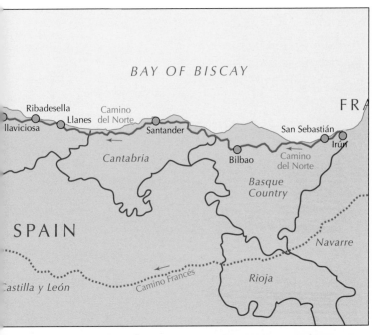

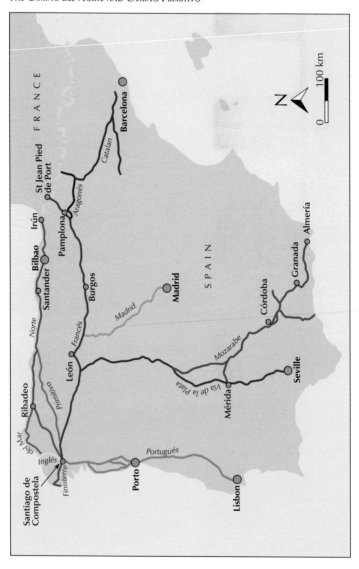

The Cathedral of Santiago de Compostela

ROUTE SUMMARY TABLES

Stage	Start	Distance (km)	Total ascent (m)	Total descent (m)	Page
	CAMINO DEL NORTE				
1	Irún	24.8	882	875	45
2	San Sebastián	19.2	544	554	55
3	Zarautz	22.6	850	856	60
4	Deba	24.2	851	771	66
5	Markina-Xemein	24.7	702	780	70
6	Gernika	31.3	930	923	75
7	Bilbao	25.2	341	356	82
8	Pobeña	16.7	390	372	88
9	Castro-Urdiales	30.9	652	671	93
10	Laredo	28.5	426	350	98
11	Güemes	14.8	189	248	103
12	Santander	30.9	449	377	108
13	Santillana del Mar	22.5	448	499	116
14	Comillas	28.9	620	537	120
15	Colombres	25.2	423	519	130
16	Llanes	20.9	338	246	135
17	Piñeres de Pría	27.3	457	559	138
18	La Isla	22	446	445	145
19	Villaviciosa	31.2	810	808	153
20	Gijón	24.7	368	369	158
21	Avilés	23.5	613	490	162
22	Muros de Nalón	35.2	997	1039	166
23	Cadavedo	15.7	233	313	173
24	Luarca	30	587	540	176
25	La Caridad	24.1	301	338	181
26	Ribadeo	28.7	803	751	187
27	Lourenzá	24.3	853	449	192
28	Gontán	21.2	261	263	196
29	Vilalba	34.5	428	423	200
30	Miraz	25.5	408	352	205
31	Sobrado dos Monxes	22	230	344	208
32	Arzúa	38.8	685	790	213
Total	**Santiago de Compostela**	**819.7**	**16,784**	**17,207**	

CAMINO DEL NORTE (cont)					
Stage	Start	Distance (km)	Total ascent (m)	Total descent (m)	Page
Prologue	Bayonne	47.3	717	723	40
	Lebaniego detour	55	2133	1636	126
	Covadonga detour	51.9	1395	1154	149

CAMINO PRIMITIVO					
Stage	Start	Distance (km)	Total ascent (m)	Total descent (m)	Page
1	Villaviciosa	27.6	592	381	222
2	Pola de Siero	16.9	164	155	227
3	Oviedo	25.8	469	621	232
4	Grado	22.8	652	495	237
5	Salas	33.6	1132	752	241
6	Campiello	27.2	1014	707	246
7	Berducedo	20.7	874	1228	252
8	Grandas de Salime	25.7	829	443	256
9	A Fonsagrada	32.4	882	1253	260
10	Castroverde	22.3	336	455	266
11	Lugo	32.7	662	533	270
12	As Seixas	28.9	480	680	275
Norte 32	Arzúa	38.8	685	790	279
Total	**Santiago de Compostela**	**355.4**	**8771**	**8493**	
Primitivo–Norte Link (Oviedo to Avilés)					
	Oviedo	29	370	593	280
Primitivo–Norte Link via Friol (Lugo to Sobrado dos Monxes)					
	Lugo	51.2	679	634	285

CAMINO FINISTERRE					
Stage	Start	Distance (km)	Total ascent (m)	Total descent (m)	Page
1	Santiago de Compostela	21	501	592	292
2	Negreira	34.1	601	492	295
3	Olveiroa	32.2	468	728	297
Total	**Finisterre**	**87.3**	**1570**	**1872**	
	Muxía extension	52.7	991	1334	300

A pilgrim on the camino after Celorio (Norte, Stage 9)

INTRODUCTION

The stunning diversity of Spain's Northern Caminos makes them as challenging to classify as they are memorable to walk. While most holidays involve a choice between trekking through mountains, lying in the sun on the beach, or engaging in a more meaningful sort of project, the Northern Caminos allow for all three. Those hungry for mountains may not find a high-level route here, but they will encounter challenging coastal ascents in the Basque Country and rugged rural tracks through Asturias. Beachcombers will find some of Europe's most popular sandy spots, such as San Sebastián, along with more isolated hideaways, accessible in some cases only to walkers. And, all who make the trek will be joined in the great human tradition of pilgrimage, unified in common cause and shared soreness, as they follow these historic pathways to sacred Santiago de Compostela.

Santiago de Compostela, whose cathedral houses the relics of Saint James, was one of three major centers of Catholic pilgrimage in the Middle Ages, along with Rome and Jerusalem. Inspired by religious zeal – and particularly the desire to connect more deeply with God through relics, such as the bones of deceased saints – pilgrims from all over the Christian world made the dangerous journey to these celebrated sites. There was no single route to Santiago: the trail began at one's doorstep. But as pilgrims approached Spain, many converged on a handful of particularly popular routes, known historically as the Caminos de Santiago or 'Ways of Saint James'.

Today those pilgrim roads have experienced a popular resurgence and are walked not just by traditional pilgrims, but by people from highly varied backgrounds. In particular, the Camino Francés, which passes through Pamplona, Burgos, and León, draws crowds from all over the world – to the point where it is often referred to as 'the' Camino de Santiago. However, other pilgrim routes, such as the Northern Caminos, have also been rediscovered, and they have a great deal to offer.

The two Northern Caminos included in this book – the Camino del Norte and the Camino Primitivo – are located north of the Camino Francés and pass through the Spanish regions of the Basque Country, Cantabria, Asturias, and Galicia. While the Camino Francés has in some ways become a victim of its own success, with huge crowds taking to its trails every year, the Northern Caminos enjoy an ideal situation. They are popular enough to offer sufficient facilities, clear routes, and a community of pilgrims, without the race for beds and lack of privacy that sometimes plagues the Francés, especially outside the busier summer months.

The Camino del Norte spans 822km, following the coast from Irún, on the French border, to Ribadeo, before cutting inland towards Santiago; the full route takes about five weeks to complete. The Camino Primitivo splits off from the Camino del Norte near

Villaviciosa and passes through Oviedo and Lugo en route to Compostela. The route is 355km and takes roughly two weeks to walk.

This book also includes an overview of the route to Finisterre, for those who wish to continue on to there from Santiago.

Catedral de San Salvador, Oviedo (Primitivo, Stage 2)

THE STORY OF SAINT JAMES

While countless pilgrimage shrines exist within the Catholic world, three cities stand out as major centers of pilgrimage. Two are obvious: Jerusalem is intimately associated with the life of Jesus, while Rome houses the relics of saints Peter and Paul, not to mention Saint Peter's Basilica. The third center, situated in an otherwise forgotten corner of Spain, is much more surprising. Santiago de Compostela, in Spain's northwestern region of Galicia, has a history built on equal parts rumor and legend.

Of Jesus's 12 apostles, perhaps less is known about Saint James (or Santiago) than any other. The brother of John and the son of an assertive mother, James is known for his temper and for being one of Jesus's first followers – and the first to be martyred. However, mystery surrounds James's life between the crucifixion of Christ and his own death. Spanish legend asserts that he brought the good word to the Iberian Peninsula, but with minimal success, winning few followers. That said, on his subsequent return to the Holy Land he fared worse; he was decapitated by Herod Agrippa in AD44.

After James's death, the story goes, his disciples smuggled his body to the coast, where it was placed on a stone boat – lacking sails, oars, and sailors – and put to sea. Amazingly, and perhaps under the guidance of angels, this boat maneuvered westward across the Mediterranean and north into the Atlantic, before ultimately making landfall at today's Padrón on the Galician coast. Once there, two disciples met the boat, took James's body, and eventually buried him in present-day Santiago de Compostela. And then, almost eight centuries passed.

In 813, the hermit Pelayo had a vision in which a star shined brightly on a nearby field. Digging there, Pelayo made a stunning discovery: the very bones of Saint James, buried and forgotten so many years earlier. The timing couldn't have been better for local Christians.

With the Moorish conquest of the Iberian Peninsula nearly complete, their armies enjoying victory after victory behind the 'arm of Mohammed', the Christian Kingdom of Asturias in northern Spain was in dire straits. However, according to legend, the tide turned at the pivotal Battle of Clavijo. As the Asturian army prepared to face the much larger Muslim force, Saint James appeared on his white horse and led them into battle, and so began the legend of Santiago Matamoros ('Saint James the Moor-killer'), one of the saint's two faces along the camino. In the other, Santiago Peregrino, his pilgrim identity, Saint James generally appears with a staff and scallop shell.

The cult of Santiago grew gradually over the next two centuries, before two major developments in the 12th century propelled Compostela to the forefront of the Christian world. First, Diego Gelmírez became the bishop of Santiago in 1101 (and archbishop in 1120), and quickly devoted his life to the aggrandizement of Compostela. Second, the 'Codex Calixtinus' emerged sometime in the 1130–40s. The first 'guidebook' to the Camino de Santiago, it included, among other things, a list of miracles attributed to Saint James, the history of the route, and a collection of practical advice for travelers, including warnings about 'evil toll gatherers' and 'barbarous' locals.

At its peak in the Middle Ages, hundreds of thousands of pilgrims from all across Europe made the journey to Santiago de Compostela. After a decline following the Reformation and a near-total collapse in numbers during the Enlightenment, the Camino de Santiago returned to prominence in the late 20th century.

THE NORTHERN CAMINOS: YESTERDAY AND TODAY

While the Camino Francés enjoys greater prominence today than the Northern Caminos, that should not suggest that the northern alternatives lack historical significance. Indeed, evidence exists of pilgrims following the coastal option in the ninth and tenth centuries. The name 'Camino Primitivo' is not meant to suggest the absence of civilization along the route, but rather the route's historical primacy.

When Pelayo of Asturias (a different Pelayo from the aforementioned hermit) halted Moorish expansion at the Battle of Covadonga in 722, he thereby preserved a sliver of northern Spain for Christianity. The Kingdom of Asturias grew gradually, experiencing its greatest success during Alfonso II's reign (791–842). During that time, the kingdom expanded into Galicia and the Basque Country, and also celebrated the discovery of Santiago's tomb.

The first pilgrims to Compostela were well aware of the persistent Muslim threat, particularly in Navarre, and thus often favored the coastal approach. Perhaps the single greatest influence on the early prominence of these routes, however, was the supreme importance of Oviedo, the Asturian Kingdom's capital. The cult of relics surrounding San Salvador de Oviedo is as old as the one surrounding Santiago. The Holy Ark kept there is said to include a fragment of the True Cross, an image of Christ, and remnants from the Crown of Thorns and Last Supper. In 1075, Alfonso VI visited Oviedo specifically to behold the Holy Ark; during his stay, he ordered the

17

Monte Igeldo and its lighthouse (Norte, Stage 2)

creation of a pilgrims' hospital. While the royal court had moved to León by this point, Oviedo's spiritual significance was reinforced by the popular pilgrimage refrain: 'He who goes to Santiago and not to San Salvador, serves the servant and forsakes the Lord.' Providing royal acknowledgement of this view, in 1222 Alfonso IX ordered all pilgrims to Santiago to pass through the Monastery of Obona near Tineo. Remarkably, many pilgrims following the Camino Francés made the lengthy detour.

Of course, not all pilgrims made the journey exclusively on foot. British and Scandinavian pilgrims, in particular, covered significant distances at sea, landing at various places along the northern Spanish coast. The British presence seems to have been particularly strong in the 14th and 15th centuries, a historical legacy preserved in

the name of the route from A Coruña, the Camino Inglés. That said, it would be erroneous to ascribe singular significance to a particular port or nationality; Scandinavian pilgrims, for example, certainly landed at Ferrol, much as English pilgrims walked from Irún or Santander.

Today, the Northern Caminos are enjoying their own resurgence in popularity. In 2017, 17,836 pilgrims on the Camino del Norte and 13,684 pilgrims on the Camino Primitivo were awarded the Compostela, granted to those who complete the pilgrimage. While those figures pale in comparison to the 180,000 who walked the Camino Francés in 2017, they reflect a significant increase in traffic along these routes, particularly the Primitivo. It's also important to remember that those statistics don't include those walkers who don't complete their pilgrimage in Santiago and receive the Compostela, so the actual number of walkers is higher.

ALONG THE ROUTES: DIFFERENT CULTURES

While outsiders might associate the Spanish with a single national identity, the truth is far different. Spanish political organization is largely decentralized, with power devolved to the regional level in the form of 17 autonomous communities. In several prominent cases, the populations of these regions share very distinctive cultures, possessing their own language and history. The Northern Caminos pass through four autonomous communities: the Basque Country, Cantabria, Asturias, and Galicia. Each is worth a closer look.

Waymark en route to Vilaserío
(Finisterre, Stage 2)

The Basque Country

The Basque Country has received significant attention because of terrorist attacks perpetrated by the Basque nationalist organization Euskadi Ta Askatasuna (ETA). That is, however, a poor representation of the Basque people and their cultural resurgence over the last few decades. Euskera, the Basque language, is taught in schools once more and most road signs are bilingual. The striking Basque flag (red background, green X, and white cross) is proudly displayed in houses and businesses. While many Basques still aspire to having a single Basque state, combining their traditional lands in both Spain and France, the Spanish Basques do enjoy a great deal of control over their community.

For the Spanish-speaking pilgrim, the spread of Euskera should be of little concern. Most Basques – and certainly those in the service sector – also speak Spanish (and many speak English as well). While towns often have distinct Spanish and Basque names (for example, San Sebastián is also Donostia), both versions are included in this guide. Besides, Euskera is a fascinating language to play with for a few days; it is historically unique, with no identifiable connection to any other language.

The Basques of northern Spain, located in the Atlantic watershed, have traditionally been great seafarers. The opening stages of the Camino del Norte pass through towns closely linked with the Age of Exploration. The seafarer of greatest fame, perhaps, is Juan Sebastián Elcano, who took over command of Magellan's fleet and completed the first circumnavigation of the globe. Elcano is commemorated with a statue in his birthplace, Getaria. In the modern era, the Basque Country emerged as an industrial power, particularly within Spain itself, where it is responsible for nearly half the country's industrial output. Nonetheless, the countryside remains very traditional, with extensive family farms.

The pilgrim's route through the Basque Country begins in Irún, a border town, separated by the Bidasoa river from French Hendaye. The first three stages generally hug the coastline, staying within a kilometer or two of the Bay of Biscay, with sweeping views of the countryside and water. From Deba, the route turns inland for the next three stages, passing around Mount Arno and through the historical town of Gernika-Lumo before arrival in Bilbao. After passing through the port town of Portugalete, the camino cuts inland for one more stage before depositing the walker on Pobeña's wonderful beach; this is the last stopping point in the Basque Country.

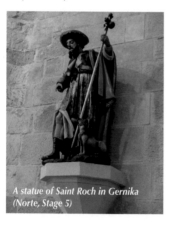

A statue of Saint Roch in Gernika (Norte, Stage 5)

Cantabria and Asturias

Like the Basque Country, the next two regions, Cantabria and Asturias, also experienced tremendous growth during the Age of Exploration. The influence of 'Indianos', emigrants who returned to Spain after making a fortune in the Americas, remains visible in the regions' architecture. That said, the story of Cantabria and Asturias goes back much further. The regions contain some of the finest Paleolithic remains in the world, including some wonderful paintings like those found in the Altamira Cave. Although both regions were conquered by Romans, the impact of their colonization is not as visible along this stretch as elsewhere on the route. The two regions returned to prominence in the eighth century. As noted, the Kingdom of Asturias became the base for the Reconquest of Spain from the Moors, and Cantabria joined in common cause soon after. Cantabria emerged as a dominant naval force around this time, behind the combined might of the Hermandad de los Cuatro Villas ('Brotherhood of the Four Towns'): Castro-Urdiales, Laredo, Santander, and San Vicente de la Barquera.

The coastal route through Cantabria and Asturias moves through a distinctive ecological setting. The ranges of the Picos de Europa and Cordillera Cantábrica press tightly against the Bay of Biscay, leaving only 25–50km between mountain and water. The steep descent and close coastline have resulted in many northward-flowing rivers, as well as a climate unique within Spain, with higher humidity and precipitation. The regions have also been indelibly marked by an emphasis on

Iglesia de Santa María de los Ángeles, San Vicente de la Barquera (Norte, Stage 14)

cattle farming, as well as the introduction of eucalyptus and pine trees, which have pushed many native species, such as oak, chestnut, and beech, to the margins.

The Camino del Norte's first major stop in Cantabria is Castro-Urdiales, before it progresses through the town's three brothers. All told, the Norte covers roughly 180 mostly flat kilometers in the region, much of it on asphalt. While the asphalt is unfortunate, it is compensated for by some of the route's finest beaches. The Río Deva marks the border between Cantabria and Asturias, with Unquera wishing you goodbye and Colombres greeting you hello.

For the first 90km of Asturias, the Camino del Norte proceeds in a similar manner to the Cantabrian route, remaining flat and brushing against the coastline with some frequency. Soon after

the market town of Villaviciosa, however, the route splits, with the Camino Primitivo forking left and the Camino del Norte continuing to the right. (It is possible for coastal walkers to follow the Primitivo into Oviedo and then return to the Norte in Avilés; this route is summarized at the end of the main route description.)

Both options bring ascents that exceed anything encountered over the previous week of walking. Along the Camino del Norte, pilgrims face a 400m climb up the Alto de la Cruz – and, almost immediately after, an equivalent descent. But, after this minor challenge, the route gradually flattens out once more, with long stretches on asphalt and passing through two prominent resort towns, Gijón and Avilés. From Villaviciosa to the Ría de Ribadeo, the Norte covers roughly 200km in

21

Calle Rivero in Avilés (Norte, Stage 20)

Asturias; the river crossing into the town of Ribadeo marks arrival in the fourth and final autonomous region, Galicia.

Meanwhile, the Camino Primitivo in Asturias runs around 200km. As on the Norte, the first stage brings an ascent to 400m. However, after a lull around Oviedo, where the Primitivo flattens out, the climb takes pilgrims significantly higher. On three different occasions, the Primitivo tops 1000m (with a fourth coming soon after, in Galicia), reaching 1146m at its highest point. Over the same stretch conditions become more rugged, and pockets of civilization become smaller and smaller. Whereas tourists and pilgrims vie for resources along the coast, few travelers other than pilgrims visit many of these villages, making the Camino Primitivo feel more central to the communities.

Galicia

The Norte and Primitivo follow different trajectories through the final autonomous region, Galicia, before reuniting shortly before Santiago de Compostela. As in the Basque Country, Galicia features a distinct nationality, the Galego people. The local language, Gallego, is immediately noticeable upon arrival in the region; note that the pilgrimage, for example, is now identified as the 'Camiño' de Santiago. Gallego is often described as a middle ground between Spanish and Portuguese. Those comfortable with either language will have no trouble communicating here.

Geographic isolation protected Galicia from too much interference by Rome (although the Roman walls of Lugo are some of the finest left in the world) and the Moors. It was shaped in many ways, however, by the earlier Celtic presence, as is visible in Galicia's very name and the many extant circular hill forts or *castros*. One such fort, the Castro de Chao Samartin, can be visited along the Primitivo, soon after Grandas de Salime.

The discovery of Santiago's remains in the ninth century launched the region into European prominence, transforming it into one of the centers of the Catholic world. But, every rise has its fall. The Protestant Reformation and related decline in the importance of pilgrimage brought several centuries of regression for Galicia, as it found itself pushed to the margins once more. The 20th century brought an abrupt return to the spotlight, with the emergence of Galicia's own Francisco Franco. Born in Ferrol, the starting point of the Camino Inglés, Franco endorsed the Camino de Santiago. Franco's death coincided with a resurgent nationalism among Galegos.

The walking conditions in Galicia are, for most pilgrims, delightful: well-worn trails, gentle streams with stone footbridges, dense forests offering shade, and traditional villages with homes built out of granite and slate, with old-fashioned *hórreos* (corn-cribs/granaries) at the front. Galicia experiences more rain than any other region in Spain, but the reward is a pervasive green, even in the middle of a hot summer. Pilgrims will notice two significant changes made to the Galician environment over the last 50 years. Eucalyptus was introduced during the Franco era. Given the rainy climate, it was believed that eucalyptus forests would thrive. And they have – perhaps too much – and now threaten many native species; there is an almost eerie quality to the absolute quiet that reigns within them. In addition, wind turbines line many mountain

Hórreo near Escamplero (Primitivo, Stage 3)

ridges, looking to translate the region's windy conditions into green energy. Many locals regard these as eyesores and threats to tourism and the local environment.

Galicia is comprised of four provinces. Both the Primitivo and Norte enter Galicia in the province of Lugo, before later moving into A Coruña. The routes through Galicia share similar characteristics, particularly as they converge upon Santiago. For the Camino del Norte, this marks the end of the coast and the beginning of a challenging stretch of walking, rising ultimately to 710m in elevation near the provincial border. The Camino Primitivo, meanwhile, has one remaining ascent of significance before descending to Lugo, the last major town before Santiago. Prior to arrival in Compostela, both routes join their more famous sibling, the Camino Francés. The Primitivo intersects it in Melide, while the Norte does so in Arzúa. The sudden change in the number of pilgrims – from a drizzle to a deluge – can be quite jarring!

23

CHOOSING YOUR CAMINO

For those starting their pilgrimage in Irún, the single biggest decision involves whether to fork south in Villaviciosa onto the Camino Primitivo or to remain on the Camino del Norte. To some extent, this decision can be distilled down to a choice between mountains and coast. The Primitivo cuts inland through the Cordillera Cantábrica and includes some significant ascents and descents between Oviedo and Lugo. Meanwhile, the Camino del Norte between Villaviciosa and Ribadeo follows relatively flat terrain through quiet coastal villages. The Primitivo is better waymarked and has more frequent pilgrim accommodation, but the Norte is not deficient in either area.

There is no clear pilgrim consensus on this point; both routes have their ardent supporters. For those walking from Irún, the authors recommend the Primitivo. After several weeks of hiking on the coast, the mountains bring an exciting change of setting, and the walker is well prepared for the rugged conditions.

That said, there are other considerations worth taking into account.

Time

Those with limited time will have to decide whether arriving on foot in Santiago and receiving the Compostela is a priority or not. If that is a priority, the minimal completion of the last 100km on foot is required. In this case, one would need to begin walking the Camino Primitivo in Lugo (102km) or the Camino del Norte in Baamonde (101.5km). If arrival in Santiago is not essential, there are many worthy

A pilgrim on the high-level route to Cadavedo (Norte, Stage 22)

stretches on the various routes that could be completed in a week or so, including Irún to Gernika-Lumo, Santillana del Mar to Ribadesella, and Oviedo to Lugo.

To complete the full Camino del Norte, walking from Irún to Santiago, typically requires at least five weeks, not counting rest days. This is true whether one chooses to remain exclusively on the Norte or transfer to the Primitivo. The Camino Primitivo, meanwhile, can typically be completed within two weeks.

Physical challenge

The most physically demanding stretches of the Northern Caminos are the opening stages of the Norte, from Irún to Bilbao, and the Camino Primitivo from Salas to Lugo. The Norte between Ribadeo and Sobrado dos Monxes also presents a challenge. But between Bilbao and Ribadeo the coastal walk is quite forgiving, rarely breaking 200m in elevation; there are some days with frequent ascents and descents, but they are manageable.

Other factors

The first week of the Camino del Norte is the most expensive stretch, passing through popular tourist destinations and offering few *albergues*, particularly outside of summer. It is quite common to spend €15–20 per night on a bed, and significantly more for a room. On the flip side, most pilgrim lodgings along the Camino Primitivo and after Gijón on the Norte continue to operate on donations or a minimal €5–8 fee.

The Primitivo is the best bet for off-road walking, with very long stretches that avoid pavement. The Norte, however, has some days on which the majority of the walking occurs on minor roads, particularly in Cantabria.

The walk from Irún to Bilbao is, in many ways, the most historically rich section of the Northern Caminos. At the same time, it draws heavy tourist attention. Those seeking parts of Spain that are off-the-beaten tourist path would be advised to seek out the Primitivo or the western half of the Norte.

WHEN TO GO

Summer is the best time to walk the Northern Caminos for several reasons. First, due to their proximity to the coast, the off-season state of the caminos can be quite soggy. Second, some of the albergues are seasonal, open only when local schools are on holiday. Third, some places, even some of the towns, are seasonal, and so they are often thriving with beach-goers when the sun shines but shut down completely for the rest of the year. That said, the caminos are drawing growing numbers of pilgrims in the summer and the facilities are getting strained, making May/June and September increasingly better options.

The off-season period along the Northern Caminos has its charms. For those in search of solitude, it can be found along the coast in March. Hotels that remain open may offer steep discounts. In theory, the Northern Caminos are viable year-round, although winter pilgrims should be prepared for driving wind and rain (and accompanying muddy trails), bitter cold, and even snow along the Camino Primitivo and the final stretch of the Camino del Norte as it veers towards Santiago.

Orio and the Río Oría (Norte, Stage 2)

PREPARATION AND PLANNING

The most important part of your preparation is the physical component, training for the rigors of the trail by doing some walking. Start slowly and build as your body allows, gradually increasing the distances covered. As you become stronger, add weight to your pack until its contents mirror what you will carry in Spain. If possible, hike on consecutive days; what might feel easy on fresh legs can be more draining on tired ones.

As you train, monitor three different areas. First, and most obvious, track how much distance you can cover comfortably, how your body responds to breaks, and what kinds of food provide you with the energy that you need. Second, keep a close eye on your feet, watching for blisters or other hot spots. Third, test your gear and clothing, making sure that your pack fits properly, the weight is manageable, and your clothes don't chafe.

Read about the Camino de Santiago and pilgrimage in general before you go. Knowing some of the history and language of the region will add meaning to your walk. Familiarity with Romanesque and Gothic architecture will help you to know where to direct your eye. Some sense of anticipated highlights will help you to plan stopping points. While there aren't many published narratives in English on the Northern Caminos, Susan Alcorn's *Healing Miles: Gifts from the Caminos Norte and Primitivo* is widely available and a compelling read. Otherwise, there is an overwhelming variety of books devoted to the Camino Francés, and these will also give you a sense of what is ahead (see Appendix C).

That said, unless your schedule is quite restrictive, try to arrive in Spain without a rigid plan for your daily itinerary. Take it easy early on. Many pilgrims arrive overflowing with energy and excitement and go too far in their initial stages. It's better to stop too soon than push too far, as the consequences of that exertion can linger in the forms of blisters, tendonitis, or other aches and pains for many days.

In addition, be wary of setting your spiritual expectations too high. Many pilgrims spend their camino waiting for their epiphany, the life-changing moment of enlightenment that they feel is promised to them on pilgrimage, only to be disappointed when it never arrives. Every pilgrim's experience is different.

BEING A PILGRIM

Making a long-distance trek as a pilgrim is a different experience in many ways from other lengthy walks. Several unique elements of the pilgrim experience are described below.

Pilgrim passport

Known as the *credenciál* in Spanish, this document identifies you as a pilgrim. It is available in many albergues, including Irún, Santander, and Oviedo, and from many camino-related groups, such as the UK's Confraternity of Saint James (CSJ) (paid-up members only) and the US-based American Pilgrims on the Camino (APOC). You will get a stamp (*sello*) each day, usually in a pilgrim hostel, although it is also possible to get stamps in bars, churches, and tourism offices (*turismos*). For most pilgrims, this becomes a treasured memento of the journey.

The Compostela

Upon arrival in Santiago, the Archbishopric will award you the Compostela, a document acknowledging your completion of the pilgrimage, provided that you meet two conditions. First, you must have your credenciál, with stamps documenting your daily progress (including at least **two** stamps per day over the last 100km). Second, you must have walked the final 100km or bicycled the final 200km. Prior to that last stretch, it is acceptable to skip ahead by motorized transportation. But the last 100km must be completed in their entirety.

Albergues

Your credenciál also gives you access to the pilgrim hostels (*albergues de peregrino*). These provide dorm-style accommodation exclusively to pilgrims, and usually include facilities to wash both self and clothes. Some also offer kitchens. Typically, the doors lock and lights are turned off between 2200 and 2300. Pilgrims may spend only one night and are expected to leave by 0800 the next

Pilgrims head past San Xurxo

morning, although exceptions are often made for ill/injured pilgrims. The price varies, typically hovering in the €5–10 range, although some albergues still operate on a voluntary donation (*donativo*) basis. Unfortunately, there are fewer of these each year, as some pilgrims equate 'donation requested' with 'free'. Pilgrim donations keep many albergues in operation for future pilgrims.

Pilgrim ethic

A popular saying in Spanish is '*Turistas manden; peregrinos agradecen*' ('Tourists demand; pilgrims give thanks'). While challenging to remember at the end of a long day, it is an important message to keep in mind. Albergues are typically run by voluntary hosts (*hospitaleros*). Often, they are supported by the local community. Waymarks are maintained by local organizations. It is easy to find fault with many things along the way, but be cognizant of how many people are giving up their time, money, and energy to make your pilgrimage possible.

GETTING THERE AND BACK

Camino del Norte: from Irún

By foot

The Voie Littorale walking route, which originates in Soulac, France, parallels the Atlantic coast for 375km to arrive at Hendaye, across the river from Irún. Some pilgrims who fly into Biarritz opt to walk from there, easing themselves into the walk on flatter terrain before crossing into Spain. The CSJ has published a guide to this route online (The Voie Littorale: Soulac to Hendaye, www.

csj.org.uk) and we include a short synopsis of the walk between Bayonne and Hendaye/Irún (see the Prologue in the Camino de Norte section).

By air

From the UK and Europe budget airlines, including RyanAir (www.ryanair.com) and EasyJet (www.easyjet.com), fly into Biarritz airport in France. From the US, it is generally most economical to fly into London or another major city and transfer to one of those flights. From Biarritz, take the 816 bus or Ouibus (biarritz.aeroport.fr/en/services/buses) to Hendaye's train station (60–75min), and then take the metro to the Irún-Colon station. Alternatively, Iberia (www.iberia.com) and Vueling (www.vueling.com) fly into San Sebastián's airport, located in Hondarribia, only 3km from Irún. Ekialdebus (www.ekialdebus.net) operates a bus connecting the airport with Irún, or you could just start walking!

By train

Irún is well connected to Spain and Europe. Spain's national line, RENFE (www.renfe.com), offers services to Irún from Barcelona (direct trains depart 0730 and 1530, 7hr, €30–70), Madrid (four daily departures, none direct, 7hr, €30–80), and other major cities. Prices are highly variable; book early for best value. EuskoTren (www.euskotren.es) links Irún with San Sebastián, with a separate train continuing on to Bilbao, although buses are often speedier for this route. France's SNCF (www.sncf.com) connects Irún with the rest of Europe, including a regular TGV service between Paris and Hendaye (five direct routes daily, 5hr).

By bus

Irún's bus station is located in front of the train station. Spain's major bus company, ALSA (www.alsa.es), offers regular service from Bilbao (2hr, €8) and Madrid (five daily departures, both from the city center and airport, 6–8hr, €39–52). Vibasa (www.vibasa.com) operates a convenient overnight bus from Barcelona Nord (departs 2235, 7½hr, €33). A wide range of bus companies covers northern Spain, so there are many other options. Check www.movelia.es or the departure bus station.

Other likely points of departure

Both Bilbao and Santander have airports, making them convenient starting points. EasyJet flies to Bilbao, as do many other major airlines. From the airport, take Bizkaibus 3247 (www.bizkaia.net) to the center (every 15min) or the Lurraldebus (www.lurraldebus.eus) to San Sebastián (every 30min, 1hr). Santander is serviced

by RyanAir and Iberia, with a bus linking the airport and the city bus station. ALSA runs buses directly from the airport to other coastal cities, including Gijón. It is also possible to reach Santander via ferry from Portsmouth and Plymouth in the UK, although this is often much more expensive.

Camino Primitivo: from Oviedo

By foot

The Camino del Salvador links Oviedo with León on the Camino Francés. The route spans roughly 120km and the CSJ has published a guide to this route online (Camino del Salvador, www.csj.org.uk).

By air

Asturias airport is serviced by EasyJet (www.easyjet.com) and Vueling (www.vueling.com), among other airlines, and is located between Oviedo and Gijón, less than 2km off of the Camino del

The approach to Santander on the ferry (Norte, Stage 11)

Norte (see Stage 21). ALSA (www.alsa. es) provides bus services between the airport and both cities (as well as Avilés).

By train
FEVE (www.feve.es) connects Oviedo with other coastal towns, from Ribadeo in the west (twice daily, 4hr, €11) to Santander in the east (twice daily, 5hr, €15). RENFE (www.renfe.com) provides service to the rest of Spain, including Madrid (three daily, 5hr, €50).

By bus
ALSA (www.alsa.es) connects Oviedo with Madrid (hourly, 5½hr, €35) and most other major Spanish cities. To reach Villaviciosa, ALSA now offers a direct service (1hr, €5).

Other likely points of departure
The other major city on the Camino Primitivo, Lugo, is accessible by train (RENFE) and bus. For the latter, ALSA again provides primary connections to most of Spain; however, local companies offer more extensive coverage of Galicia. In particular, Empresa Freire (www.empresafreire.com) links Santiago airport and Lugo (every 2hr, 2hr).

Getting back from Santiago de Compostela

By air
Lavacolla (Labacolla) airport, just outside of Santiago, is well connected with Spain and the rest of Europe, offering multiple routes operated by RyanAir, EasyJet, and Air Berlin (www.airberlin.com). Although Iberia sometimes advertises a special discounted fare for pilgrims with Compostelas, their prices rarely rival that of a ticket on one of the budget airlines. Flights from A Coruña airport go to many different European destinations,

By train
RENFE runs a daily service at 1006 from Santiago to Hendaye; from there, connections to Paris and other European towns are possible. Six trains run daily to Madrid (5-6hr, €30–80). If you have time, returning along the coast on FEVE can be a nice way to 'retrace' your steps.

By bus
ALSA is once again the best bet.

EQUIPMENT

Remember that you will have to carry everything you take, every day. The guiding principle is to pack light, focusing on what is absolutely necessary and cutting everything else. As the caminos pass regularly through towns, it will be possible to restock or acquire new supplies as needed.

Footwear
Walkers passionately debate whether shoes or boots are superior. Modern cross-trainers typically provide a great deal of support and comfort, without the weight and bulkiness of boots, and are advisable for most. If you prefer boots, make sure that they are broken in prior to departure. Outside summer, it is worth considering waterproof shoes, although these have their downsides, most notably a loss of 'breathability' that tends to result in hotter feet. In addition, bring a pair of sandals suitable for albergue showers and post-walk strolls around town.

The Caños de San Francisco fountain in Avilés (Norte, Stage 20)

Sleeping bag

Those walking in the summer who don't get cold too easily should consider bringing a sleep-sheet (sheet sleeping bag). Silk sleeping bag liners weigh little and suffice for many. However, if you do not fit in those categories, a sleeping bag will be necessary. Look for an ultra-lightweight +5°C bag.

Rucksack

Pack size will be determined in large part by your sleeping-bag decision. Those who opt for a sleep-sheet could walk the camino with a pack as small as 30 litres. With a sleeping bag, something in the 45 litres range may be needed. Regardless, a good fit is critical. Look for a pack that is properly sized for your torso and keeps the weight on your hips.

Clothing

Aim for two or three sets of clothes (shirt/top, socks, underwear) – one or two in your pack and one on you – along with two pairs of shorts/pants (trousers). Avoid cotton. Synthetic clothing wicks moisture from the body, dries quickly, and packs light. Finally, bring a warm outer layer. In the off-season, a long-sleeved/legged base layer is recommended as well.

Poncho

Walking on the coast, the weather can be unpredictable, and rain is more likely than it is inland. A good poncho will cover both person and pack, and can be donned quickly. Otherwise waterproof clothing and a rain cover for your pack will do. If you're walking outside of summer, you may prefer more extensive rain-gear.

Water

Personal preference will determine the choice of either a bottle or hydration bladder, but make sure to have at least a litre of water with you at all times, and more on certain stretches.

31

Pack towel
A synthetic, chamois-style towel packs lighter and smaller than a normal towel and dries faster.

Basic first-aid kit
Bring small amounts of most first-aid essentials. It's easy to buy more if you run out. Make sure to carry a good supply of foot-care materials, including Compeed, moleskin, or another similar product to treat blisters.

Flashlight/headlamp
Essential for late-night bathroom runs, early-morning packing, and pre-sunrise walking.

Toiletries
Limit these to the essentials.

Other gear worth considering
A hat, sunglasses, camp pillow, notepad/pen, eating utensils and bowl, digital camera, trekking poles, Spanish–English dictionary, and maps.

ACCOMMODATION

Albergues, providing dorm-style accommodation exclusively for pilgrims, on a first-come, first-served basis, are available in many towns and villages along the Northern Caminos. That said, they are not as plentiful as their equivalent along the Camino Francés, and some – especially in the Basque Country – are seasonal, operating only during peak months. Pilgrims walking outside of summer will need to be prepared to make use of other options. Of course, all pilgrims are welcome to stay in any manner of accommodation; some find the albergues to be a central part of the experience, while others need additional comfort at night in order to regroup for the next day's walk. Whenever possible, a range of options are presented for each stage in this guide, but other possibilities can always be found at the local tourism office.

While the Spanish classification system for beds is not always on the mark, generally places identified as a *fonda* or *pensión* are designed for travelers on a budget. Furnishings and facilities are often a bit at the scruffier end of things. That said, great deals can be had. Another option for inexpensive lodging, especially in larger towns, is a youth hostel (*albergue juvenil*) or tourist hostel (*albergue turístico*), both of which are open to all travelers but may offer special rates for pilgrims. Those looking for more amenities will want to target *hostales* or *hoteles*. The distinction between the two is not always clear, although hoteles are typically stand-alone facilities with a receptionist available at all hours, while hostales fill only part of the building and provide guests with keys to their room and the building. The price is likely to be determined by the number of stars attributed to the facility.

Remember that the Camino del Norte in particular passes through popular holiday areas, so beds can be booked up far in advance in summer, and some places are closed all together in the winter. Albergues de Peregrinos generally operate on a 'first-come, first-served' basis, but if you hope to sleep anywhere else, particularly in the summer months, it is wise to reserve ahead, at least a couple of days.

Albergues in Maariz (Norte Stage 27),

Bodenaya (Primitivo Stage 5)

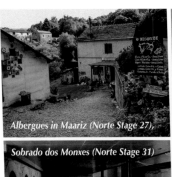

Sobrado dos Monxes (Norte Stage 31)

Lourenzá (Norte Stage 27)

FOOD

A pilgrim's culinary options are shaped in large part by the walking schedule and restaurant opening hours. In the morning, pilgrims can count on finding croissants and *cafés con leche*. Later in the day, those in need of something more substantial can ask for *bocadillos* – large sandwiches filled with a range of options, including ham (*jamón*), sausage (*chorizo*), cheese (*queso*), and omelette (*tortilla*). The *tortilla española* (egg and potato omelette) is a particularly filling snack on its own or in a bocadillo. *Tapas* – bite-sized appetizers, served both hot and cold – can be an excellent option for an evening snack.

A typical sit-down meal will involve a meat dish (pork and lamb are common in the north), a side dish, and bread. Vegetables are rarer, generally appearing in salads or soups. Fish is more abundant along the coast and in Galicia. *Paella*, a saffron-infused rice-based dish with seafood, can be an excellent option throughout the north. Regional specialties include *marmitako* (fish stew) in the Basque Country, *fabada Asturiana* (white beans, pork, and blood sausage) in Asturias, and *pulpo* (octopus) in Galicia.

The greatest food-related challenge for many is the Spanish meal schedule. Outside of cities, bars in the north rarely open before 0800. Lunch, the major daily meal, is served between 1300 and 1500. Dinner presents the biggest difficulty, as it commonly begins around 2100, making it harder to finish eating before the albergue curfew. Pilgrim-friendly bars and restaurants will serve earlier, but this varies greatly from town to town.

Some albergues have kitchens, where pilgrims can prepare their own meals. Groceries and supermarkets are accessible on most days, although some planning may be necessary, as they are not always located in the same towns as the albergues. Most shops and supermarkets, except in cities, close during siesta, so typical opening hours are from 0900 to 1300 and from 1600 to 2000. Almost every supermarket closes on Sunday.

POSTAL SERVICES

Most post offices (*correos*) in Spain are open weekdays from 0830 until 1400. Some reopen in the afternoon and on Saturday mornings. Stamps can also be purchased from tobacco shops. The 'poste restante' system allows pilgrims (and everyone else) to send packages ahead, which comes in handy if you find yourself with unnecessary gear in your pack. While sending the gear home might be very expensive, mailing a package to Santiago is generally quite affordable. It is also an excellent way to receive care packages from home.

To mail a parcel poste restante, ask in the post office about Lista de Correos. If you do not have packing materials, most offices can provide these. On the mailing label, address the parcel to yourself, underlining your surname. Under your name, write 'Lista de Correos', followed by the postal code, town name, and province. Postal codes can be found on the www.correos.es website. When you retrieve your package, make sure to take photo identification. The post office will generally hold packages for two weeks for free, charging more for additional days, but it is wise to reconfirm current policy when mailing.

Monasterio de Cornellana

TELEPHONES AND INTERNET

Payphones are becoming an endangered species, but some still exist. Telephone cards can be purchased from tobacco shops; note that different cards are often needed for local and international calls. Instructions for making international calls are provided on each card. To call internationally, dial 00, wait for a new dial tone, and proceed with the country code, area code, and number. Spain's country code is 34; this can be dropped from numbers when you are calling within the country. Larger towns also have *locutorios* (call centers), which offer cheap international calls and internet connections. Most internet cafés have closed, likely as a consequence of the proliferation of smartphones; if you need an internet-connected terminal, your best bet is the local *biblioteca* (library), which often has a small computer lab. Bring your passport to check in.

More and more pilgrims are bringing their mobile phones with them on the camino. The most expensive way to do this is usually to activate an international package with your home provider. A more budget-friendly option is to purchase a prepaid SIM card in Spain. Provided that your mobile phone is unlocked, you can put the Spanish SIM card in and immediately have a local number – and, by extension, local calling rates. Most companies, including Vodafone and MoviStar, have a very affordable starter pack available; credit can later be added online, by phone, and in many supermarkets. The cheapest approach, though, is to put your phone on airplane mode and use it exclusively as a wifi device, making calls home through FaceTime or Skype and texting through WhatsApp, or similar programs.

OTHER LOCAL FACILITIES

Spanish **banking** hours are limited, typically running from around 0900 until 1400, Monday to Friday. Some banks open on Saturday morning. Almost every town has an ATM for withdrawing euros. Traveler's checks can be difficult to cash and are discouraged. **Pharmacies** are available in most towns and maintain a similar schedule to supermarkets. Medications, even basic items such as ibuprofen, are only available from pharmacies. Churches in most sizable towns hold **mass** on weekday and Saturday evenings, usually around 2000, as well as midday on Sundays. Ask in the albergue or listen for the bells. In all parts of the Northern Caminos, it is possible to **ship your pack ahead**. Your best bet is the service offered by the Spanish postal service, Correos, available April–October (www.elcaminoconcorreos.com). Expect to pay €4–5 per day.

WAYMARKING, ROUTE-PLANNING, AND MAPS

With occasional exceptions, waymarking on the Northern Caminos is reliable. Trusty yellow arrows (*flechas amarillas*) painted on trees, signs, rocks, and other physical landmarks guide you through the countryside and most towns. In cities, the arrows are often replaced with scallop-shell markers embedded in the sidewalk. In Galicia, concrete markers

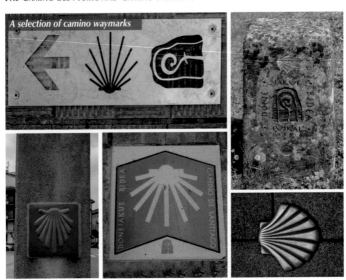

A selection of camino waymarks

complement the arrows, appearing at least every 500 meters. With this reassurance, you should not have to clutch this book tightly each step of the way, nor should you count on it for turn-by-turn directions.

Nonetheless, it is advisable to review each day's route before starting. Look in particular for several potential complications. First, there are multiple stretches where the camino splits, especially along the Norte, with two (or three) possible options available. In some cases, only one of these options is clearly marked. In others, the yellow arrows steer walkers towards the most direct route, while the red/white stripes associated with the European GR footpaths offer a more scenic alternative. You will want to anticipate these crossroads to ensure that you follow

your desired course. Second, there are some relatively long stretches without food or water. Plan your day to avoid unnecessary difficulties. Finally, be advised that the Northern Caminos continue to be refined, as efforts are made to move more of the walk from pavement and onto footpaths. You may encounter waymarks that lead you in an unexpected direction. Study them carefully, evaluate your options, and make an informed choice. It is always wise to seek updated information from albergue hosts (hospitaleros).

The most useful single overview map of the Northern Caminos is the Northern Spain Adventure Map (#3306) published by National Geographic and available from most online bookstores. The Caminos del Norte and Primitivo routes are highlighted (as is the Camino

Francés). Scaled to 1:350,000, this is helpful for seeing the big picture, but not for turn-by-turn navigation.

The Spanish Mapas Militares (Serie L) are the best bet for more detailed route-finding assistance, designed on a 1:50,000 scale. The downside is that this is a much more expensive option, requiring you to purchase many individual map sheets to fully cover your route. In the authors' experience, these are not necessary. The Mapas Militares are available from The Map Shop in the UK and can be ordered online.

GPX

GPX tracks for the routes in this guidebook are available to download free at www.cicerone.co.uk/1014/GPX. A GPS device is an excellent aid to navigation, but you should also carry a map and compass and know how to use them. GPX files are provided in good faith, but neither the author nor the publisher accept responsibility for their accuracy.

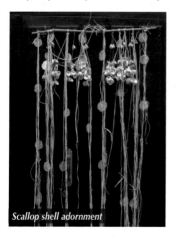

Scallop shell adornment

USING THIS GUIDE

This guidebook has broken the different routes into stages. With rare exceptions, each stage ends in a town or village with a pilgrim albergue. However, these stages are simply recommendations and should not be considered the 'official' way of organizing the route. Listen to your body: if you're struggling, stop earlier; if you're flying, enjoy it. Listen to your heart: if the beauty of a place strikes you, stick around. And listen to your fellow pilgrims: they may have excellent advice to offer.

The box at the start of each stage provides key information to help you assess the day ahead, including ratings for terrain and route-finding on a 1–5 scale. The figure for terrain indicates how physically demanding the stage is, with 1 corresponding to an easy walk and 5 to a very challenging trek. It is important to note that the difficulty rating does not factor in the day's distance. The route-finding rating indicates the challenge posed by the day's waymarking and presence of alternative routes. If you see a 1 or a 2, you can safely put away this book and trust the waymarks. Anything higher suggests that there are some problematic stretches, or important route choices to make. The box also lists all albergues on that stage, but not other accommodation options. Look through the full stage description for that information.

Key towns and villages along the route are shown in boxes in the route description (the distance from the previous key town/village is given after the heading). The boxes include information on accommodation and facilities, as well as a short summary of features of interest.

With three different languages spoken along the Northern Caminos – Castilian, Euskera (Basque), and Gallego (and Asturian making strides of its own!) – it is challenging to achieve a single, consistent approach to place names. In this guidebook, place names have been dealt with as follows. In the Basque Country, both the Castilian and Euskeran versions of town names are included when they are significantly different. In Galicia, names generally follow the Gallego spelling to reflect what is seen on street signs and maps. The similarity between Gallego and Castilian in most cases makes it easy to draw connections (for example, 'Palas do Rei' and 'Palas de Rey'). Geographical features and other vernacular terms are often presented in both Spanish and English to facilitate not only their identification but their use as directional aids.

This guide includes all pilgrim albergues in operation at the time of writing (late 2018), and a range of selected hotels, hostels, and other viable options. All accommodation listings include price, phone numbers, and (when needed) address. Additional information includes the number of beds available, meals served, and the presence of cooking facilities, washer/dryer (W/D), and internet (@). Opening hours are included if they are notable. Please note that prices can change quickly or by season, and are often higher when booked through an online service; always confirm in advance.

Each stage of the route in this guide is accompanied by a map at 1:100,000 scale with the exception of the detour tracks on the Camino Covadonga and the Camino Lebaniego. The maps use a

A statue in Santiago's Hostal dos Reis Católicos (Norte, Stage 32)

red line for the main route description and a red dashed line for any alternative routes described. All place names in **bold** in the text are also included on the maps. Where a distance appears in brackets, that figure relates to the distance from the previous town/village that is highlighted in brackets.

N followed by a number (eg N-634) denotes a major Spanish highway, while regional roads are often identified by the first two letters of the province followed by a number (eg AS-235).

Sources of useful information on transport and other practicalities are listed in Appendix A. There is also a glossary of key terms in Spanish and Euskera (Appendix B), and some recommended further reading (Appendix C).

Finally, please keep in mind that despite the authors' best efforts, some information in this guide will go out-of-date almost as quickly as it's printed. Please check www.northerncaminos. com for route updates and book corrections. We are grateful to all readers for updates from the trail.

THE CAMINO DEL NORTE

Santiago waymark (Stage 32)

INTRODUCTION

The Camino del Norte is the longest route in this guidebook. From the city of Irún, located on the French border, the Norte follows the coast for the better part of 620km. Upon reaching Galicia, it turns inland, with 150km of trails bringing pilgrims to the Camino Francés in Arzúa, 40km before Santiago de Compostela. The highlights are strikingly diverse – hilltop bluffs overlooking the ocean; waymarked walks on sandy beaches; albergues in medieval monasteries; cosmopolitan cities with dramatic cathedrals and stunning art museums... the list goes on, but you'll just have to walk it to see it all. For added variety, pilgrims can divert from the Camino del Norte in Villaviciosa (Stage 19), complementing the coastal walk with the Camino Primitivo's mountainous terrain.

PROLOGUE: THE VOIE LITTORALE
Bayonne to Irún/Hondarribia

Start	Bayonne cathedral
Finish	Albergue de Peregrinos, Irún
Distance	47.3km
% unpaved	28.7%
Total ascent	717m
Total descent	723m
Terrain	2
Route-finding	3
Pilgrim accommodation	Bayonne, Guéthary, Ciboure, Hendaye, Irún

While the Camino del Norte begins in Irún, pilgrims would have joined it from much farther afield, and some coming on foot from France would have followed the Voie Littorale along the coast to Spain. Some of today's pilgrims are also drawn to the idea of starting in French territory, for a few reasons. First, it aligns nicely with budget flights arriving in Biarritz – you could even walk out the airport's front door and begin your journey. Second, while the Norte's initial stages are quite strenuous, this is an easier walk, helping you to get your legs under you. Finally, it's quite lovely! However, plan for some high prices; even a coffee may cost three times what it would in Spain.

As this is a skeletal route summary, we do not include accommodation suggestions here, but the most up-to-date list of pilgrim-specific options can be found on www.xacobeo.fr. St-Jean-de-Luz provides a fantastic place to break the walk, though it lacks pilgrim-specific accommodation.

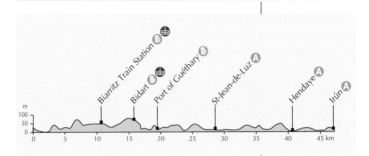

Leaving Bayonne's cathedral (pilgrim information desk Mon–Sat 0900–1145, 1500–1800), proceed eastward to the River Nive. Soon after, the riverside walkway diverges from the main road; near that point, you'll encounter your first camino (chemin) waymark. 2.8km from the cathedral, turn right, away from the river (two other chemins continue straight, so don't be confused by conflicting waymarks). Skirt the edge of **Anglet** (1.5km) and then loop around **Biarritz Airport**, arriving at **Biarritz train station** (6.3km) (bars, grocery, bakery). ▸ Proceed past **Mouriscot Lake** (marked turn to Biarritz youth hostel) and then follow a series of busier roads to the coast, arriving in **Bidart** (5.7km) (bars, grocery, bakery, turismo) soon after.

Those walking or arriving by taxi directly from the airport would come in from the right at this point.

The Voie Littorale near Bidart

From Bidart, you have two options. The 'official' chemin veers inland, passing Bidart's church and then following a series of mostly minor, paved roads to St-Jean-de-Luz. This approach spans 12.8km (500 meters more than the coastal route). We prefer the coastal approach, following yellow markings indicating the 'Sentiere Littorale.' Pass through the port of **Guéthary** (3.1km) (additional bars/restaurants, turismo uphill) and around the **Paul Jovet Botanical Garden** (5.2km).

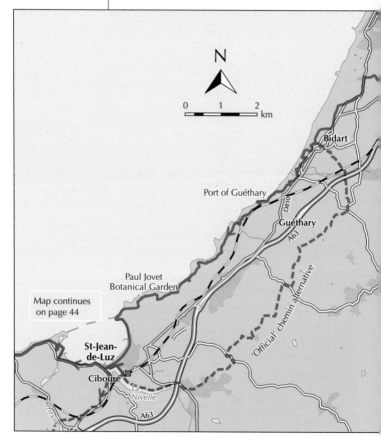

Map continues on page 44

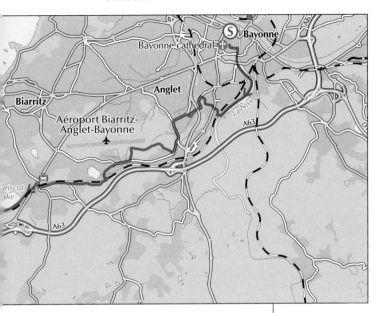

Finally, join an elevated promenade past St-Jean's spectacular beaches, before turning inland at the lighthouse and proceeding into the center of **St-Jean-de-Luz** (4km) (all facilities).

Once again, you have two options from St-Jean-de-Luz to Hendaye, with the 'official' chemin veering inland once more and the 'Sentiere Littorale' remaining on the coast. The routes diverge on the other side of the Nivelle River in St-Jean, with the 'official' chemin turning left just before the Église Saint-Vincent, while the coastal alternative continues along the riverside. The 'official' route spans 17km, largely bypassing Hendaye. As before, we prefer the coast. After passing through the neighboring village of **Ciboure** (3km), the route generally follows a footpath running parallel to (and sometimes directly alongside) the **D912** highway. After passing through the grounds of the **Centre de Vacances Haicabia** (5.1km), the route leaves the highway behind and has a lovely final approach to **Hendaye** (all facilities). At the **Casino d'Hendaye** (4.2km), you can decide to walk into Irún or catch the ferry to Hondarribia.

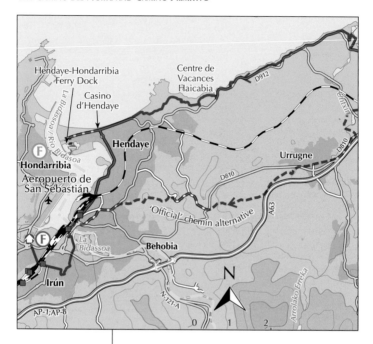

Ferry bypassing Irún

It is an option to continue straight from the casino, turning left six blocks later on Place du Port and proceeding to the passenger ferry dock (1.1km), which provides regular transport to **Hondarribia**. Yellow arrows start at the dock, leading 900 meters into the center, where it is possible to continue directly to join the Camino del Norte after Irún. Alternately, one could walk into Irún (4.4km) or even take a local bus.

To proceed into Irún on foot, turn left and follow D912 (or, more enjoyably, veer one block to the right and follow the riverside walkway). There are no waymarks on this stretch, but the highway leads past Hendaye's train and metro stations. Soon after, fork right to cross the old Pont Saint Jacques. Yellow arrows begin on the bridge, leading you through Irún to the **Albergue de Peregrinos** (6km).

STAGE 1

Irún to San Sebastián

Start	Albergue de Peregrinos, Irún
Finish	Albergue La Sirena, San Sebastián
Distance	24.8km
% unpaved	43.9%
Total ascent	882m
Total descent	875m
Terrain	5
Route-finding	3
Pilgrim accommodation	Irún, Pasajes de San Juan, San Sebastián

The Camino del Norte's first stage may also be its most spectacular, offering incredible views of both land and sea. Leaving Irún, a short riverside walk transitions to an ascent to the Guadalupe Sanctuary. From there, pilgrims are advised to take the high-level route, which follows a ridgeline high above the Bay of Biscay, passing Neolithic dolmens, medieval towers, and castle ruins before descending to Pasajes de San Juan. A small passenger boat shuttles you across the port. More uphill awaits, leading over another ridge before ultimately – and impressively – San Sebastián appears below. However, many route options exist so be sure to find the best fit; alternative approaches from Hondarribia are included at the end.

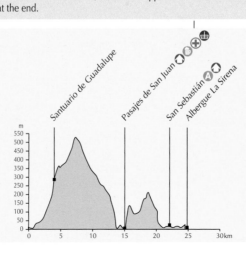

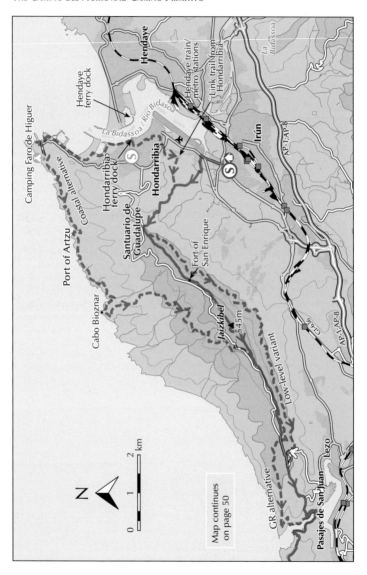

Hendaye

Hendaye train/metro stations

Link trail from Hondarribia

La Bidassoa

Hendaye ferry dock

Irún

AP-1/AP-8

Camping Faro de Higuer

La Bidassoa / Río Bidasoa

Coastal alternative

Hondarribia ferry dock

Hondarribia

Santuario de Guadalupe

Port of Artzu

Fort of San Enrique

Cabo Bioznar

Jaizkibel

545m

Low-level variant

CL-456

AP-8

AP-1/AP-8

N

0   1   2 km

Map continues on page 50

GR alternative

Lezo

Pasajes de San Juan

46

IRÚN

All facilities, RENFE station. Albergue de Peregrinos Jakobi (donativo, 60 beds, kitchen, breakfast, open Mar–Oct, credenciáles, c/Lesaka 1, tel 640 361 640). Albergue Juvenil Martindozenea remains closed in 2019 (€17–22, includes breakfast, meals available, kitchen, @, Avda Elizaxto 18, tel 943 621 042), Pensión Bowling (singles €30–50, doubles €40–60, c/Mourlane Michelena 2, tel 943 611 452), Pensión Lizaso (doubles €30–50, @, c/Aduana 5, tel 943 611 600).

Irún lies across the Río Bidasoa from French Hendaye. As a border town, it has been a frequent site of diplomatic wrangling. Franco and Hitler met across the river at Hendaye rail station. In exchange for Spanish support, Franco demanded significant territorial promises, none of which Hitler was willing to concede. Hitler was bored by the general and skeptical of Spanish military capability; Spain thus remained neutral throughout World War II. However, the dissolution of Franco and Hitler's relationship came too late for Irún, which had seen its historic core obliterated by German bombers (at Franco's behest) during the Spanish Civil War. Because of this, most of Irún today is modern.

▶ From the albergue return to the adjacent roundabout and take the second right. After crossing the Amuteko Canal, turn left and join a pedestrian track. A series of minor paved roads leads you past the Ermita de Santiago (fountain), where the route from Hondarribia joins from the right, before transitioning to a dirt track uphill to

To reach Irún's Albergue de Peregrinos from the train/bus station, follow Estación Kalea to Zubiaurre Kalea and turn left. Proceed downhill to a major roundabout and take the first right. The albergue is on your left.

SANTUARIO DE GUADALUPE (4KM)

Bar behind church (unreliable hours). Fountain water is not potable.

This small 16th-century church offers sweeping views of the Bidasoa valley. When nearby Hondarribia was besieged in 1638, the Virgin of Guadalupe supposedly protected the town for 69 days. Every 8 September, locals visit this sanctuary to commemorate her.

Throughout the rest of this stage, camino-specific yellow arrows and GR-specific red/white stripes frequently overlap,

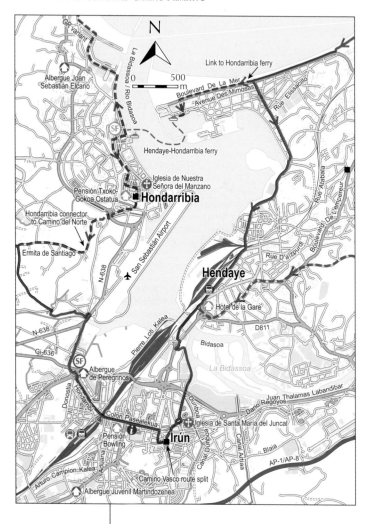

sometimes following the same trails and at other times split-ting. Both lead to San Sebastián; the GR is often more spec-tacular and, not coincidentally, longer.

Shortly after the church, the camino splits, with a sign informing 'Alpinist pilgrims' to keep straight on, and all oth-ers to turn left.

Low-level variant

For an easier walk, turn left when the route splits after Santuario de Guadalupe onto the dirt road. Keep straight on, with views of the Spanish interior and frequent tree cover, for 5.1km. Turn right and proceed for 4.2km, ignor-ing the marked left to Leto. Soon after, join GI-3440 (and the higher route). This route is 1.4km longer than the high-level option.

We recommend the high-level route continuing straight on, up a very steep ascent. While the route is certainly challenging, this brutal first climb is not representative of the more undu-lating walk that follows. After 1km, reach the first of Mount Jaizkibel's five (formerly six) towers, built during the 19th-cen-tury Carlist Wars. Proceed along the ridge, passing additional towers and an ancient dolmen. After 3km, reach the ruined **Fort of San Enrique** atop the mountain. Follow the ridgeline around a radio tower before descending to the highway. ▸

From GI-3440, turn onto a single-lane road. After 2.7km, descend steps into **Pasajes de San Juan**. Arrows pro-vide direct access to the albergue.

It is possible to turn right off of the highway soon after, following the GR: a more scenic – and strenuous – route which adds 1.6km to your approach to Pasajes. It is not recommended in poor weather or for people with fear of heights.

PASAJES DE SAN JUAN/PASAIA DONIBANE (10.6KM)

Bars, restaurants, pharmacy. An Eroski supermarket is located 400 meters to the left of the west dock. Albergue de Peregrinos Santa Ana (donativo, 14 beds, opens 1600, Apr–mid Oct, tel 618 939 666).

Originally two towns, Pasajes and San Juan were founded in 1180–1203, and unified in the 19th century. A long-prominent port, Pasajes hosted the Spanish naval fleet, the Escuadra Cantábrica, for 400 years and built part of the Spanish Armada. Victor Hugo lived at Donibane 63, near the plaza and currently home to the turismo. The 15th-century **Iglesia de San Juan Bautista** features a baroque altarpiece and the image of Santa Faustina Martir, a gift from Pope Leo XII.

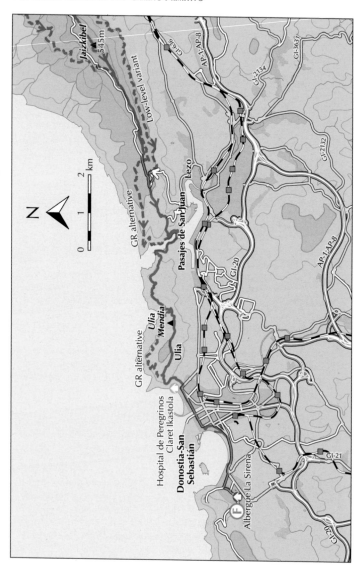

Take the small pedestrian ferry across the port (70c/person). On the other side, the camino splits again. Our route turns right, along the coastal promenade. Near the end, turn left and ascend steep steps to the old lighthouse. Take a footpath until turning right onto Faro Pasealekua.

Shortly before another lighthouse, the Faro de la Plata, turn left onto a footpath and proceed 1.6km. Then, the route splits again. The camino turns left, for a direct approach that follows a paved road into a parking lot, crosses it, and then joins a footpath towards San Sebastián's outskirts. ▶ Merge with c/Zemoria and descend the steps – you're now in San Sebastián, but some 4km stand between you and Albergue La Sirena! Turn right on c/Nafarroa (seasonal Hospital Claret Ikastola on your right), and then left along the beach promenade. Cross the Puente de Zurriola and continue across the peninsula. Rejoin the promenade and proceed all the way to the beach's end. Turn left onto c/Satrustegi, then fork left on Paseo de Igeldo. Keep straight on to Albergue Juvenil La Sirena to end the stage in

Alternatively, follow the GR right for a longer, coastal approach that adds 1km and rejoins the camino before town.

SAN SEBASTIÁN/DONOSTIA (10.2KM)

All facilities, RENFE and EuskoTren stations, Central Bus Station located on Pio XII Square. Hospital de Peregrinos Claret Ikastola (donativo, 60–75 beds, open 1500, July–Aug only, credenciáles, Avda de Nafarroa 1), Albergue Juvenil La Sirena (€15–21, 100 beds, kitchen, @, W/D, Paseo de Igeldo 25, 943 310 268), Albergue Juvenil Ulia, located on-route before San Sebastián (€15–18.75, 54 beds, kitchen, meals available, @, W/D, tel 943 483 480), Pensión Loinaz (singles/doubles €50–80, triples €75–105, quads €90–120, W/D, @, c/San Lorenzo 17, tel 943 426 714), Pensión La Perla (singles €30–60, doubles €40–72, includes breakfast, tel 943 428 123), Pensión Anne (doubles €40–60, Esterlines Kalea 15, tel 943 421 438), Hotel Niza (singles €59–69, doubles €72–175, breakfast available, @, Zubieta Kalea 56, tel 943 426 663).

This is one of Europe's most stunning beach cities. Probably founded by Basques, it later hosted a Roman fort and a monastery before becoming a Navarrese military stronghold. Frequent conflicts between France and Spain left a mark on San Sebastián. The most serious threat came in the Peninsular War, when Napoleon's forces took the town and the Duke of Wellington besieged it for months. The British finally broke through and celebrated by looting the town for a week. Ultimately, only two churches and 35 houses escaped this clash; the population

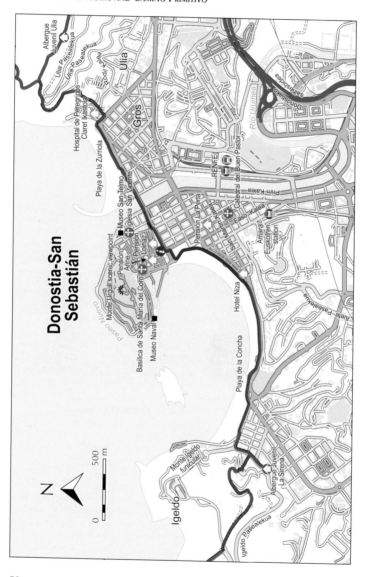

Donostia-San Sebastián

Albergue Juvenil Ulia

Ulia Pasealekua

Zodi-Yades

Uria Pasealekua

Ulia

Gros

Hospital de Peregrinos Claret Ikastola

Playa de la Zurriola

RENFE

Río Unimea

Donostiako

Catedral del Buen Pastor

Prim Kalea

Museo San Telmo

Iglesia San Vicente

Pensión La Perla

Monte Urgull/scenic viewpoint

Pensión Anne

Pensión Loinaz

Kalea

San Martin Kalea

Easo-Kalea

Amara Euskotren Station

Aiete-Pasealekua

Paseo Nuevo

Basílica de Santa María del Coro

Museo Naval

Hotel Niza

Playa de la Concha

Monte Igeldo funicular

Igeldo

Albergue Juvenil 'La Sirena'

Igeldo Pasealekua

N

0   500   m

was halved. San Sebastián has been burned to the ground a dozen times over its history, and thus most buildings date from the 19th century. The oldest section of town, the Parte Vieja, can be found beneath Monte Urgull.

San Sebastián's most impressive sights are natural ones: two fantastic beaches flanked by prominent hills. The larger beach, **Playa de la Concha**, is capped on its west side by the Miramar Palace. Meanwhile, Monte Igeldo looms over the **Playa de la Zurriola**, with a great park on top (tired pilgrims can ride the funicular). The other hill, Monte Urgull, preserves a rich history, including the **Castillo de Santa Cruz de la Mota** (1530) and a British cemetery from the Peninsular War.

Human-made highlights include the 19th-century **Catédral del Buen Pastor**, a neo-Gothic structure modeled after Cologne's cathedral. Built out of sandstone, it has three large naves and a 75m tower (0800–1230 and 1700–2000). The **Iglesia San Vicente** (1507) is a fine Gothic structure with a striking altarpiece. The **Basilica de Santa María del Coro** has a long history, but its current exterior is more recent. A legend states that the Virgin del Coro's image was in the church's choir, but a lazy clergyman, tired of the uphill climb to reach it, decided to steal the image. However, he was immobilized as he tried to leave the building. The **Museo Naval (Untzi Museoa)** shares the history of Basque seafaring (c/Paseo del Muelle 24, Tue–Sat 1000–1400 and 1600–1900; Sun 1100–1400). Finally, the **Museo San Telmo** (€6, Tue–Sun 1000–2000), located in the 16th-century Dominican monastery of San Telmo, contains a number of golden murals documenting Basque history. It also includes three works by El Greco and Rubens.

San Sebastián and Monte Igeldo

Alternative routes from Hondarribia

Some pilgrims prefer to start from Hondarribia instead of Irún and this is easy to do. Yellow arrows originate from the pedestrian ferry dock (from Hendaye) and proceed inland to the c/de Santiago, where the route turns left. After a slightly tricky intersection, forking left across Harresilanda Kalea and then back to the right uphill, proceed into the center of the old town. The Arma Plaza, roughly 900m from the dock, offers excellent views, houses the turismo, and borders the cathedral. The route now departs the old town, crosses a roundabout, and then turns right on Zumardi Kalea. Cross another roundabout, navigating towards a small set of steps (easily missed) directly ahead on the other side. Once atop those stairs, quiet, well-marked roads lead to the **Ermita de Santiago** and the 'official' camino from Irún. This walk covers 2.8km.

It is also possible to take an entirely different approach from Hondarribia, following a GR that hews closer to the coastline. From the dock, proceed north (with the river on your right), wrapping inland briefly around a large port, before returning to the coast. After a second port, the first red/white marks appear, calling for a left turn uphill. Roughly 4km from the dock, you arrive at a lighthouse with restaurants and **Camping Faro de Higuer**. This is your last chance at water until Pasajes, so load up. The next 7km is a glorious stretch of coastal walking, passing the old **Port of Artzu**, which was used by Romans and once the site of a wheat and corn mill. Turn inland at **Cabo Bioznar**; the ascent is quite strenuous over the next 6km as you climb to intersect the camino, roughly 1km after the Fort of San Enrique. All told, this walk spans 17.1km between Hondarribia and the camino, with 5.4km still separating it from Pasajes.

STAGE 2
San Sebastián to Zarautz

Start	Albergue Juvenil La Sirena, San Sebastián
Finish	Albergue de Peregrinos, Zarautz
Distance	19.2km
% unpaved	31.3%
Total ascent	544m
Total descent	554m
Terrain	4
Route-finding	2
Pilgrim accommodation	Orio, Zarautz

After yesterday's brilliant walk, today might feel like a minor let down. Sea views are not as plentiful and beach access is limited to the start- and end-points, while facilities remain equally limited. However, the comparison is unfair; this remains an enjoyable walk, with long sections stretching across rolling green hills. Short ascents out of San Sebastián and Orio mark the major challenges. These are tamer than yesterday's climbs, but may feel harder given those exertions.

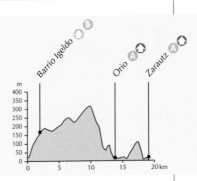

From the albergue on Paseo de Igeldo, head west on Marbil Bidea, shortly before the youth hostel. Proceed uphill, watching for waymarked shortcuts leading up stairs, including one off a hairpin turn, before passing right through a parking lot. After a stint on the old Carretera de Orio, fork right into

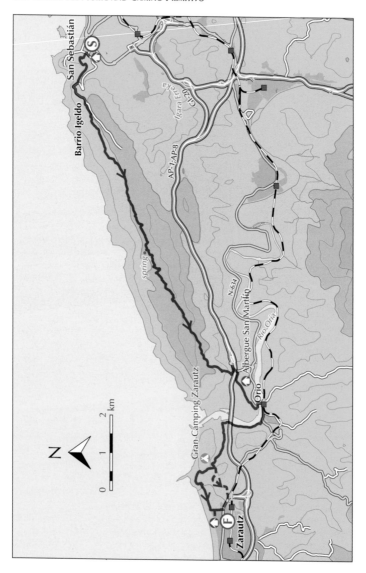

BARRIO IGELDO (2KM)

Pensión/Restaurante Buenavista (doubles €32–72, meals available, @, tel 943 210 600), Pensión Tximistarri (doubles €25–60, @, tel 943 218 801). Camino info, water, and sello left by a 'friend of the camino' at a roadside kiosk.

Continue straight on Marabieta Bidea before transitioning to a well-marked footpath and dirt roads. After 5.2km you reach a trailside **spring** offering cool, fresh water. Keep straight on for 5.1km through countryside, descend under the AP-8, and turn right uphill onto Ermitarako Bidea. The albergue is ahead on the left, shortly before

ORIO (11.6KM)

Bars, restaurants, and grocery shops. Albergue San Martín (€10, 20 beds, kitchen, meals, washing machine, open Mar–Oct, tel 617 118 689), Albergue Juvenil Txurruka (€12–15, 112 beds, includes breakfast, @, tel 943 830 887), Pensión Xaloa (singles €46–57, doubles €61–83, c/Estropalari 26, tel 943 131 883).

The well-preserved port town of Orio has long been an important pilgrimage stop. Ferdinand and Isabella declared in 1484 that pilgrims could not be charged for ferrying across the Río Oria. Orio's residents were ardent Republicans in the Spanish Civil War and suffered following Franco's victory. Today, the town is recognized for its weightlifters and surfers. Its Plateresque **Ermita de San Martín de Tours** has a long, covered porch ideal for breaks on a hot day. The 17th-century **Iglesia de San Nicolás de Bari** is connected to a neighboring building by a pedestrian bridge that spans the camino. The baroque structure replaced an earlier church from which the graves remain, visible under newer benches.

Turn left in front of the Iglesia de San Nicolás, descend to the waterfront, and cross the bridge. Turn right, following N-634 and then forking right to remain on the waterfront. After passing under the AP-8 expressway and the Albergue Juvenil, turn inland. Follow a minor road to **Gran Camping Zarautz** (bar, Albergue de Peregrinos – €5, 14 beds, kitchen, tel 943 831 238). We suggest turning right onto a coastal variant immediately after the campsite, following red/white stripes. ▶ This leads to a paved pedestrian track that offers stunning views of the old Malla Harria iron-loading dock and warehouse before descending to a beachfront promenade. At

To follow the 'official' camino, continue straight, descending to N-634, which leads into Zarautz, roughly 300 meters shorter.

Zarautz's golf course, ignore waymarks calling for a left turn – continue straight, with the course to your left and beach to your right. After the golf course, take the first left and then turn right at the next corner. Two blocks later, turn left on Zinkunegi Kalea. The **Albergue de Peregrinos** is one block ahead, to your right on Zumalacárregui Kalea.

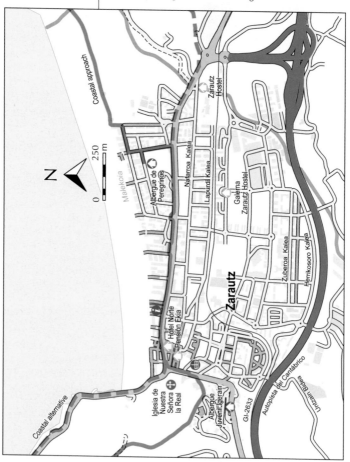

Orio's Ermita de San Martín de Tours

ZARAUTZ (5.6KM)

All facilities. **Albergue de Peregrinos** (donativo, 60 beds, open 1600, July–Aug, c/Zumalakarregi 16, tel 943 830 990), **Albergue Juvenil Igerain** (€15–21, includes breakfast, open Feb–Nov, @, tel 943 415 134), **Galerna Zarautz Hostel** (€21, 18 beds, includes breakfast, tel 943 010 371), **Zarautz Hostel** (€20–28, 24 beds, includes breakfast, open Mar–Dec, kitchen, W/D, @, Avda Gipuzkoa 59, tel 943 833 893), **Pensión Ekia** (singles €55–80, doubles €65–90, Elizaurre Kalea 3, tel 943 010 664), **Hotel Norte** (doubles €49–89, includes breakfast, @, c/ Amezti 1, tel 943 832 313).

This important shipping town historically was home to whalers and great explorers, and Magellan's ship, *La Vitoria*, was built here. International attention came in the 20th century with the Belgian royal family's decision to summer here in the Palace of Narros. It has the region's longest beach (2.8km) and, not coincidentally, its population triples during summer months. The **Iglesia de Nuestra Señora la Real** contains the tomb of 'the pilgrim'. The church was targeted in 1586, when a Genoese pilgrim stole a number of artifacts. However, he was captured, drawn and quartered, and displayed on the camino (nothing remains today).

STAGE 3
Zarautz to Deba

Start	Albergue de Peregrinos, Zarautz
Finish	Albergue de Peregrinos, Deba
Distance	22.6km
% unpaved	57.5%
Total ascent	850m
Total descent	856m
Terrain	5
Route-finding	3
Pilgrim accommodation	Getaria, Azkizu, Zumaia, Deba

This stage offers a happy balance between beach towns, sea views, and quiet hills. Leaving Zarautz, the pilgrim can choose between a higher inland route and a lower coastal option. After Getaria, the routes rejoin and jut inland through Azkizu before returning to the beach in Zumaia. An outstanding jaunt along a rugged coastline follows, although pilgrims can also opt for an inland, higher-level approach. Enjoy the beach in Deba tonight, as you won't return to the coast for several days.

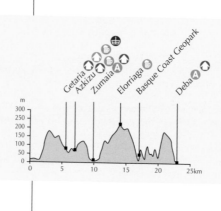

Follow N-634 to Zarautz's end, where the camino splits. Turn left for the recommended higher-level route. ▶ Shortly after, turn right uphill along a medieval road and proceed through vineyards overlooking the bay. After 4.3km, arrive at Kanpaia Aterpeatxea. To visit Getaria, follow the road right downhill for 400 meters. Otherwise, turn left.

Turn right for the coastal option, which continues along N-634 to Getaria and is roughly equivalent in length.

GETARIA (5.5KM)

Bars, grocery stores. **Kanpaia Aterpetxea** (€12, 30 beds, open Mar–Oct, breakfast available, W/D, c/San Prudentzio Auzoa, 28-Bajo, tel 695 711 679), **Hostel Txalupa** (€25, 14 beds, private rooms, breakfast available, tel 688 856 146), **Pensión Getariano** (singles €40–75, doubles €55–95, triples €75–135, tel 943 140 567).

Getaria is another important fishing town with a history of whaling and exploring. Basque navigators were quite popular on Portuguese and Spanish ships. The most famous example, Getaria's own Juan Sebastián Elcano, took over Magellan's fleet after Magellan was killed and completed the globe's first circumnavigation. He is still honored today, and every four years, townspeople re-enact his heroic return. The 13th-century **Iglesia de San Salvador** hosted Elcano's baptism and contains his (empty) tomb. It has several distinctive and curious elements, including a tilted floor, a menorah on the back wall, and a chapel and crypt accessible by the alley.

Follow dirt roads and paved tracks through undulating hills to

AZKIZU (1.8KM)

Agote Aundi has a pilgrim menu and small albergue (€15, includes breakfast, open all year, W/D, @, tel 659 634 103).

Azkizu has one of the oldest Christian churches in Gipuzkoa, the **Iglesia de San Martín de Tours**, noted for its Gothic masonry. A key is obtainable from a neighbor.

Descend to N-634, cross the Ría Urola, and follow steps to the dock. Turn left and continue across a second bridge into

ZUMAIA (3.1KM)

All facilities. Albergue de Peregrinos Convento San José (donativo, 35 beds, open Easter–mid Oct, W/D, @, San Jose Kalea 1, tel 600 280 375), Albergue/ Agroturismo Santa Klara (€25 for B&B, free laundry, €35–55 for rooms, located 1.3km after town, tel 943 860 531), Pensión Goiko (singles €30–45, doubles €45–57, c/Erribera 9, tel 943 860 078), Hotel Zumaia (singles €60+, doubles €80+, c/Alai Auzategia 13, tel 943 143 441).

Set on the Ría Urola, Zumaia developed around a 13th-century monastery, and was a frequent target for piracy. By the 16th century, the town had 136 houses, 70 within the walls. Zumaia's beaches are set on the longest continuous rock strata in the world, over 100 million years old. The **Museo Zuloaga** (visits upon request, tel 677 078 445), former home of Basque painter Ignacio Zuloaga, includes pieces by Goya, El Greco, and Zurburán (and, of course, Zuloaga). The 15th-century **Iglesia de San Pedro** features a gargoyle-lined entrance and Juan de Antxieta's Romanist altarpiece (note the monumental, energetic human figures, including Saint Peter in his chair). The building exemplifies the late Gothic style, with pointed arches and a star vault over the apse.

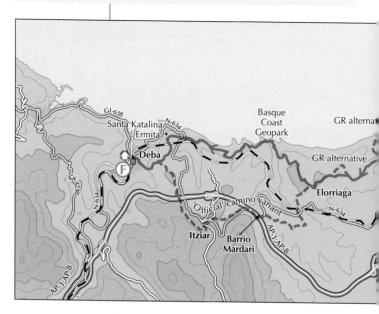

Continue straight uphill, forking right soon after on a single-lane road that becomes a gravel track. ▶ After 3km, pass through a park with toilets and then continue along the grassy footpath toward

For a more scenic approach, turn right along the Ría Urola and then left on the far side of Plaza Amaia. GR waymarks appear and lead out along the coast. This rejoins the 'official' route 2.5km later and is 1.1km longer.

ELORRIAGA (3.7KM)

Bar.

Small village founded in the 10th century. **Ermita de San Sebastián** features a Romanesque baptismal pool.

The route splits immediately before Elorriaga. The right turn onto the GR is recommended for an approach that, while more strenuous, offers some of the Norte's most dramatic coastal scenery. A steady descent leads 2.5km through a small copse of pine and around a lonely house before arriving at the **Basque Coast Geopark**, famous for its geological Flysch deposits, which preserve 60 million years of history.

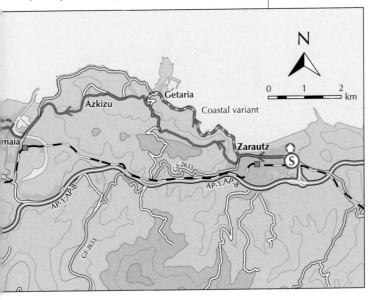

Basque Coast Geopark

The route spends the next 1.3km running alongside this coastline, before turning inland for a series of tough ascents. The walk proceeds along a former railway track (now covered with gravel), past a water treatment plant and the **Santa Katalina Ermita** (fountain), before rejoining the 'official' camino shortly before Deba.

'Official' camino variant

From Elorriaga, proceed along quiet country roads, first crossing N-634 and then joining it in **Barrio Mardari** (Restaurante/ Agroturismo Santuaran Bekoa – singles €39, doubles €55, meals available, tel 943 199 056) before crossing AP-8/E-80. Fork right off N-634 downhill onto a footpath. Then ascend sharply to N-634 for a third time. Continue straight into

ITZIAR (5.3KM)

Bars, grocery store. Hotel Kanala (singles €56–69, doubles €76–89, triples €83–96, tel 943 199 035).

The 16th-century **Santuario de Nuestra Señora de Itziar** preserves the image of the Virgin of Itziar – one of the Basque region's most important – in its niche.

Follow a generally flat cement track out of town before transitioning to a series of minor roads. Turn left at a T intersection with a footpath, rejoining the recommended GR route soon after for the final approach to Deba. This route is 300m longer.

Soon after the routes rejoin, fork right onto a long stretch of cobblestones. ▶ Turn right at the end of the descent, then fork left to arrive at the Plaza de Foruen. If staying in the albergue, proceed first to the tourist office, where registration is mandatory. To reach the albergue, continue straight through Plaza de Foruen, turn left in front of the railroad tracks, and proceed to the far side of the train station in the center of

Those with sore knees could stay on the road instead, following old waymarks to the elevator!

DEBA (8.5KM)

All facilities. **Albergue de Peregrinos** (€5, 56 beds, open all year, W/D, @, registration in turismo, or with Policia Municipal when the turismo is closed, tel 943 192 452), **Pensión Zumardi** (singles €50–60, doubles €60–85, pilgrim discounts, breakfast available, Marina Kalea 12, tel 943 192 368).

Founded in 1343 by Alfonso XI, Deba maintains its original layout. Like its neighbors, its past was devoted to whales and trade, while its present focuses on tourism. At its peak, Deba had three pilgrim albergues. Its must-see **Iglesia de Santa María** (open 0900–1300) is one of the region's finest churches. The Gothic entrance is the highlight. Six apostles flank each side, while 38 angels, virgins, and martyrs adorn the frieze. The Annunciation, Visitation, Birth, and Epiphany are narrated on the tympanum. The cloister is also a masterpiece designed to perfect classical proportions.

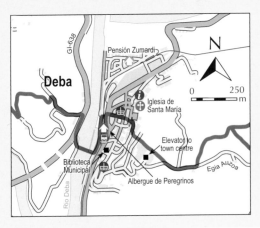

STAGE 4
Deba to Markina-Xemein

Start	Albergue de Peregrinos, Deba
Finish	Albergue de Peregrinos, Markina-Xemein
Distance	24.2km
% unpaved	70.2%
Total ascent	851m
Total descent	771m
Terrain	5
Route-finding	1
Pilgrim accommodation	Ermita del Calvario, Markina-Xemein

Say goodbye to the coast for a few days. From Deba, the camino heads for the interior of Vizcaya, climbing over the Collado de Arno, some 500m higher than Deba. With extensive stretches of dirt roads and footpaths passing through densely forested hills, this stage's scenery and climate differ dramatically from those of the preceding days. Markina-Xemein also offers a much less touristed stopping point. Alternatively, consider walking a little farther to where the monks of Zenarruza (Stage 5) provide hospitality. Plan ahead: it is rarely possible to buy food or drink along this route.

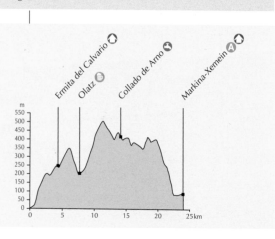

Cross the Río Deba and turn right. ▶ The well-marked route begins on paved roads before transitioning to dirt tracks. In past years, waymarks here have been vandalized, but the problem seems resolved. After a brisk climb, arrive at

As of late 2018, the bridge in Deba center is closed for repair, so a detour requires an additional 1km out and back to cross the river.

ERMITA DEL CALVARIO (4.3KM)

Fountain behind church, restaurant (nights only). **Izarbide Aterpetxea**, 600 meters after restaurant (€13, 32 beds, open Mar–Oct, kitchen, meals available, W/D, @, tel 655 459 769).

Across from the restaurant is the old *probadero*, where oxen tested their strength by dragging rocks over cobblestones.

Keep straight on the paved road, which quickly becomes a dirt track to

OLATZ (3.4KM)

Taberna (erratic hours). Fountain at town entrance.

This picturesque village has a small church.

Continue straight along the road for 2.8km. Transition to a footpath, running uphill through a lovely forest to

COLLADO DE ARNO (5.7KM)

Covered fountain on left.

This is basically a small cluster of houses on the border between Guipúzcoa/Gipuzkoa and Vizcaya/Biscay.

Turn right at the T-junction, following the dirt road. Proceed 7km along a mix of dirt roads, footpaths, and occasional paved stretches. Finally, you begin a long, rocky descent into Markina-Xemein. Proceed around the town's outskirts, passing the **Ermita de San Miguel de Arretxinaga** and the **Iglesia de Santa María de la Asunción**, before finally

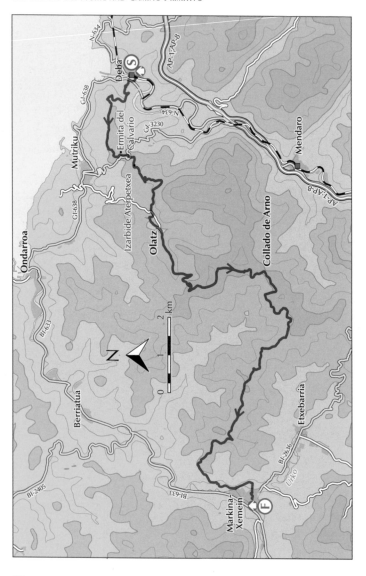

entering the historical center. The albergue is located shortly before the end of town.

MARKINA-XEMEIN (10.8KM)

All facilities. **Albergue de Peregrinos** in the Convento de los Padres Carmelitas (donativo, 40 beds, open Apr–mid Oct, washing machine, c/Carmen 5, tel 609 031 526), **Albergue Intxauspe** (€12, 20 beds, open Apr–Oct, meals available, tel 652 770 889) located outside of Markina's center but the hospitaleros will pick pilgrims up at the entrance to town, **Albergue/Pensión Pitis** (€12, doubles €35, open all year, kitchen, @, Karmengo Plaza 11, tel 657 727 824), **Hostal Vega** (Abesua Kalea 2, tel 946 866 015).

Paleolithic remains have been found in the area. The town coalesced around a fort in 1355, reflecting its strategic value as a border post. Born of conflict, it enjoyed little peace, with Napoleon, the Carlist Wars, and the Spanish Civil War all wreaking havoc on the region. However, today Markina-Xemein is called the 'University of Pelota' because of its many *pelota* (court games) champions. It features several notable churches, including the hexagonal **Ermita de San Miguel de Arretxinaga**, founded in the 11th century around three Megalithic stones.

Three megalithic stones fill the Ermita de San Miguel de Arretxinaga in Markina

STAGE 5
Markina-Xemein to Gernika-Lumo

Start	Albergue de Peregrinos, Markina-Xemein
Finish	Albergue Juvenil Gernika
Distance	24.7km
% unpaved	52.6%
Total ascent	702m
Total descent	780m
Terrain	5
Route-finding	2
Pilgrim accommodation	Ziortza-Bolibar, Zenarruza, Munitibar, Olabe, Mendata, Gernika-Lumo

The route from Markina meanders alongside a small creek before turning towards the village of Ziortza-Bolibar and the picturesque Monastery of Zenarruza. From there, it parallels the highway, but with sufficient separation to allow for quiet walking. The tree cover thins the farther west you travel, as do the stopping points, but arrival in Gernika-Lumo makes the trek well worthwhile, as it is one of the most historically significant towns on the camino.

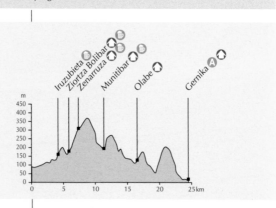

Proceed straight towards BI-633. Turn left on a pedestrian track, which soon leads under the highway and then onto a trail alongside the Río Artibai. Re-emerge on a paved road into

IRUZUBIETA (3.9KM)

Two bars/restaurants.

Turn right on a minor road and then join a footpath, crossing the tree-covered hillside. Descend the hill, cross BI-2224, and fork right into

ZIORTZA-BOLIBAR (2.2KM)

Bar, grocery, bakery. **Albergue Usandi** (€12, 20 beds, open Mar-Oct, kitchen, W/D, @, tel 637 054 023).

The ancestral homeland of Simón Bolívar, founded in the 11th century. Although his ancestors departed Spain four generations before his birth, he is commemorated with the **Casa-Museo de Simón Bolívar** (open 1000–1300). The name 'Bolibar' is Basque for 'windmill valley'. The **Iglesia de Santo Tomás** is a typical fortress-temple.

Re-cross the highway and return to the hillside. Follow the medieval road to the Albergue Ziortza Beitia and then continue into

MONASTERIO DE ZENARRUZA (1.3KM)

Medieval monastery with **Albergue de Peregrinos** (donativo, 20 beds, meals provided, tel 946 164 179). Shortly before the monastery is the **Albergue Ziortza Beitia** (€12, 24 beds, doubles €50, bar/restaurant, W/D, tel 946 165 722).

Legend holds that an eagle brought a skull here from the Gerrikaitz ossuary, prompting the monastery's construction. It was first documented in 1082, although the 14th-century Gothic church came later. Cistercians took over the monastery in 1988. It is a serene spot for rest or reflection, with a large covered porch, impressive altar, and evocative cloister. The tympanum and altarpiece are impressive; the former features El Salvador between two trumpet-bearing angels, while the latter details the Virgin's life with a Santiago Peregrino towards the bottom.

The entrance to the Monasterio de Zenarruza tells the story of its origin

The camino to
Iruzubieta

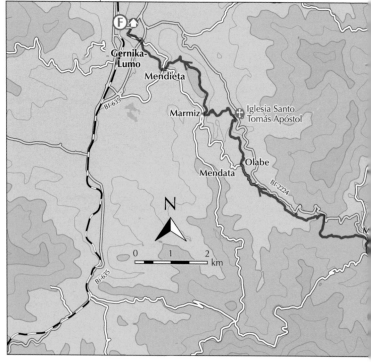

Leaving the monastery, return to the hills once more, following a rocky footpath with a couple of steep drops, now 'improved' with a series of wooden staircases. Descend a series of steps to the rural road leading into

MUNITIBAR (4KM)

Two bars, grocery shop, pharmacy. **Albergue Lea** (€15, 10 beds, open all year, W/D, Herriko Plaza 3, tel 615 721 807), **Casa Rural Garro** (doubles €45+, tel 946 164 136).

Leave town on BI-2224, then turn left on a minor road uphill, before following a series of footpaths and minor roads. After 5.4km, turn right into the village of **Olabe** (Albergue Andiketxe – €12, 20 beds, meals available, kitchen, W/D, tel 946 253 150). ▸ Further on, ascend to the impressive **Iglesia Santo Tomás Apóstol** before looping back to a footpath along the river. Just before intersecting BI-3224 in **Marmiz** make a sharp right and follow a minor road uphill. Cross the highway in **Mendieta** and wrap behind the church to the right.

Turn left here for a detour to Mendata's Albergue Municipal Artape (€7, 36 beds, closed Mon–Tue, open Apr–Oct, tel 946 257 204).

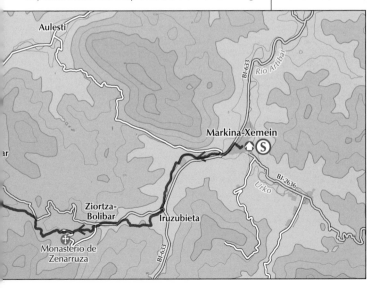

Finally, join BI-3224 and enter Gernika. Turn right for the youth hostel, 150 meters away, or left to follow the camino into the center of

GERNIKA-LUMO (13.3KM)

All facilities. **Refugio de Peregrinos** (donativo, 35 beds, Aug only, Zearreta Kalea 11, in the Colegio Allende Salazar, tel 609 031 526), **Albergue Juvenil Gernika** (€18, 70 beds, includes breakfast, open all year, kitchen, W/D, @, Kortezubi Bidea 9, tel 946 126 959), **Hotel Boliña** (singles €40+, doubles €45+, Barrenkalea 5, tel 946 250 300), **Hotel Akelarre** (singles €38–43, doubles €48–56, Barrenkalea 5, tel 946 270 197).

For centuries, the Lords of Vizcaya gathered under Gernika's oak tree to swear loyalty to the nation's *fueros* (charter). Later, when the Basques joined Spain, Spanish kings traveled there to reiterate their commitment to Basque liberties. However, Gernika is known internationally primarily because of two men: Franco and Picasso. As the Spanish Civil War languished in a bloody stalemate, Franco faced heavy pressure to produce results. He shifted focus to the Basque Country. Although Franco's military was outdated, he had Hitler and Mussolini's modern air forces available, carrying with them a brutal new kind of war. On a market day in 1937, the German Condor Legion pummeled Gernika with incendiary explosives before passing a second time to strafe the fleeing townspeople. The town was destroyed and thousands were killed. Aghast, Picasso took up the brush and produced one of his most famous works, which shares the town's name. Intended as a warning of the destructive power of new technology and the savagery of the fascist militaries, its message went largely unheeded.

As a result of the bombing, today's Gernika is a modern city, with few historic buildings. However, a sapling of the old oak survives in the park surrounding the **Casa de Juntas** (1000–1400 and 1600–1900, closes earlier in off-season), the seat of the Vizcayan Provincial General Assembly. It includes an exhibit on Basque government and culture. Even more compelling is the **Museo de la Paz de Gernika** (€5, Mar–Oct, Tue–Sat 1000–1900, and Sun 1000–1400, reduced hours in off-season, closed Jan), which goes beyond the bombing to examine 20th-century efforts at peace and justice.

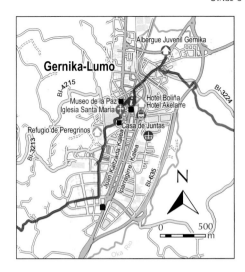

STAGE 6

Gernika-Lumo to Bilbao

Start	Albergue Juvenil Gernika
Finish	Plaza de Unamuno, Bilbao
Distance	31.3km
% unpaved	25.6%
Total ascent	930m
Total descent	923m
Terrain	4
Route-finding	2
Pilgrim accommodation	Eskerika, Larrabetzu, Lezama, Bilbao

This stage connects two of the Camino del Norte's more famous stops. The first half is quite enjoyable. Warm up by climbing 300m in the first 5km. Descend to the highway, then steel yourself for more uphill walking, leading to the Altos de Morga and Aretxabalgane. Arrival in Goikolexea spells the end of the day's most pleasant walking, as it is followed by a long, straight, flat stretch of highway.

From Zamudio, one more ascent awaits, the completion of which promises impressive views of Bilbao – and a long, paved downhill into the dynamic city. Note that the distance listed here brings you into Bilbao's Casco Viejo, where many accommodation options are clustered, but others are still as far as 4km to 5km across town.

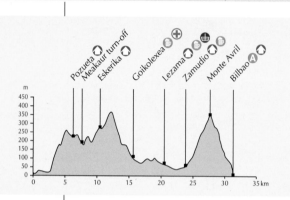

Brown street signs, labeled 'Donejakue Bidea', mark the camino through Gernika.

◄ From the albergue, return to the T-junction and keep straight on Kortezubi Bidea. Turn left on Ocho de Enero Kalea, then right towards the *ayuntamiento* (town hall). Proceed up stairs through the town hall, turn left past the Escuelas Publicas, then turn right around the Casa de Juntas. Proceed through a residential neighborhood, before an ermita signals Gernika's abrupt end, 2.3km from the hostel. A pleasant walk follows, along wooded tracks. Skirt the village of **Pozueta**, where Albergue Caserio Pozueta is located (€18, 7 beds, includes breakfast, kitchen (€1 charge), @, tel 696 565 318). Cross under BI-2121 to arrive at

MEAKAUR TURN-OFF (7.6KM)

No facilities. To reach Albergue Turístico Meakaur (€16, 62 beds, meals available, W/D, @, tel 944 911 746) turn right on BI-2121 and walk 2km.

The small **Iglesia de San Esteban** contains Roman remains.

The next section involves multiple sharp climbs, crossing the Altos de Morga and **Aretxabalgane**. A house in **Eskerika**, 2.8km from the Meakaur turn-off, offers the only chance to refill water bottles before Goikolexea. ▶ Continue along a series of minor paved roads, dirt roads, and footpaths, ultimately descending into

Turn right here for Albergue Eskerika (€14, 20 beds, breakfast available, kitchen (€1 charge), open Apr–Oct, tel 696 453 582).

GOIKOLEXEA (8.2KM)

Bar, pharmacy.

Like Gernika, Vizcayan lords gathered here for loyalty oaths. The Gothic **Iglesia de San Emeterio y San Celedonio** honors two Roman legionnaires martyred for their Christian faith. In 1991, restoration revealed several murals of great artistic significance.

Keep straight on BI-3713 before forking right into

LARRABETZU (1.4KM)

Bar, grocery. Albergue de Peregrinos Larrabetzu (donativo, 20 beds, open Apr–mid Oct, microwave, W/D, Askatasunaren Enparantza 1, tel 609 031 526).

Founded in 1376 by Prince Juan and ravaged by fire in 1830, today's town is largely the post-fire neoclassical incarnation. The 18th-century **Iglesia de Santa María** includes a Greek cross and a 15th-century statue of Our Lady.

Continue along BI-3713 (later merging with BI-737) to

LEZAMA (3.4KM)

Bars, restaurants, supermarket. Albergue de Peregrinos (donativo, 20 beds, open Jun–Sep, W/D, in Centro Civico, tel 609 031 526), Casa Rural Matsa (doubles €41–120, open all year, @, situated 1.5km off-route, c/Aretxalde 153, tel 944 556 086).

Lezama is known for its three famous towers – Basabil, Arechavaleta, and Lezama – which speak to its medieval military significance. The **Iglesia de Santa María de Lezama** is a good rest stop.

And, yet again, continue straight along BI-737 to

ZAMUDIO (3KM)

Bars, restaurants, supermarket. Pensión Udondo (singles €45, doubles €55–60, c/ Mungialde 3, tel 946 564 909).

Turn left at the end of town, proceeding uphill. Cross the roundabout, fork right, and cross the expressway. From there, dirt tracks and minor roads lead uphill to

MONTE AVRIL (4.8KM)

An enjoyable park offering excellent views of Bilbao.

Continue downhill. Cross BI-631 (the 'GR-228' variant described in Stage 7 begins here) and wind around the **Basílica de Nuestra Señora de Begoña**. Descend the Calzada de Mallona, a long series of steps leading into the **Plaza de Unamuno** in the heart of Bilbao's Casco Viejo.

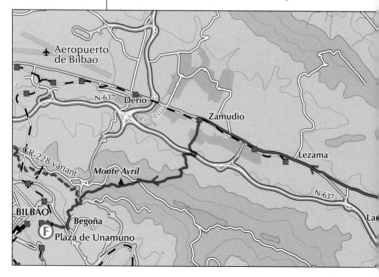

Nuestra Señora
de Begoña

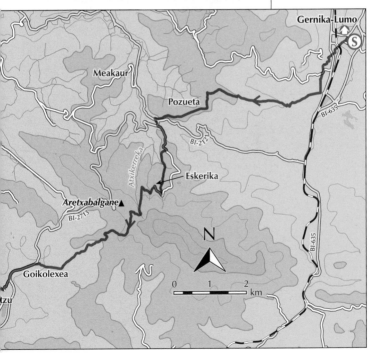

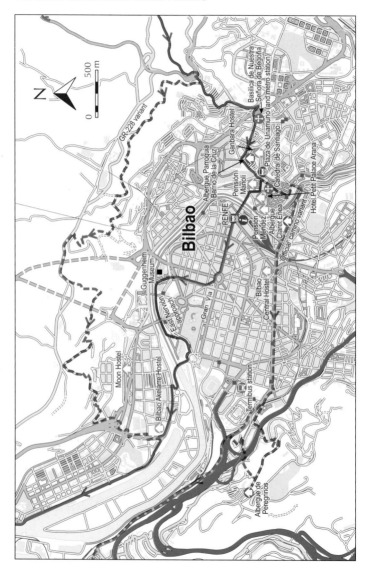

BILBAO (2.9KM)

A major city with all facilities and services. RENFE and EuskoTren stations, Termibus station located near San Mames. Bilbao airport is accessible by Bus A3247. **Albergue de Peregrinos** is hospitable but on the far, far side of town (donativo, 40 beds, open Apr–mid Oct, communal meals, c/Kobetas 60, tel 609 031 526). By contrast, **Albergue Parroquia Barrio de la Cruz** is at the entrance of the city (donativo, 22 beds, open mid Jun–mid Sep, tel 687 529 627). **Albergue Claret Enea** (€11, 20 beds, open May-Oct, includes breakfast, kitchen, W/D, Plaza Corazón de María, tel 946 510 171). Many youth hostels, including: **Ganbara Hostel** located in the old town (€18, 62 beds, includes breakfast, kitchen, W/D, @, tel 944 053 930), **Bilbao Central Hostel** (€16–23, 40 beds, includes breakfast, kitchen, W/D, @, c/Fernández del Campo 24, tel 946 526 057), **Moon Hostel** (€10+, 83 beds, kitchen, @, c/Luzarra 7, tel 944 750 848), **Bilbao Akelarre Hostel** (€15+, 36 beds, includes breakfast, kitchen, W/D, @, tel 944 057 713). **Pensión Manoli** (singles €36, doubles €42, c/Libertad 2, tel 944 155 636), **Pensión Mendez** (doubles €35, c/Santa Maria 13, tel 944 160 364), **Hotel Petit Palace Arana** (doubles €120–40, Bidebarrieta 2, tel 944 156 411).

Today, Bilbao is a center of Spanish industry, insurance, and banking, which has led to a significant influx of non-Basques. From its founding in 1300, it was destined to be a place of economic importance, given its strategic position on the Río Nervión, connecting the Basque country with Castile. Despite sound thumpings from Napoleon's forces and during the Carlist Wars, 19th-century Bilbao was changed most markedly by the Industrial Revolution. Thanks to its extensive natural resources, including iron mines, forests, and the potential for abundant water power, Bilbao enjoyed a boom in shipbuilding and steel mills.

The Gothic **Basílica de Begoña** was the first landmark seen by sailors as they approached the city, and feels more monumental than Bilbao's cathedral, given its three naves, massive entryway, and bell tower (containing 24 bells). Vibrantly restored paintings on the life of the Virgin line the walls. The basilica was damaged in the Spanish Civil War, when a bomb exploded in one of the building's doorways; speculation placed the blame on a Franco supporter. The historic center, known as the Seven Streets, radiates out from the **Catédral de Santiago** (1000–1300 and 1700–1930). The original cathedral was largely destroyed by fire in 1571; its replacement features a variety of styles, including a Renaissance porch, Gothic cloisters and main doors, and a neo-Gothic façade and tower.

Bilbao's **Guggenheim Museum** (€7.50–13, Tue–Sun 1000–2000) is the major highlight, although the building – wonderfully designed by Frank Gehry and built in 1997 – exceeds in quality anything on display within it. The eclectic contemporary collection is primarily comprised of exhibits on loan from other Guggenheim holdings.

STAGE 7
Bilbao to Pobeña

Start	Plaza de Unamuno, Bilbao
Finish	Albergue de Peregrinos, Pobeña
Distance	25.2km
% unpaved	2.9%
Total ascent	341m
Total descent	356m
Terrain	1
Route-finding	5
Pilgrim accommodation	Barakaldo, Portugalete, Pobeña

What will it be? The direct, riverside jaunt that takes you through Bilbao's tourist-friendly, downtown core? A longer walk through the city's gritty, industrial heart? A high-level alternative that is more demanding but offers magnificent views? Or maybe the metro is calling your name. Options abound as you consider the approach from Bilbao to Portugalete; from there onward, though, there is but one: the bike/pedestrian track leading downhill to the coast and the lovely beaches of Playa de la Arena and Pobeña.

There is a fifth option – if you are not a stickler about walking every step, consider taking the metro from Bilbao to Portugalete. It's quick, cheap, and easy, and there's a station at Plaza de Unamuno.

From Bilbao to Portugalete, there are four routes to consider and we describe three below, briefly summarizing the fourth. ◀ We favor the East Nervión approach, as it is the shortest and also passes Bilbao's most scenic spots. Leave the 'official' camino in **Plaza de Unamuno**, turning right on Sombrereria Kalea and then right again on c/del Correo. Cross the Puente de Arenal and continue straight on Gran Vía past the **RENFE station**. Turn right in Plaza Eliptica onto Alameda Recalde and proceed to the **Guggenheim Museum**. Turn left on the riverfront walkway. Cross the next pedestrian bridge, turn left, and continue straight for 1.5km. Fork right on Morgan Kalea, just before Puente Euskalduna, skirting the roundabout. The **Bilbao Akelarre Hostel** is ahead on the right. After the hostel, fork left to remain on Morgan Kalea.

Follow the Nervión for 8.4km. Upon reaching **Las Arenas**, take the famous **Puente Colgante** across the river (40c/person or €5 via the elevated footbridge). On the other

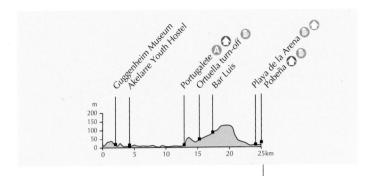

side, proceed inland one block, turn left, then right on Casilda Iturrizar Kalea in **Portugalete**. Rejoin the other routes here.

'Official' camino variants
While longer and mostly through urban sprawl, this approach offers a nuanced portrait of greater Bilbao – with immigrant-heavy neighborhoods, industrial suburbs, and striking glimpses of a working river economy. Follow the yellow/blue scallop shell plaques straight out of Plaza de Unamuno on c/de la Cruz, then fork right on Dendarikale, passing the **Catédral de Santiago**. Turn left at a T-junction, then right across the Puente de San Antón. Turn right on c/Bilbao la Vieja (also the N-634), which becomes c/San Francisco. Cross the railroad and then continue through Plaza Zabálburu. The road is now c/Autonomía; in time, it becomes Avda de Montevideo (also the N-634). You arrive at a route split 3.1km from Plaza de Unamuno. Fork right to continue on the camino; fork left to proceed 1.5km to Bilbao's **Albergue de Peregrinos**, following a waymarked route uphill. This route continues along N-634, and 2.5km later it passes through **Zorrotza** (bars, supermarket, Pensión Zorroza 1 – doubles €40–50, c/Fray Juan 11, tel 94 972 430). After crossing the Ría Cadagua, fork right onto c/Zumalakarregi and enter **Barakaldo**. Soon after the Lutxana Barakaldo metro station, turn left (fountain in park on left), climb to the overpass, and then cross back over, entering a pedestrian-only zone above the river. Following a pleasant off-road stretch, cross a pedestrian bridge, briefly follow a minor paved road, and then join BI-3739. This leads into **Sestao**

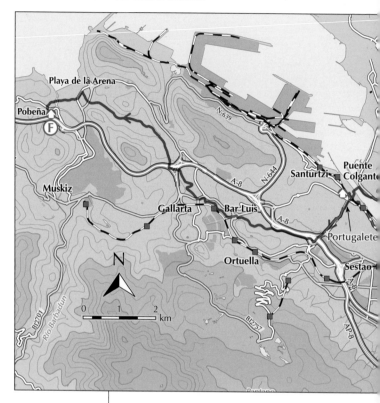

(bars, supermarket, Pensión Tres Concejos – singles €19, doubles €32, tel 658 412 795). Continue and soon after entering **Portugalete**, fork right to the church and then continue straight to rejoin the other routes on Casilda Iturrizar Kalea. This route is 1.5km longer than the East Nervión approach.

The other 'official' camino continues straight past Bilbao's **Albergue de Peregrinos** and then swings wide to the west before turning north towards Portugalete. This route spans 20km, but offers a convenient breaking point in **Barakaldo**, 12km from the Plaza de Unamuno (Albergue del Polideportivo de Gorostiza – donativo, 16 beds, open Jun-Sep, kitchen, tel 687 529 627).

GR-228 (Anillo Verde) variant

For those hoping to avoid the urban realm, this is your best shot. Backtrack along the camino from Plaza de Unamuno for 1.9km, watching for the red/white stripes marking a left turn onto Estrada Mendiarte, shortly before crossing the BI-631 expressway. The next 6.9km offers some of the most stunning views you can get of Bilbao, with the Guggenheim front and center, and it's nearly all off-pavement, following footpaths and dirt roads. It's also much more work, with considerably more ups and downs than the other options.

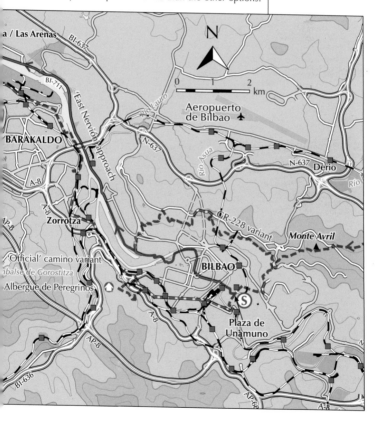

The GR brings you to Morgan Kalea and the **Akelarre Youth Hostel**, where you can join the East Nervión approach, described above. This route is 4.6km longer than the East Nervión.

From where the routes rejoin on Casilda Iturrizar Kalea in Portugalete, you can reach Portugalete's Albergue de Peregrinos by turning onto c/Martín Fernández Villarán and proceeding 200 meters. The albergue is in the polideportivo on the right.

PORTUGALETE (13.2KM)

All facilities. Last supermarket before Castro-Urdiales. Seasonal Albergue de Peregrinos in Polideportivo Zubi Alde (donativo, 30 beds, open Jun–Sep, c/Pedro Heredia, tel 944 729 320), Albergue Bide Ona (34 beds, €12, open all year except for Dec holidays, microwave, W/D, @, tel 946 038 630), Pensión la Guía (singles €22–30, doubles €32–40, free laundry, @, c/Virgen de la Guía 4, tel 944 837 530), Hostal Santa María (singles €25–36, doubles €30–42, c/Salcedo 1, tel 944 722 489).

Today Portugalete is a thriving suburb, with an active commercial center. First documented in 1249, but undoubtedly much older, Portugalete contains the remains of early walls and a tower. Its highlight is the **Basílica de Santa María**, built as Columbus set sail for the New World and then expanded over time. Although a prototypical Gothic building, the Renaissance is visible in the central altarpiece. The Santiago Chapel has a bold Santiago Matamoros.

Proceed uphill first along Casilda Iturrizar Kalea and then Avda de Carlos VII (enjoy the moving sidewalks!). Keep straight on out of town and over the A-8. After 2km, skirt the edge of the sprawling town of **Ortuella** (bars and restaurants off-route). Continue along a pedestrian/cyclist track, reaching Bar Luis after 2.3km. The track continues to wind gradually downhill to

PLAYA DE LA ARENA (10.8KM)

Bars/restaurants. Apartamentos La Arena (singles €35+, doubles €55+, triples €70+, kitchen, tel 946 365 454).

The Puente Colgante in Portugalete

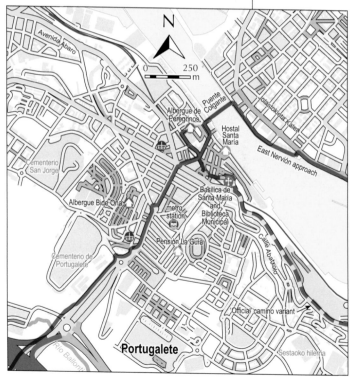

Turn left along the road, then through a beachside park. Alternatively, it is possible to disregard the waymarks and follow the beach. Regardless, keep straight on towards and across the pedestrian bridge. The camino splits after the bridge. Fork right up a flight of stairs to continue walking or continue straight for the albergue in

POBEÑA (1.2KM)

Bars/restaurants. **Albergue de Peregrinos** (donativo, 22 beds (+20 in summer), open 22 Apr–8 Oct, W/D, tel 609 031 526), **Apartamentos Mugarri** (doubles €60, kitchen, Plaza de Pobeña, tel 617 038 292).

STAGE 8
Pobeña to Castro-Urdiales

Start	Albergue de Peregrinos, Pobeña
Finish	Albergue de Peregrinos, Castro-Urdiales
Distance	16.7km
% unpaved	12.3%
Total ascent	390m
Total descent	372m
Terrain	3
Route-finding	4
Pilgrim accommodation	Ontón, Castro-Urdiales

This stage begins – following a surprisingly long flight of steps – with a stunning walk along the coastal hillside. A recreational path follows the trackbed of the former railroad that carried iron ore to waiting ships. Towards the path's end, you can still see the old *descargadero* (wharf), where the ships were loaded. Soon after, choose between two possible routes to Castro-Urdiales, either a direct approach that is half-highway and half-coastal footpath, or a longer trek along quiet roads.

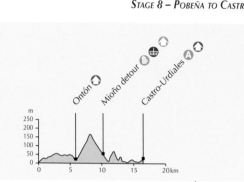

Backtrack to the waymarked steps and ascend. Follow the pedestrian track, offering impressive views. Shortly after a tunnel, curve inland, pass under the A-8, and descend to

ONTÓN (6KM)

Albergue Tu Camino (€6, 25 beds, open all year, breakfast available, kitchen, @, tel 645 985 269), Hotel El Haya is 2km before town, waymarked off the camino (meals available, tel 942 879 306).

Climb to N-634, where the route splits. We advise ignoring a waymarked left turn onto CA-523, instead continuing straight along N-634. After 4.2km, 500 meters before arriving in **Mioño** (bars, grocery store, and Hospedería Los Tres Caños – doubles €55–70, breakfast, tel 942 879 658), turn right onto a dirt road. Descend to the coast and follow a road around the beach before turning left uphill. ▸

Those who prefer to enter Mioño can rejoin here by following a minor road.

The ascent quickly pays dividends, as it flattens out and offers outstanding views. Finally join the beach promenade outside **Castro-Urdiales** and follow it directly to the center. The albergue is on the far side of town.

'Official' camino variant
From N-634 in Ontón, follow yellow arrows left onto CA-523. This route mixes highways, occasional dirt roads, and a long stretch along a paved cycling track, although there is little to see. From the fork, it proceeds: 1.2km to **Baltezana** (bars), 5.3km to the old train station of **Otañes** (the route does not enter the town proper), 2.4km to **Santullán**

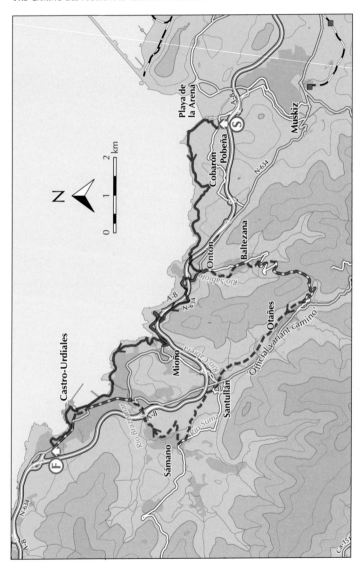

(bar, panaderia), 2.1km to **Sámano**, and 4.5km to the albergue in **Castro-Urdiales**. This route is 6.2km longer than the recommended approach.

The Iglesia de Santa María de la Asunción in Castro-Urdiales

The camino through Castro-Urdiales is poorly waymarked, with inconsistent old arrows and stickers. The simplest approach is to follow the promenade to the church and castle. Fork left uphill towards the **Iglesia de Santa María de la Asunción**. Descend to the other side of town and remain along the coast, continuing to the last beach. Fork left along the adjacent plaza, turn left at the end, and then left again on c/el Sable, leading towards the Plaza de Toros. The albergue is behind the bullring.

CASTRO-URDIALES (10.7KM)

All facilities. **Albergue de Peregrinos** (€5, 16 beds, kitchen, tel 620 608 118), **Pensión Ardigales 11** (singles €42–56, doubles €58–78, triples €75–98, meals available, @, c/Ardigales 11, tel 942 781 616), **Pensión La Mar** (singles €35–48, doubles €48–65, triples €65–80, c/la Mar 27, tel 942 870 524), **Hostéria Villa de Castro** (singles €35–45, doubles €50–65, triples €60–75, quads €70–95, kitchen, c/Los Huertos 2, tel 650 483 650).

A long-inhabited area, with human remains dating to 12000BC and a Roman milestone outside the Iglesia de Santa María. A Templar castle stood here, although little remains; its ruins serve as the lighthouse's base. The town suffered at the hands of the French in the Peninsular War.

The **Iglesia de Santa María de la Asunción** is a must-see. It holds a dominant position overlooking town and water. One of the Norte's finest Gothic churches, its exterior is spectacular, with buttresses flying in all directions. Strange iconography on the main entrance's frieze harkens back to Templar time, with rabbits kissing oxen, dragons eating serpents eating birds, and so on. Inside, a cross from the Battle of Las Navas de Tolosa – the turning point in the Reconquista – is on display (M–F 1000–1200 and 1600–1800, Sa 1000–1200).

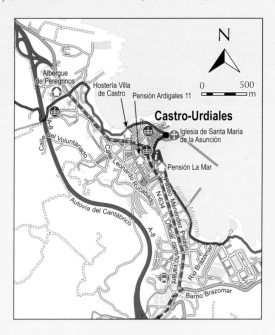

STAGE 9

Castro-Urdiales to Laredo

Start	Albergue de Peregrinos, Castro-Urdiales
Finish	Plaza Capuchín, Laredo
Distance	30.9km
% unpaved	24.8%
Total ascent	652m
Total descent	671m
Terrain	3
Route-finding	4
Pilgrim accommodation	Islares, El Pontarrón de Guriezo, Liendo/ Hazas, Laredo

For those with the time and energy, today's longer route offers some of the greatest variety of the Norte's first half. From Castro-Urdiales to Islares, the route meanders along gentle hills with sweeping coastal vistas. After a short and unavoidable stretch along N-634, the route turns inland, and the sea is replaced by craggy hilltops and wide green valleys. It is terrain that simultaneously uplifts and makes one feel very small! Finally, the route rises back out of the valley of Liendo, before depositing tired walkers on Laredo's sandy beach. A highway variant offers walkers a more direct alternative.

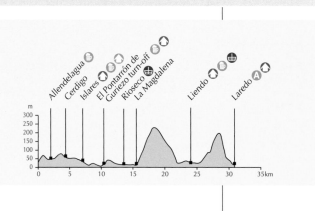

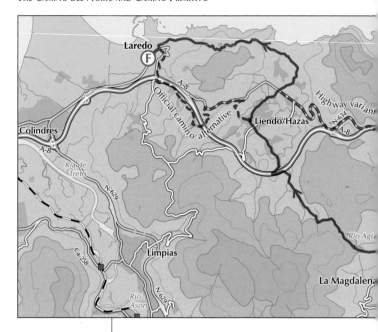

Proceed inland, following a minor road through **Allendelagua** (bar) and **Cerdigo**. Transition to a footpath leading through excellent coastal terrain to

ISLARES (7.2KM)

Bar/restaurant. **Albergue de Peregrinos** is closed for 'bureaucratic' reasons. **Camping Playa Arenillas** offers beds to pilgrims (€10, restaurant and grocery, tel 942 863 152), **Hotel Arenillas** (singles €30–35, doubles €45–55, located on the highway, tel 942 860 766).

Here are the 16th-century **Iglesia de San Martín** and the ruins of the 16th-century **Hospital de la Vera Cruz**.

Walk to the end of Islares then follow N-634 to **El Pontarrón de Guriezo**. Before town, but immediately after passing under the A-8, the camino splits.

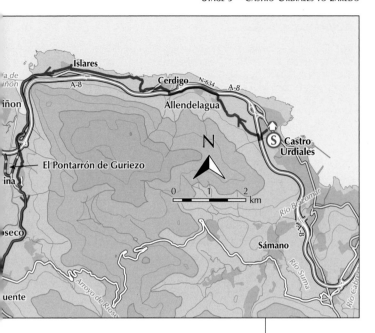

The waymarked route forks left uphill. Follow minor roads into **Rioseco** (bar, supermarket, Posada Fernanda – singles €29–32, doubles €41–45, includes breakfast, tel 942 850 315). Continue along flat roads through **El Puente** and **La Magdalena**. ▶ Turn right, soon transitioning to dirt roads, which lead most of the way to **Liendo**, where the albergue is immediately after the church.

Highway variant
From the fork after the A-8, continue on N-634 into **El Pontarrón de Guriezo**, which has a bar and **Albergue de Peregrinos** (donativo, 14 beds, key from bar, tel 942 850 061). Continue on N-634 for 6.4km. Upon reaching CA-501, turn left and proceed 1.2km to enter **Liendo**, making this route 4.7km shorter than the recommended approach. Alternately, it is possible to bypass Liendo, turning right on CA-501 and continuing directly to Laredo, shaving an additional 2.4km from this stage.

Online reports indicate that the waymarked route now bypasses La Magdalena, saving 2.7km, but we can't confirm this.

LIENDO/HAZAS (16.4KM)

Bars, restaurants, supermarket. **Albergue de Peregrinos** (€8, 16 beds, open all year, kitchen, W/D included, tel 682 074 723), **Posada La Torre de la Quintana** (doubles €68–86, open Mar–Oct and Dec, Barrio de Hazas 25, tel 942 677 439).

This is a sprawling community set in a valley where dense fog is common in the morning.

The 'official' camino from Liendo to Laredo, via Tarrueza, is waymarked (continuing straight past the church in Liendo) and 1.2km shorter, but entirely paved and a much-inferior walk.

Leaving Liendo, those following the recommended approach will turn right at the church, fork left, and then keep straight on. Cross N-634 and fork right, then left. This becomes a footpath, leading above Laredo and offering excellent views, before descending into the town's compact historic core. ◀ Turn left on c/Santa María (Iglesia de Santa María on your right), then right on c/Emperador, and proceed directly into the Plaza Capuchín in

LAREDO (7.2KM)

All facilities. Two **Albergue Privados** open all year: **El Buen Pastor** (€13, 20 beds, kitchen, c/Fuente Fresnedo 1, tel 942 606 288) and **Casa de la Trinidad** (€10, 23 beds, kitchen, c/San Francisco 24, tel 942 606 141). **Hotel El Cortijo** (singles €40–52, doubles €62–68, c/González Gallego 3, tel 942 605 600), **Hostal Ramona** (singles €20, doubles €30, open mid-Mar–Nov, pilgrim discounts, free laundry, @, c/Alameda de España 4, tel 942 607 189).

An important Roman site, known as Portus Luliobrigensium, and the location of a naval clash with the Celtiberians. The town grew around the Monastery of San Martín, receiving its charter and walls from Alfonso VIII. Allison Peers noted in 1928 that the church featured the following sign in three different locations: 'It is forbidden to spit in the House of God.' Today, it is Cantabria's biggest resort town. The 13th-century **Iglesia de Santa María de la Asunción** features five naves. A gift from Charles V, two eagle-shaped lecterns, is on display.

The coastal approach to Laredo

The next stage involves taking the Laredo–Santoña ferry, which makes its first run at 0900. Early risers might prefer sleeping in Santoña (see Stage 10). The boat shuts down entirely in the winter, during which pilgrims must either follow the interior route or take a local bus (the A3 or A4) around the bay.

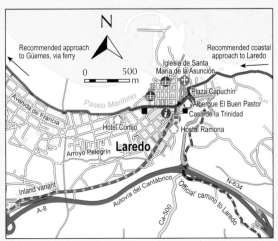

97

STAGE 10
Laredo to Güemes

Start	Plaza Capuchín, Laredo
Finish	Albergue La Cabaña del Abuelo Peuto, Güemes
Distance	28.5km
% unpaved	12.3%
Total ascent	426m
Total descent	350m
Terrain	1
Route-finding	3
Pilgrim accommodation	Santoña, Colindres, Gama, San Miguel de Meruelo, Güemes

Start your morning on the beach in Laredo before catching the ferry across to Santoña. After a short walk through town, return to the coast for one of the Norte's nicest stretches, crossing the Playa de Berria, cutting over the scrub-covered hill, and then continuing across yet another beach, the Playa de Trengandín. The second half of the day moves from sand to pavement, following quiet country roads to Güemes's wonderful albergue. Alternatively, pilgrims can consider an inland variant, bypassing the ferry and the coast.

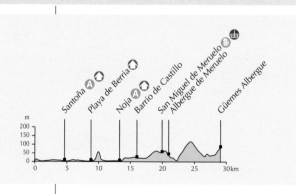

In Laredo's Plaza Capuchín, the camino splits. ▸ We recommend continuing straight across Plaza Capuchín on c/de López Seña, then joining the beach promenade. At the peninsula's end, follow signs to the **Laredo-Santoña ferry** (€2, Jul–Sep every 10min 0900–2000, May/Jun/Oct 0900–1800, Mar–Apr and Nov–early Dec 0900–1400, closed 12 Dec–Feb, tel 675 874 742). The boat pulls up to the beach, close to a small shelter, and takes you to

The inland variant is summarized at the end of the stage. Look for small blue waymark stickers through town.

SANTOÑA (4.8KM)

All facilities. Albergue La Bilbaina (€20, 40 beds, includes breakfast, W/D, @, Plaza San Antonio, tel 942 661 952), Albergue Juvenil de Santoña (€7.50, 68 beds, meals available, W/D, @, Crta Santoña-Cicero, tel 942 662 008), Hospedaje La Tortuga (singles €48–70, doubles €65–108, closed Jan, c/Juan de la Cosa 39, tel 942 683 035).

Santoña is another town with medieval, monastic origins, although only the **Iglesia de Santa María del Puerto** remains. Columbus's *Santa María* was built here, and the town was also the home of his second trip's cartographer, Juan de la Cosa. Towards the quay's end, a large fort remains from the Peninsular War.

Continue straight from Santoña's dock, first along c/Santander, then c/Cervantes, and finally c/Sanjurjo. Join CA-907, pass the prison, and then proceed to the end of **Playa de Berria** (Hostal Berria – singles €37–49, doubles €59–69, tel 942 660 847); turn right onto the beach. Alternatively, take the second right after the prison and join the beach sooner.

At the end of the beach, climb the **Punta del Brusco**. ▸ Another impressive beach awaits; spend up to 1km walking along it before joining the adjacent road, following this into the center of

This is a steep ascent and can be quite difficult in inclement weather; if you find conditions unsafe, you can bypass it by remaining on CA-907, turning right on CA-141 and right again on CA-147, which will return you to the coast.

NOJA (8.7KM)

All facilities. Albergue Noja Aventura (€10, 94 beds, open all year, kitchen, W/D, tel 609 043 397) located near the beach before town, Hotel Las Olas (doubles €75–140, Playa Trengandin 4, tel 942 630 036), Hostería Los Laureles (doubles €58–85, c/Las Viñas 14, tel 942 630 000).

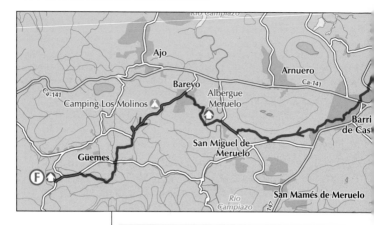

Noja is a modern beach town with many restaurants, great views, and a pleasant central plaza.

It is possible to follow the coast entirely from Noja to Galizano on the Senda del Litoral, bypassing Güemes, though we haven't scouted this. A new Albergue de Peregrinos in Isla/Arnuero (donativo, 28 beds, open all year, communal meals, kitchen, W/D, tel 658 547 270) offers an overnight stop.

Ascend the main road, passing many bars and restaurants. ◄ Turn left at the first major intersection. Pass the church and curve right through the roundabout, around the turismo. Fork left, then right, and then take a soft left. Arrows improve in frequency and reliability from here, although the route remains primarily roadbound. Rural roads lead to **Barrio de Castillo**, where the two routes reunite, and then continue to **San Miguel de Meruelo**.

Inland variant

This option avoids the ferry and has two albergues. Unfortunately, it is almost entirely on highways, not scenic, and longer. From the Plaza Capuchín in Laredo, follow N-634 4.2km to **Colindres**, which has all facilities (Hospederia El Puerto – singles €35, doubles €55, c/del Mar 29, tel 942 650 828 and Albergue de Peregrinos – €5, 18 beds, c/Heliodoro Fernández, tel 942 674 000). Keep straight on along N-634 and then follow yellow arrows 2.4km to **Adal-Treto** (bar, Hotel Las Ruedas – singles €45–55, doubles €55–65, tel 942 674 422), 2.1km to **Cicero**, and an additional 5.4km to **Gama** (bars, a supermarket, and Albergue de Peregrinos – €4, 12 beds, key from Bar Los Yugos, tel 942 642 065).

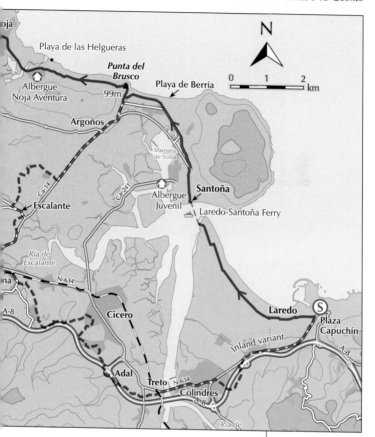

Take **CA-148** for 2km to **Escalante** (all facilities), and then CA-450 for 4.6km to **Argoños** (bars, grocery, Hostal Argoños – singles €30–44, doubles €35–55, breakfast available, tel 942 626 015), rejoining the coastal route soon thereafter, at the end of Playa de Berria. This route is 13km longer than the coastal option, although it's possible to shorten it considerably by following CA-450 for 4km out of Escalante, crossing CA-147, and rejoining the camino in Barrio de Castillo.

Albergue de Meruelo

SAN MIGUEL DE MERUELO (6.5KM)

Bars and grocery store located off-route.

After passing the **Iglesia de San Miguel**, proceed down-hill and join CA-454, turning left at town's end. Descend to the Puente de Solorga and arrive soon after, 1.5km from San Miguel's center, at the **Albergue de Meruelo** (€12–15, 36 beds, meals available, W/D, @, open mid Mar–Oct (closed indefinitely), tel 699 486 444). Keep straight on into **Bareyo**, fork right through town, then left onto CA-447 towards **Camping Los Molinos** (bar/grocery). Follow a series of minor roads and highways to

GÜEMES ALBERGUE (8.5KM)

Albergue La Cabaña del Abuelo Peuto offers excellent hospitality (donativo, 85 beds, communal meals, W/D, @, tel 942 621 122). The hospitalero, Ernesto Bustio, is fascinating and generous, and the community has joined with him to care for pilgrims and other wanderers. Posada Rural Valle de Güemes (doubles €33–50, open all year, laundry service, meals available, @, tel 609 480 553).

STAGE 11

Güemes to Santander

Start	Albergue La Cabaña del Abuelo Peuto, Güemes
Finish	Albergue de Peregrinos, Santander
Distance	14.8km
% unpaved	52.7%
Total ascent	189m
Total descent	248m
Terrain	1
Route-finding	2
Pilgrim accommodation	Santander

Arrival in major cities generally presents a problem on pilgrimage, as industrial sprawl and unconstrained urban growth combine to produce unpleasant walking conditions that can span many kilometers. Santander offers a rare, enjoyable exception. From Güemes, the camino leads straight to the coast, where a footpath parallels the cliff's edge, eventually delivering you straight into Somo. From there, the ferry takes you the rest of the way, offering a refreshing capstone. Pilgrims seeking a more direct route can bypass the coast and follow the highway from Galizano to Somo.

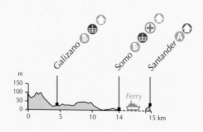

It's all highway to start: follow CA-443 for 3.5km, turn left on CA-141, and then right on CA-440, leading into

GALIZANO (4.5KM)

Bar and grocery. Posada El Solar (doubles €75–115, meals, tel 942 505 292), Hotel La Vijanera (doubles €55–77, includes breakfast, c/La Canal 1, tel 942 505 373).

A pilgrim hospital was documented here in 1620.

Alternatively, it's possible to take the old route to Somo, continuing straight on CA-440, returning to CA-141 and then following it onward. It's 2.6km shorter, but not scenic at all.

From Galizano, turn right onto CA-441, to arrive on the coast after 1km. ◄ From there, follow dirt roads and minor footpaths – as well as a long stretch on the beach – along the coastline all the way to Somo, enjoying incredible views. As you approach Somo, leave the beach past a bar and proceed inland along c/de las Quebrantas. Turn right on Avda Trasmiera and then fork right on c/Peñas Blancas. Turn left at the waterfront; the ferry dock is on your right.

SOMO (9.5KM)

Bars, restaurants, and grocery stores. Hotel Alemar (doubles €40+, c/Reguril 44, tel 942 510 601), Hotel Las Dunas (singles €40–60, doubles €50–80, Avda las Quebrantas 5, tel 942 510 040), Hostal Meve Mar (singles €30, doubles €45, c/La Fuente 2, tel 942 510 279), Hotel Pinar Somo (singles €25–40, doubles €45–60, triples/quads, pilgrim discount, surfing classes, tel 942 510 615).

A comfortable port town, Somo is great for a quiet break before bustling Santander.

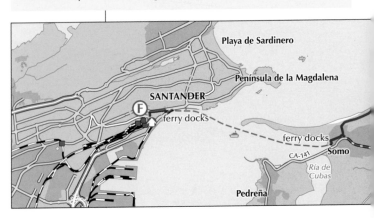

Take the ferry to Santander, which costs €2.80 (Mon–Fri runs every half-hour 0820–1955, weekends hourly 0955–1955). From Santander's dock, turn left along the waterfront, watching for waymarks in the sidewalk. Turn right, crossing through the Jardines de Pereda, then turn left on the other side. Turn left on c/Rúa Mayor (a complicated intersection with two possible left turns – this is the second). The albergue is on your left.

SANTANDER (0.8KM)

Albergue de Peregrinos Santos Martires (€12, 40 beds, kitchen, W/D, open 1500, credenciáles, c/Ruamayor 9-11, tel 942 219 747). Three hostels: **Santander Central Hostel** (€21–29, 40 beds, open Mar–Oct, kitchen, @, c/Calderón de la Barca 4, tel 942 377 540), **Hostel Santander** (€19–29, 20 beds, open all year, W/D, Paseo de Pareda 15, tel 942 223 986), **Hostel Allegro** (€21–25, 20 beds, includes breakfast, open all year, kitchen, @, c/Alta 42, tel 679 484 589). **Plaza Pombo B&B** (doubles €35–80, triples €65–95, includes breakfast, c/Hernan Cortes 25, tel 942 212 950), **Hospedaje Magallenes** (singles €29–49, doubles €39–69, c/Magallenes 22, tel 942 371 421), **Pensión Plaza** (singles €32–40, doubles €43–64, triples €60–76, c/Cádiz 13, tel 942 212 967), **Hostal Cabo Mayor** (singles €35–65, doubles €45–65, c/Cadíz 1, tel 942 211 181), **Hostal del Carmen** (singles €29–39, doubles €39–55, triples €57–75, c/San Fernando 48, tel 942 230 190).

Santander is the third major city on the Camino del Norte and the capital of Cantabria. Founded by Romans, it became a major medieval port, exporting wine,

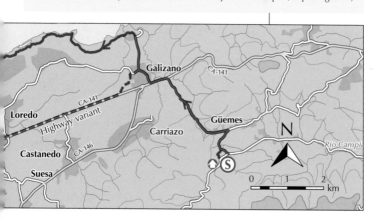

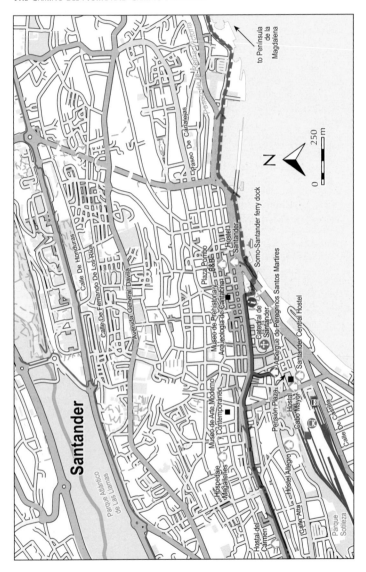

olives, fish, and wool. It emerged as an important Catholic destination, as pilgrims gained indulgences by visiting the relics of Saints Emeterio and Celedonio. Like San Sebastián, Santander gained prominence for beached royalty – in this case, Queen Isabel II chose to summer here in the 1860s, hoping the sea air would improve her health. After World War I, it became *the* fashionable summer spot for Madrileños.

Santander knows disasters. In 1893, a ship full of dynamite exploded in the harbor, killing 500 and destroying the surrounding area. A fire broke out in 1941, starting in the Archbishop's Palace and consuming much of the old center. The result is a modern waterfront, certainly enjoyable but perhaps lacking in atmosphere. Most vacationers and locals make a beeline for the Sardinero district, which features two excellent beaches and the Belle Epoque casino.

The **Catédral de Santander** comprises two 13th-century Gothic churches (Mon–Fri 1000–1300 and 1600–1930, Sat 1000–1300 and 1630–2000, Sun 0800–1400 and 1700–2000). The upper church has a 14th-century cloister that was rebuilt after the 1941 fire. The lower church of El Santísimo Cristo serves as the crypt and contains the original furnace box that held the patron saints' skulls. They have since been encased in silver and are now carried in festival processions. A glass floor covers Roman remains. The **Museo de Prehistoria y Arqueologia de Cantabria** holds a collection of prehistoric artifacts. The highlights are copies of regional cave paintings and a small collection of Roman *stellae* (€5, Tue–Sat 1000–1400 and 1700–2000, closes earlier in off-season). In addition, the **Museo de Arte Moderno y Contemporáneo (MAS)** houses a collection of European art from the last five centuries, headlined by Goya's portrait of King Fernando VII (reopening in 2019).

The cloister in Santander's cathedral

STAGE 12
Santander to Santillana del Mar

Start	Albergue de Peregrinos, Santander
Finish	Albergue Municipal, Santillana del Mar
Distance	30.9km
% unpaved	1%
Total ascent	449m
Total descent	377m
Terrain	1
Route-finding	5
Pilgrim accommodation	Santa Cruz de Bezana, Boo de Piélagos, Requejada, Santillana del Mar

While the walk into Santander is lovely, the same cannot be said of the exit. Indeed, this is one of the drearier legs of the Camino del Norte – flat, paved, and with little to see. Two significant shortcuts are recommended, cutting unnecessary kilometers from the official route, in order to reach Santillana del Mar sooner. Santillana's perfect medieval center and nearby prehistoric cave art make the trek well worthwhile. Those with plenty of time can consider an unmarked, coastal alternative between Santander and Boo (see the end of this stage).

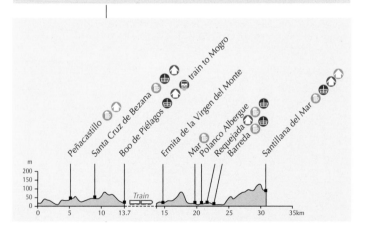

Backtrack to c/de Calvo Sotelo and turn left. The route generally proceeds in a straight line out of town, with this road becoming N-611. After 5.1km, arrive in **Peñacastillo** (bar, Hotel San Millán – singles €30–40, doubles €40–50, tel 942 345 677) and turn right. Cross the railroad, turn left, and soon after join CA-301, which leads into

SANTA CRUZ DE BEZANA (9KM)

Bar, grocery. **Albergue La Santa Cruz** (donativo, 14 beds, open all year, confirm in off-season, communal meals, located across expressway at Avda Cruz 22, tel 659 178 806), **Albergue Nimon** (€15, 10 beds, open Mar–Oct, includes breakfast, kitchen, c/Ramón Ramírez 2, key from Cafetería Nimon, tel 635 451 714), **Hotel Alcamino** (offers a pilgrim special: room, dinner, and breakfast for €43–59, soon after town, tel 942 765 976).

The **Iglesia de Santa Cruz** is worth a quick visit, if open.

▸ The camino follows a series of minor roads, continuing straight on Avda de la Mompia, turning left on Avda de los Condes, crossing the railroad, and then forking right through a major roundabout onto CA-304. Fork right again, re-cross the railroad, and arrive at the train station in

BOO DE PIÉLAGOS (4.7KM)

Grocery, FEVE station. **Albergue Piedad** (€12, 16 beds, one double for €30, breakfast and W/D included, kitchen, @, tel 680 620 073), **Hostería de Boo** (pilgrim discounts, Barrio San José 1, tel 942 586 231).

The next section poses a dilemma. The nearby Ría de Mogro, looming just past Boo, was traditionally a minor concern for pilgrims. A ferry shuttled walkers across, and while boat operators were irreputable fellows, no unnecessary kilometers were added. Today, though, the ferry is long gone.

For many years, modern pilgrims simply walked across the railroad bridge. Whereas five years ago this was encouraged by locals, it is now actively discouraged and we can't recommend it. Beyond the safety concern, bridge-crossers may be fined by the police. Those rejecting all advice to the contrary will follow the camino out of Boo, proceeding

Online reports indicate that the 'official' camino now deviates southward, bypassing Boo and proceeding through Arce and Oruña before rejoining the 'old-old' (two permutations back) camino in Mar. We cannot recommend this approach yet and note that it is 6.2km longer than our suggested route.

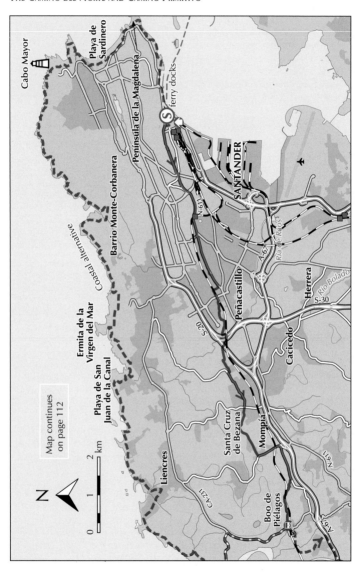

Cabo Mayor

Playa de Sardinero

Peninsula de la Magdalena

ferry docks

SANTANDER

Barrio Monte-Corbanera

Coastal alternative

Ermita de la Virgen del Mar

Playa de San Juan de la Canal

Peñacastillo

Herrera

Cacicedo

Liencres

Santa Cruz de Bezana

Mompia

Boo de Piélagos

Map continues on page 112

N

km

0 1 2

Albergue La Santa Cruz

along a minor road parallel to the railroad. As the road curves left, away from the tracks, transfer to the railroad. From here, carefully follow the tracks across the bridge, arriving at Mogro station. Leaving Mogro station, yellow arrows immediately reappear, calling for a left turn on CA-232, and then forking right on CA-322 uphill to the **Ermita de la Virgen del Monte**. This route spans 1.5km.

Instead, most pilgrims now take the train from Boo to **Mogro**, and we advise this approach. Trains run every half-hour on weekdays and hourly on weekends, and the journey just takes two minutes. Pilgrims will then follow the route above 700m to the ermita.

Pilgrims who must walk every step can follow the 'official' camino south from Boo towards **Puente Arce**, following suburban roads, before turning back north on the other side of the river and giving back all of the distance just earned. The 16th-century bridge (6.1km from Boo) and surrounding neighborhoods are pleasant, with bar/restaurants and a supermarket available, but all told, the walk is a frustrating 9.1km to **Ermita de la Virgen del Monte**, near Mogro, where the two routes converge.

From the ermita, you once again have options. The 'official' camino turns right from the ermita, but an older route continues directly along the road and is considerably shorter.

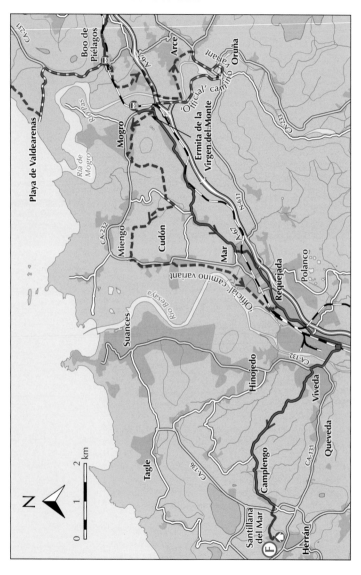

'Old' camino route

We recommend disregarding the waymarks and continuing straight on CA-322, past the ermita. Formerly the waymarked camino, the old yellow arrows have been systematically covered with gray paint. Nonetheless, the arrows are unnecessary, as the route follows the highway directly to **Mar** (bar). At that point, arrows reappear. Turn left at the main intersection. Soon after, join N-611, walking past Polanco's albergue and then arriving in **Requejada,** rejoining the other route.

'Official' camino variant

Follow yellow arrows leading directly away from the ermita along a single-lane road into **Mogro** and then over small hills towards the Río Saja Besaya. Pass through **Cudón** (bar, Posada La Victoria – doubles €65–95, includes breakfast, c/ Mies de Abajo 40, tel 942 577 723) and then join the pipeline trail. Turn left uphill, cross the railroad, and proceed into Requejada. This route is 4.1km longer than the 'old' camino route.

REQUEJADA (7.8KM)

Bars, grocery, bakery. **Albergue de Peregrinos Clara Campoamor** (€5, 12 beds, open all year, keys from Bar El Puerto, tel 942 082 416), **Albergue Regato de las Anguilas** in neighboring Polanco (€5, 6 beds, keys from nearby house).

Follow N-611 to

BARREDA (1.3KM)

Bars, supermarket.

Saint Francis is said to have stayed in the House of Calderón on his rumored pilgrimage to Santiago.

Continue straight through Barreda, then turn right and cross the railroad and river, before forking right through a roundabout in **Viveda**. Follow CA-340 through gentle hills, then turn right on a minor road leading into Santillana del Mar. After passing the church, turn left into the Museo Jesús Otero; the albergue is located behind it.

SANTILLANA DEL MAR (8.1KM)

Bars, restaurants, grocery store. **Albergue Municipal Jesús Otero** (€6, 16 beds, open 1600, tel 942 840 198), **Albergue El Convento** (€12–16, 36 beds, open 1200 year-round, includes breakfast, @, c/Antonio Niceas 2, tel 680 594 138), **Casona Solar de Hidalgos** (bed €10–15, singles €25–44, doubles €30–55, Plaza de Santo Domingo 5, tel 942 818 387), **Camping Santillana** (€10, restaurant and grocery, W/D, has bungalows for pilgrims, located after town, tel 942 818 250), **Hospedaje Santillana** (singles €30–60, doubles €40–70, c/Los Hornos 14, tel 942 818 803), **Casa del Organista** (singles €49, doubles €60, closed mid Dec–mid Jan, W/D, @, c/Los Hornos 4, tel 942 840 352).

One of the most picturesque stopping points on the Camino del Norte is this wonderfully preserved medieval village – all cut rock and tourist kiosks. In the Middle Ages, Santillana experienced great success thanks to wool and linen production, making nobles out of its residents. It has since enjoyed a string of celebrity residents and visitors, including the Marqués de Santillana, the Archduchess of Austria, and even Jean-Paul Sartre, who called it the most beautiful village in Spain. It also gained acclaim as picaresque hero Gil Blas's home. Its transformation into a popular tourist stop is quite recent. Only 40 years ago cows filled the ground floor of local homes; now souvenir shops have taken their place.

The 12th-century **Colegiata de Santa Juliana** is a must-see (€3, Tue–Sun 1000–1330 and 1600–1930, reduced hours in off-season). The cloisters are spectacular, finely crafted Romanesque works. One section even has preserved its paint. The impressive capitals depict biblical and hunting scenes. Inside the church, highlights include the altar made of Mexican silver and the sepulcher of Saint Juliana, who was martyred by Diocletian and whose remains have been protected in Santillana since the sixth century. That said, the church's back wall does not inspire a great deal of confidence.

The famous **Cueva de Altamira**, a UNESCO World Heritage site featuring Paleolithic cave art, is located 2km from the center. The real cave is closed to tourists, but a near-perfect replica has been built to host visitors. It is well worth a visit, but reservations are necessary (€3, Tue–Sat 0930–2000; Sun 0930–1500, shorter hours in off-season).

Coastal alternative between Santander and Boo
Those hoping for a more scenic approach have an excellent alternative, but it's much, much longer and completely without waymarks. Proceed east from the ferry dock in Santander and wrap around the city's coastline for 4.7km, cutting inland to nip across the Magdalena peninsula and then skirting **Playa de Sardinero**. Leaving the city, the route winds

around the Mataleñas golf course (1.1km), the **Cabo Mayor lighthouse** (1.3km, bar/restaurant), and a football pitch (1.1km), ultimately emerging in sparsely-settled, open terrain, following footpaths right along the ocean's edge. 9.3km later, arrive at the Playa de la Virgen del Mar, a good spot for a break with the imperial-chique Bambara Tavern, Camping Virgen del Mar (grocery), and the **Ermita de la Virgen del Mar**, which has an enviable location. Another good option for a rest is just 2.1km further, at the **Playa de San Juan de la Canal** (bars/restaurants, Posada La Morena – doubles €60–90, tel 942 588 041, tel 676 888 446, Hospedaje Costa San Juan – doubles, bungalows, tel 942 579 580).

Santillana del Mar's Colegiata de Santa Juliana

Climb the hill at the end of the beach – some of the best views of the walk are just ahead! The cliffside walk leads you past the Covachos and Arnía beaches, before jutting inland to the most complicated wayfinding part of the walk, as it passes along the edge of **Liencres** (4.2km). After descending from the cliff, follow the road uphill from the Portio beach, turning right soon after the road curves left. Turn left at a T-junction, away from the coast. At the next T, turn right. ▸ Follow this road until just before the coast, turning left down a street lined with beach houses, which quickly becomes a dirt track. Continue along the coastline for 4.6km to reach the large parking lot for the **Playa de Valdearenas** (bar, toilets, fountain at main entrance to parking lot). Follow the road away from the beach (pedestrian footpath running parallel) and then turn right on CA-231, which leads directly to **Boo**. All told, this walk spans 31.7km.

To reach the center of Liencres (all facilities, Hotel Calas de Liencres – singles €40–65, doubles €60–90, tel 942 588 093), turn left instead.

STAGE 13
Santillana del Mar to Comillas

Start	Albergue Municipal, Santillana del Mar
Finish	Albergue de Peregrinos, Comillas
Distance	22.5km
% unpaved	14.2%
Total ascent	448m
Total descent	499m
Terrain	3
Route-finding	2
Pilgrim accommodation	Caborredondo, Cóbreces, Comillas

While you will rarely escape pavement today, there is much to enjoy. Grassy fields yield sprawling vistas, broken periodically by church towers. San Martín de Cigüenza is a pleasant surprise – a small town with a stunning church and peaceful river. The next stop, Cóbreces, lights up with color, a true novelty after so many stone buildings. Finally, Comillas signals your return to the coast, and features some of the most impressive architecture on the Camino del Norte.

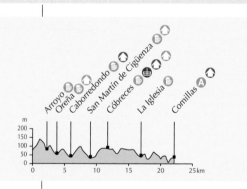

Turn left from the albergue, turn right on c/las Lindas, then fork right out of Plaza de Ramón Pelayo on c/Hornos. The route transitions from paved roads to dirt tracks, taking you past **Camping Santillana** and then three small towns: **Arroyo**

(bar), **Oreña** (bar, Hospedaje Oreña – doubles €35–50, triples €45–65, includes breakfast, tel 655 943 983, Posada La Aldea – doubles €40–60, includes breakfast, tel 942 716 091), and **Caborredondo** (bar, Albergue de Peregrinos Izarra – €6, 20 beds, open Mar–Oct, kitchen, W/D, tel 628 428 167). Keep straight on CA-920 through town, cross CA-131, and fork right on a country road. Descend into

SAN MARTÍN DE CIGÜENZA (9.1KM)

Bar. Posada Cigüenza (doubles €50–70, tel 942 890 759).

The 18th-century **Iglesia de San Martín de Tours** features a baroque façade, comprised of two massive symmetrical towers flanking a central arch.

Leaving Cigüenza, rejoin CA-353 and follow it to the edge of Cóbreces near Albergue El Pino. From here, the camino splits, allowing you to: 1) continue on the highway, passing Albergue Viejo Lucas before arriving at the church, or 2) turn right onto a minor road through the hills. The routes are equidistant – 900 meters – and reunite at the church in

CÓBRECES (3KM)

Bar, grocery, bakery. Albergue de Peregrinos (€5, 30 beds, open all year, in the Cistercian Abbey, tel 942 725 017), Albergue El Pino (€15, 12 beds, open mid Mar–Oct, includes breakfast, kitchen, @, tel 620 437 962), Albergue Viejo Lucas (€14, 158 beds, singles €20, doubles €34, triples €48, open Mar–Nov, includes breakfast, free W/D, @, tel 625 483 596), Posada Las Mañanitas (singles €32+, doubles €45+, triples/quads, c/Antoñan 88, tel 942 725 238). Towards the beach: Pensión Bellavista (doubles €45–65, triples €55–75, tel 942 725 221), Hotel Sanmar (singles €40–65, doubles €50–85, includes breakfast, @, tel 659 381 972).

A comfortable stop (with far more albergue beds than Comillas), dominated by two large, pastel-colored buildings – the red **Iglesia de San Pedro Advíncula** and sky-blue **Abadía Cisterciense de Viaceli**. The former is a striking neo-Gothic structure with two prominent towers and an octagonal dome. A monument to pilgrims stands behind it. The abbey, one of Spain's first concrete buildings, is distinctive for its rows of pointed windows. Those staying in the abbey's albergue are invited to vespers.

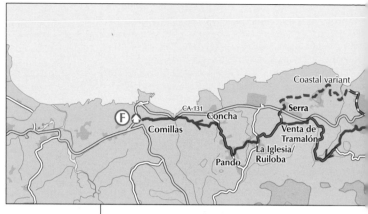

The Abadía Cisterciense de Viaceli in Cóbreces

From the church of Cóbreces, you once again have two options, roughly equal in length. We prefer the inland approach, which passes behind the church and includes some medieval tracks – a very pleasant and shady jaunt into **Venta de Tramalón** (bar). In Venta, briefly join CA-131 before promptly forking left onto a dirt road leading to a cemetery; turn onto a paved pedestrian track and

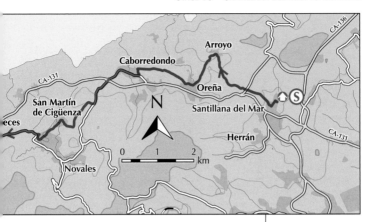

reunite with the other route. ▶ Continue past Camping El Helguero (**bar**) and proceed into **La Iglesia/Ruiloba** (**bars**). Keep straight on towards the monastery of **Pando** and the village of **Concha**. Leaving Concha, the minor road soon becomes a dirt track, ultimately joining CA-131 outside of Comillas. Turn left onto c/Calvo Sotelo and proceed into the center; turn right at the T-junction to proceed uphill for the albergue.

COMILLAS (10.4KM)

All facilities. **Albergue de Peregrinos** (€5, 20 beds, open Apr–mid Sep, kitchen, c/Barrio la Peña, tel 942 720 033), **Hotel Solatorre** (doubles €40, triples €55, quads €70, @, tel 942 722 480), **Pensión La Aldea** (doubles €40–50, c/La Aldea 5, tel 622 244 323), **Hostal Esmeralda** (singles €40–60, doubles €50–80, c/ Antonio López 7, tel 942 720 097).

Comillas boomed in the 19th century when the Barcelonan aristocracy started summering here – and brought their architects along. The local shipping magnate, Antonio López, made a fortune from the Cuban slave trade, bought the title of Marquis de Comillas, and married the daughter of Barcelona's richest man. With

For the coastal variant, descend CA-353, turn left briefly on CA-131, then turn right soon after. Once at the beach, follow a pedestrian walkway to a parking lot, then join a road leading inland. Turn right on CA-131 in Serra and then left immediately after, soon rejoining the other route at a cemetery.

money to burn, the marquis became Antoní Gaudí's primary patron, and Gaudí left his mark in Comillas.

The **Capricho de Gaudí** was entirely his own creation. Built as the marquis's summerhouse, it is a stunning combination of iron, brick, and ceramic, displaying Spanish and Arabic influences. Sunflowers are prominent on this surrealist structure. Gaudí assisted with the general design and furnishings of the **Palacio de Sobrellano**, which is more properly attributed to Joan Mortorell. An impressive neo-Gothic building, this dominates the left hill as you follow the camino out of town. The interior is considered even finer than the exterior, particularly the grand salon. Regular tours run daily (€3). Gaudí also contributed to the **Capilla-Pantéon**, which holds the crypts of the marquis's two sons.

Opposite the Palacio de Sobrellano is the equally impressive **Seminario Pontificio**, which was founded in 1883 for the training of priests and acclaimed for its music school and choir. Sadly, it has remained vacant since 1964, when the papal university was moved to Madrid. Check out the gargoyles carved over the main stairway.

Although easily reached today, Comillas long enjoyed its isolation. Its residents reveled in that timelessness, noting: 'Comillas will be Comillas / For ever and ever. Amen.'

STAGE 14
Comillas to Colombres

Start	Albergue de Peregrinos, Comillas
Finish	Plaza Ibáñez y Posada, Colombres
Distance	28.9km
% unpaved	12.5%
Total ascent	620m
Total descent	537m
Terrain	3
Route-finding	2
Pilgrim accommodation	Serdio, Unquera/Bustio, Colombres

The last stage in Cantabria brings with it a day of great variety, with some notably different architectural styles, small villages and a larger town (San Vicente de la Barquera), several river crossings and a great beach section. Arrival in Colombres marks your entry into Asturias, a region that feels a little more rugged and wild than the others on this route. Pilgrim-specific accommodation is more limited tonight, especially in the summer, so plan ahead.

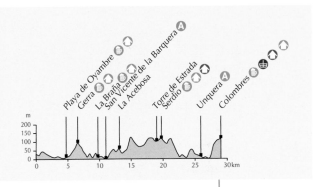

Keep straight on CA-135, which soon merges with CA-131, passing most of Comillas's great sights on the way. Cross the Ría de la Rabia and Río Capitan, turning right immediately after (very limited waymarks) toward

PLAYA DE OYAMBRE (4.9KM)

Bar. **Hotel Pájaro Amarillo** (doubles €55, breakfast available, tel 942 720 917).

Keep straight on to **Gerra** (bar, **Pensión Oyambre** – doubles €20–40, quads €47–58, tel 942 746 082) and **Playa de Merón**. Climb uphill, then fork right downhill into the beach town of **La Braña** (**Hotel Don Ramón** – singles €40+, doubles €50+, tel 942 712 426). ▸ Follow CA-364 along the river inland, then join N-634 and cross the Ría de San Vicente and cross the bridge into

It is also possible to join the beach in Merón and follow this directly to La Braña.

SAN VICENTE DE LA BARQUERA (6.7KM)

All facilities, but the albergue is now closed. **Pensión Liebana** (doubles €30–45, closed 28 Jan–9 Mar, @, c/Ronda 2, tel 942 710 211), **Hotel Cantón** (doubles €35–70, c/Padre Ángel 8, tel 942 711 560), **Hotel Luzón** (singles €30–45, doubles €50–70, closed Jan, @, Avda Miramar 1, tel 942 710 050). Uphill, leading out of town: **Pensión Alto Santiago** (doubles €42–65, tel 942 710 121), **Hotel Azul de Galimar** (singles €50–70, doubles €60–80, tel 942 715 020).

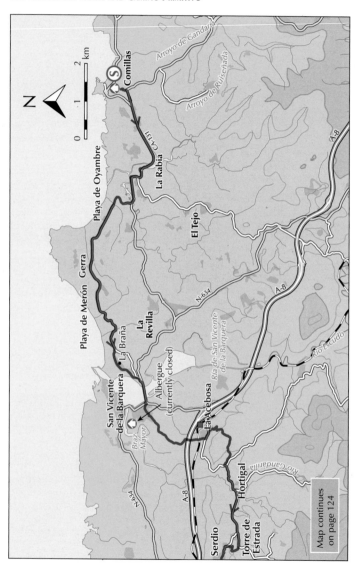

Map continues
on page 124

122

*San Vicente de
la Barquera*

Another fishing/resort town, San Vicente is dominated by the ruins of its eighth-century **Castillo del Rey** (€2, July–Aug 1030–1400 and 1630–2000, reduced hours and closed Mon in off-season). Although the town boomed in the Middle Ages, it was devastated by fires; its prominent Jewish Quarter was wiped out in 1483 and a 1636 blaze devoured most of what remained. The 13th-century Gothic **Iglesia deSanta María de los Ángeles** holds the tomb of Inquisitor Antonio del Corro. The statue of del Corro is regarded as one of the finest pieces of Renaissance funerary art. Classical music aficionados will recognize Schubert's 'Ave María', played in the bell tower every quarter-hour (exhausted locals suggest this was the work of a town enemy).

Proceed uphill, along the Camino de las Calzadas. Cross the A-8 expressway and railroad tracks before reaching a T-junction in **La Acebosa**. Turn left and then wrap around the hillside before joining CA-843. Pass through tiny **Hortigal**, then continue along the highway to the 12th-century **Torre de Estrada**. Turn right and follow minor roads into

A double waymark, for the Camino del Norte and the Camino Lebaniego

SERDIO (7.7KM)

Bar. **Albergue de Peregrinos** (€5, 16 beds, open all year, tel 664 108 003), **Posada La Torre** (doubles €42–55, tel 942 718 462), **Hostería El Corralucu** (doubles €45, tel 942 718 566).

Fork right at the church leaving Serdio. Later, fork left onto a dirt road and follow this 2.3km to **Muñorrodero** (bar, Posada de Muño – doubles €45+, tel 942 718 058). Waymarks for the pilgrimage to Santo Toribio de Liébana call

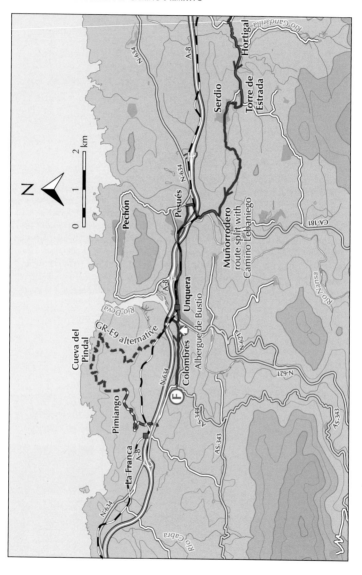

for a left. ▶ Instead, fork right, join CA-181, and proceed into **Pesués** (bars, Hostal Baviera– singles €20–25, doubles €30–40, includes breakfast, tel 942 718 180). Turn left, cross the Ría de Tina Menor, and turn left again, winding uphill through a small neighborhood. Fork onto a dirt road alongside the train tracks, later joining a minor highway into

UNQUERA (7.5KM)

All facilities, FEVE station. Bar La Granja has cheap rooms for pilgrims (singles €15, doubles €25, tel 942 717 074). A new albergue is located across the river: Albergue de Bustio (donativo, 12 beds, breakfast, @, 607 812 610). Hostal Río Deva (singles €19–29, doubles €32–38, c/San Felipe Neri, tel 942 717 157), Hotel Canal (singles €23–40, €39–66, tel 942 717 101), El Rincón de Bustio, located across the river (doubles €80–100, tel 985 412 525).

A small town with few sights, but it does provide the best opportunity to resupply between San Vicente and Llanes.

Continue straight across the Río Deva, arriving in the autonomous region of Asturias. ▶ Cross the road and climb a cement track. Pass **Albergue El Cantu** before sloping downhill into the central plaza in

COLOMBRES (2.1KM)

Bars, restaurants, and grocery stores. Albergue El Cantu (€12, 120 beds, may be filled with groups in high season, meals available, tel 985 413 026). On the highway after town: Pensión Oyambre (doubles €30, tel 985 412 242), Casa Junco (singles €33, doubles €50, triples €60, breakfast available, tel 985 412 243).

While Indianos architecture – a style popular with locals who made fortunes in the New World – is prevalent throughout Asturias, Colombres features some exemplary cases of it. Of particular interest is **La Quinta Guadalupe**, a marvelous blue edifice that houses the **Museo de la Emigración** and **Los Archivos de Indianos**.

The sixth-century Monasterio de Santo Toribio is said to house the largest piece of the True Cross. The pilgrimage route is 55km with albergues along the way: a brief route description is included after this stage.

Or you can take the GR-E9: immediately after crossing the Deva, turn right along the riverside walkway. GR waymarks pick up soon after, following an 8.8km loop past the Ermita de San Emeterio and Cueva del Pindal, a spectacularly-situated cave featuring prehistoric paintings (€3, open Wed–Sun, 1000–1700, reservations essential, tel 608 175 284). The GR rejoins the camino shortly before La Franca.

DETOUR: THE CAMINO LEBANIEGO
Muñorrodero to Santo Toribio de Liébana

Start	Muñorrodero
Finish	Monasterio de Santo Toribio
Distance	55km
% unpaved	42.4%
Total ascent	2133m
Total descent	1636m
Terrain	5
Route-finding	2
Pilgrim accommodation	Cades, Lafuente, Cicera, Cabañes, Potes

While pilgrims to Santiago recognize the importance of Rome, Jerusalem, and Santiago as pilgrimage sites, Santo Toribio de Liébana joins them as one of five Christian sites that are empowered to bestow perpetual indulgences. Its preeminence stems from the monastery's possession of the largest piece of the True Cross, which was first brought to the Iberian Peninsula in the fifth/sixth century and then relocated from Astorga to the Liébana Valley when Moors invaded northern Spain. It was a good hiding place – for reasons that will become immediately apparent as you make this walk, climbing to the edge of the Picos de Europa. Over time, as the region re-stabilized, the monastery emerged as a major pilgrimage site.

The Lebaniego route splits from the Camino del Norte in Muñorrodero, just after Serdio, although waymarks for the route (a red cross paired with a red arrow) parallel those of the Norte as early as San Vicente. Serdio has an albergue, so that might make it a good spot to sleep before tackling the Lebaniego. Plan carefully for food as opportunities for resupply are sorely lacking between San Vicente and Potes.

From **Muñorrodero**, the route follows a pedestrian track alongside the Río Nansa and then transitions to the 'Senda Fluvial,' a purpose-built, riverside footpath with green/white markings. There's a great cave along the way, and then a deeper/calmer part of the river with a small waterfall near the end. Arrive at a T-junction on a paved road 9.2km from Muñorrodero.The Lebaniego turns right. ◀

If you turn left here, after 10min you will reach Camijanes (bar), where food is available.

The Lebaniego crosses the Nansa on a large Romanesque bridge and then passes **El Solaz de los Cerezos** (doubles €55–90, quads €60–95, kitchen, tel 666 592 400). This next section is much hillier, winding through **Cabanzón** (2.1km),

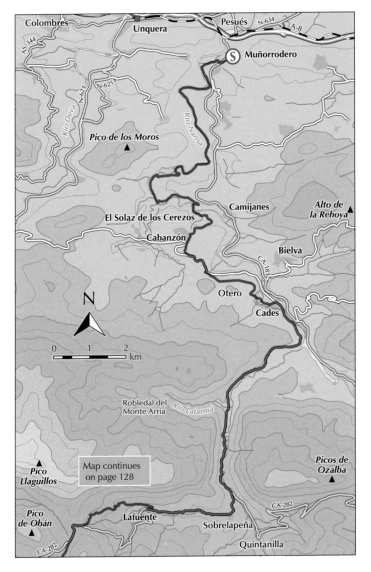

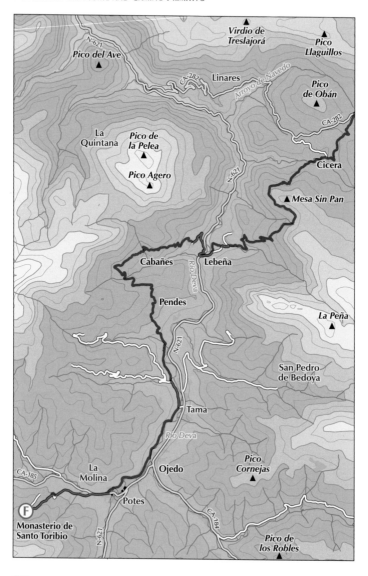

along the edge of **Otero** (1.9km), and then into **Cades** (1.8km), which has both a restaurant and Albergue de Peregrinos (€8, 24 beds, open all year, meals available, tel 680 179 113). From there, you face a lengthy stretch along a minor highway, climbing steadily through an increasingly narrow gorge, ultimately leading to the edge of **Lafuente** (10.2km). Soon after passing the Iglesia de Santa Juliana, the route turns right. However, continue straight for 700 meters to stay in the village's Albergue de Peregrinos (€7, 20 beds, open all year, meals available, tel 638 148 170).

Monasterio de Santo Toribio de Liébana

The walk now enters its most strenuous section, with two significant ascents in the next 8km, followed by a descent that gives back all of that elevation, and then some. The initial climb leads to **Cicera** (5.4km), which has a bar, a restaurant, and an Albergue de Peregrinos (€5, 20 beds, open all year, kitchen, tel 679 530 105). A harder trek follows, gaining over 300m in roughly 2km and then dropping into **Lebeña** (7.5km), which has a stunning 10th-century church, the Iglesia de Santa María de Lebeña.

The remainder of the walk stays within close proximity of the Río Deva. Pass through **Cabañes** (4.3km) Albergue de Peregrinos – €15, 56 beds, includes breakfast, dinner available, must call 2–3 days in advance, @, tel 626 813 080), **Pendes** (2.9km) (cheese shop), and then arrive at the edge of **Tama** (3.5km). The route continues straight, but bars/restaurants are accessible across the Deva. The riverside trail ultimately brings you to **Potes** (3.3km), where there is an excellent Albergue de Peregrinos (€5, 60 beds, kitchen, key from turismo, tel 942 738 126) and all facilities. To reach Santo Toribio, follow the highway out of town and then turn left roughly a kilometer later. A final ascent leads to the **Monasterio de Santo Toribio de Liébana** (2.9km), where visits are possible (1000–1300, 1600–1900). You'll need to backtrack on foot to Potes or arrange for a taxi. To return to the Camino del Norte, there is regular bus service between Potes and Unquera.

STAGE 15
Colombres to Llanes

Start	Plaza Ibáñez y Posada, Colombres
Finish	Albergue La Casona del Peregrino, Llanes
Distance	25.2km
% unpaved	62.7%
Total ascent	423m
Total descent	519m
Terrain	2
Route-finding	4
Pilgrim accommodation	La Franca, Buelna, Pendueles, Llanes

After many pavement-intensive days, this stage is a relief, with significant time spent on coastal footpaths and dirt roads. This requires some attentive walking, however, as the 'official' camino remains highway-bound much of the time. With natural marvels vying for your attention – the Picos de Europa to your left, the sea to your right, and (for a time) the *bufones* all around you – it's easy to lose track of the route, so be careful! Llanes is the trendiest, hippest stop along this stretch of the Norte, with many highlights to enjoy.

In Asturias, the waymarkers indicate the direction you should turn based on where the lines in the shell converge, but this is reversed when you reach Galicia!

With your back to the church at Colombres, walk out of the back-right corner of the plaza and continue to proceed in a westward direction out of town. ◄ After a short off-road stretch, arrive at a T-junction. Waymarks point in both directions; both options are roughly 1.3km in length. Neither is notably superior, but the right fork gets you off the highway and passes two bars soon after. The routes rejoin on N-634, proceeding into

LA FRANCA (3.1KM)

Bar, grocery. **Albergue Renacer** (€15, 10 beds, open all year, includes breakfast and W/D, tel 678 169 939), **Albergue Triskel** (€15, 12 beds, open Feb-mid Dec, includes breakfast, W/D, @, tel 688 804 747), **Camping Playa de la Franca** (€15, beds in bungalows, tel 985 412 222).

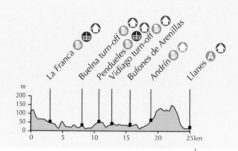

Fork left after town, following a footpath through a pleasant off-road stretch before returning to N-634. While the 'official' camino follows the highway, newer yellow arrows point to a superior approach, crossing the highway and proceeding towards the coast, rejoining the 'official' route in Pendueles. This is recommended in good weather. ▶ 2.9km later, the route skirts **Buelna**; turn left and proceed 250m to reach the village (bar, Albergue de Peregrinos – €10, 60 beds, doubles €30, open Mar–Nov, meals available, W/D, tel 985 411 218). Otherwise, continue onward to

The highway approach is 1.1km shorter and passes directly by Buelna's albergue.

PENDUELES (7.3KM)

Bar, grocery, Albergue Aves de Paso (donativo, 14 beds, open Apr–Sep but closed on Fri, W/D included, tel 617 160 810), Albergue Turístico Casa Flor (€20, includes bed, dinner, and breakfast, 15 beds, open Mar–Sep, W/D, tel 650 431 982), Bar Castiellu (doubles €25, closed Dec, W/D, tel 639 881 604).

Only the church remains from the **Monasterio de San Acisclo**.

The 'official' camino returns to N-634 and proceeds largely along the highway into Llanes. That is not advisable. A more pleasant option follows the GR E-9, described here. Watch for the red/white stripes and turn accordingly. This route leads towards the coast, almost exclusively along dirt roads. Pass **Camping La Paz** and its secluded beach, then skirt the edge of **Vidiago** (Albergue El Caserón de Vidiago – €10, 18 beds, open Mar-Oct, meals available, W/D, @, tel 985 404 446) and N-634, before continuing to

BUFONES DE ARENILLAS (5KM)

An impressive geological feature: cracks have formed within the rock cliff, allowing for eruptions of seawater as high as 20m. Proceed with caution through the *bufones* and remain on trails.

Follow the footpath for 3.4km. Join a paved road in **Andrín** (bar, La Casona de Andrín – doubles €70–80, tel 985 417 250). Cross the small town, ascend to the highway, and turn right, passing a scenic viewpoint. From here, you have two options – a highway approach or a more scenic route along the GR E-9. We recommend the latter, which offers better views and is mostly off-road. From the scenic viewpoint, follow the red/white stripes across the highway and proceed 3km to the **Ermita del Cristo del Camino**. Turn right and return to paved roads. Pass the turn-off for first the Albergue La Senda del Peregrino and then Albergue La Portilla, continuing straight into **Llanes**, and rejoining the other route on AS-263.

Highway variant

Alternatively, follow LLN-2 into **Cue** (bar, Pensión Castañu – doubles €30–50, tel 985 401 454, Pensión Paulina – doubles €15–35, tel 985 401 168), then turn right on LLN-1 towards

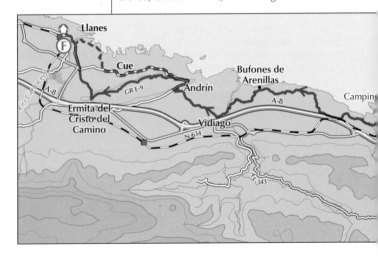

the Playa de Toró. Turn left and follow a coastal road to
AS-263 in **Llanes**. Turn right onto AS-263, rejoining the GR.
This route is 800 meters shorter.

Cross the Río Carrocedo and curve left. For **Albergue La
Casona del Peregrino**, turn right at the sign for Hotel Don
Paco in

LLANES (9.8KM)

All facilities. Five private hostels: Albergue La Casona del Peregrino (€15, 56
beds, open all year, includes breakfast, c/Colegio la Encarnación 3, tel 985 402
494), Albergue La Estación (€11–16, 34 beds, open Mar–early Dec, kitchen,
W/D, tel 985 401 458), Albergue Juvenil Juventudes (€10, 82 beds, open all
year, meals available, c/Celso Amieva 15, tel 985 400 770), Albergue La Senda
del Peregrino (€15, 24 beds, open Mar–Oct, includes breakfast, located in
La Portilla neighborhood at entrance to town from the GR, tel 985 404 486),
Albergue La Portilla (€15, 48 beds, open Mar–Sep, also in La Portilla, tel 616
460 183). Pensión Los Pinos (doubles €40–70, Avda Las Gaviotas 28, tel 985
401 116), Hotel Posada del Rey (singles €35–85, doubles €50–103, pilgrim
discounts, c/Mayor, tel 985 401 332), Hotel Sablon (doubles €36–59, open Mar–
Oct, @, c/la Moría 1, tel 985 400 787).

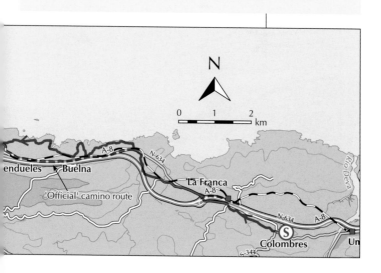

The port of Llanes

A lively town, popular with tourists thanks to its wonderful location, nestled between the coast and the Picos de Europa. Llanes has enjoyed a long history, as evidenced by the surviving remnants of its 800-year-old city walls. The town celebrates two major events from the 16th century with commemorative plaques: the visit of Emperor Charles V in 1517 and the contribution of 65 men and three ships to the Spanish Armada. Beaches are the major attraction, but find time for a look at the **Cubos de la Memoria**, which honor the city's seafaring tradition, located in the port and visible on the walk from Cue.

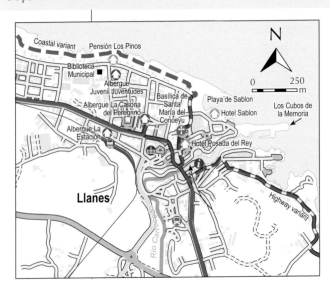

STAGE 16

Llanes to Piñeres de Pría

Start	Albergue La Casona del Peregrino, Llanes
Finish	Albergue Casa Rectoral, Piñeres de Pría
Distance	20.9km
% unpaved	45.1%
Total ascent	338m
Total descent	246m
Terrain	1
Route-finding	2
Pilgrim accommodation	Playa de Poo, Celorio, Villahormes, Piñeres de Pría (and Cuerres)

Today provides more evidence that monastery builders had excellent taste in building sites. First in Celorio and then again near the Playa de San Antolín, monasteries lurk within range of beaches, close enough to enjoy the fresh sea air but with sufficient distance to allow for grassy fields and a quiet sentry of tall trees. The rest of the walk offers a mix of road and trail, small villages and open countryside, and generally flat conditions that make for easy going. Piñeres de Pría, along with neighboring Nueva and Cuerres, offer a mix of affordable accommodation options.

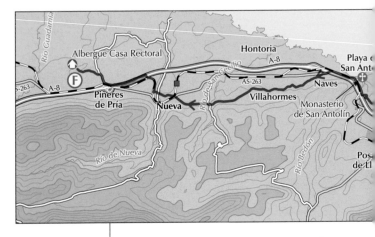

For a far more pleasant walk, proceed to the Playa del Sablon in Llanes, climb the steps to an elevated, grassy track, and follow the coastline to the far side of Poo, descending to the Farola del Mar hotel and rejoining the camino soon after. This approach is 1.6km longer.

◀ Keep straight on AS-263 out of Llanes, before following a series of minor tracks into

PLAYA DE POO (2.4KM)

Bar, grocery. **Albergue Llanes** (€10–15, 23 beds, open all year, W/D, @, c/de la Playa 36, tel 985 403 181), **Albergue La Cambarina** (€12–15, 16 beds, open mid Mar–Oct, kitchen, W/D, Plaza de los Higos 128, tel 635 739 837), **Hotel El Camin** (singles €55–80, doubles €60–130, includes breakfast, tel 985 402 301), **Hotel La Farola del Mar** (doubles €55–90, meals available, tel 985 401 250).

At the town's end, turn right and then fork left soon after onto a footpath (the coastal route rejoins here). Follow a series of minor roads into

CELORIO (3.1KM)

Bars/restaurants, grocery, pharmacy. **Albergue Las Palmeras** (€12.50–15, 20 beds, closed Jan, meals available, Barrio Abajo 120, tel 638 287 065), **Pensión Costa Verde** (beds €11.50, doubles €25–40, tel 648 277 347), **Hotel Moran**

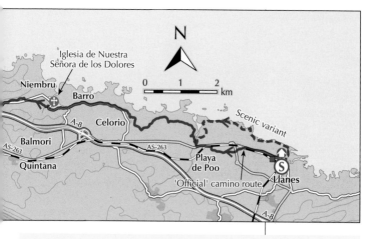

Playa (singles €40–65, doubles €50–90, Avda de la Playa 5, tel 985 401 107), **Hotel Miracielos** (25% pilgrim discount, breakfast and laundry included, pilgrim menu, @, tel 699 976 921), **Hotel Gavitu** (Barrio Abajo, tel 985 400 588).

The **Monasterio de San Salvador** had a pilgrim refuge in the 12th century.

Cross a pair of beaches in Celorio and then follow the highway out of town, leading through **Barro** (bars). After crossing the Ría de Barro, and before reaching the picturesque **Iglesia de Nuestra Señora de los Dolores**, turn left onto a footpath. A pleasant walk leads to the ruined **Monasterio de San Antolín** and the eponymous beach. Follow a mix of single-lane and dirt roads through **Naves** (bar) and **Villahormes** (Albergue Villahormes – €10–15, 24 beds, open all year, W/D, tel 671 692 095). After another long, straight stretch, descend to AS-263, and cross to the bar's right into

NUEVA (12.1KM)

Bars/restaurants, grocery. **Pensión San Jorge** (singles €35–50, doubles €45–65, pilgrim discounts, tel 985 410 285), **Hotel Cuevas del Mar** (doubles €55–75, Plaza de Laverde Ruiz, tel 985 410 377).

Iglesia de Nuestra Señora de los Dolores

Rejoin the highway, cross under the expressway, and continue straight into Piñeres de Pría, passing the bar and casa rural. A final ascent leads to the Iglesia de Pría and its neighboring Albergue Casa Rectoral.

PIÑERES DE PRÍA (3.3KM)

Bar (no food). **Casa Rural La Llosa de Cosme** (€10, 10 beds, includes breakfast and W/D, open all year, kitchen, tel 609 861 373), **Albergue Casa Rectoral** (€6, 36 beds, open May–mid Sep, kitchen, tel 617 942 141).

STAGE 17
Piñeres de Pría to La Isla

Start	Albergue Casa Rectoral, Piñeres de Pría
Finish	Iglesia de Santa María de Tona, La Isla
Distance	27.3km
% unpaved	33.8%
Total ascent	457m

Total descent	559m
Terrain	2
Route-finding	1
Pilgrim accommodation	Cuerres, San Esteban de Leces, La Vega, La Isla

The camino returns to the coast in a big way today, passing three excellent beaches and finishing on a fourth – a final burst of sandy glory before Primitivo-bound pilgrims take leave of the sea. Try to make time in Ribadesella to see its prehistoric cave art and be sure to grab a snack for the road, as opportunities for food are limited between there and La Isla.

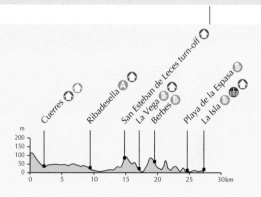

Pass to the left of the neighboring church and cemetary, continuing straight to tiny

CUERRES (2.4KM)

Albergue Casa Belén (donativo, 8 beds, communal meals), Albergue Reposo del Andayón (donativo, 10 beds, open Mar–mid Oct, communal meals, W/D, @, tel 639 677 933), Hotel Rural Aldea del Trasgu (singles €50–75, doubles €65–85, includes breakfast, tel 985 861 504).

Take a peek at the 15th-century pilgrims' fountain.

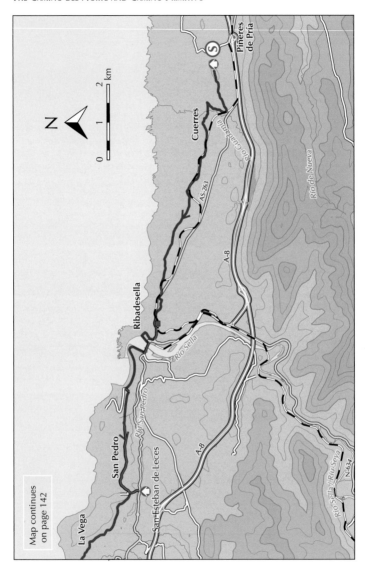

The route follows quiet tracks, weaving back and forth across the railroad, before two short stretches on AS-263. Finally, fork right downhill and then right again, into Ribadesella. The camino leads northeast through the old town to the Iglesia de Santa María Magdalena.

RIBADESELLA (7KM)

All facilities. **Albergue Juvenil Ribadesella** (€21, 56 beds, open all year, includes breakfast, W/D, @, c/Ricardo Cangas, tel 985 860 421), **Pensión Arbidel** (singles €30–40, doubles €40–80, triples €60–85, c/Oscura 1, tel 985 860 141), **Hotel Argüelles** (doubles €35–50, c/del Sol, tel 985 861 810), **Hotel Marina** (singles €35–58, doubles €55–83, triples €65–98, c/Gran Via 36, tel 985 860 050), **Hotel Derli Sella** (singles €30–40, doubles €40–65, triples/quads, breakfast available, c/El Picu, tel 985 860 092), **Habitaciones Ribadesella** (beds €17, c/Manuel Caso de la Villa 38 5a, tel 642 762 155).

Conquered by Romans during Augustus's rule, Ribadesella traditionally marked the border between the Astures and Cantrabras tribes. Today's town, however, was founded in 1270 by Alfonso X and developed around whaling. Like other strategically significant locations, Ribadesella suffered badly during the Peninsular War, the Carlist Wars, and the Spanish Civil War. Its highlight, the **Cuevas de Tito Bustillo**, echoes the region's more distant past. Unlike Santillana del Mar's Altamira Caves, where tourists can visit only a replica cave, these are the real thing. Regular guided tours lead deep underground through stalactites to a room filled with 15,000–20,000-year-old paintings depicting deer, horses, bison, and more. Reservations are essential (€7.34, open Mar–Oct, Wed–Sun, 1015–1700, tel 985 185 860).

The port of Ribadesella

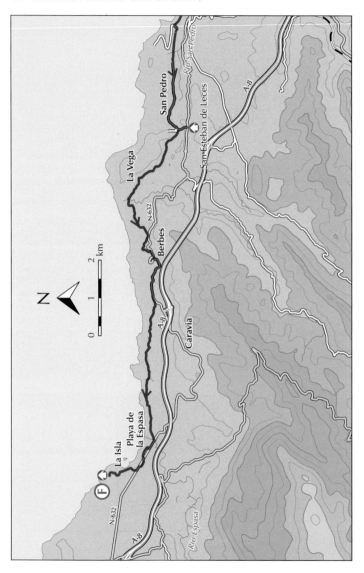

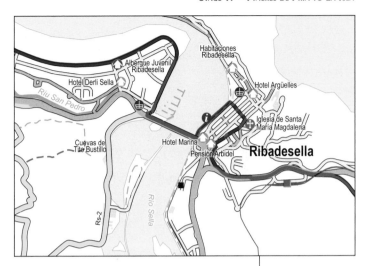

Cut to the waterfront and cross the Río Sella, then follow the beachfront promenade. Follow minor roads through the San Pedro neighborhood, proceeding gradually uphill. At a marked intersection, the camino splits. Keep straight on to continue, or turn left and proceed 300 meters to the albergue in

SAN ESTEBAN DE LECES (5.5KM)

Albergue de Peregrinos (€6, 38 beds, open all year, kitchen, tel 985 857 611, take-away food service available).

Backtrack to the camino and keep straight on, turning right at a T-junction towards the coast and the village of

LA VEGA (2.2KM)

Bar. Albergue Tu Casa (donativo, 7 beds, open Mar–Oct but closed Fri, communal meals, tel 984 100 746).

The **Ermita de la Magdalena** dates to the 18th century.

An attempt to run a pilgrim hospital here was undermined by scheming, bickering town officials in the Middle Ages.

Pilgrims who would prefer to bypass La Isla can continue straight, as the route to Colunga forks left soon after.

The 'Camino Real' after Berbes

Turn left immediately before the beach, joining a medieval road uphill. After a pleasant, coastal walk, cross N-632 in **Berbes** (bar). ◄

After some time on N-634, turn right onto a footpath, the 'Camino Real,' for an abrupt ascent followed by an equally jarring drop, leading to the lovely **Playa de la Espasa** (bars). Follow N-632 away from the beach, zigzagging off both sides, before turning right onto c/Teldiz. ◄ The coastal walk leads into La Isla. The albergue is located on the outskirts, near the coast, but is waymarked.

LA ISLA (10.2KM)

Bars, grocery. **Albergue de Peregrinos** (€6, 25 beds, open all year, closed in 2018 for repairs, kitchen, W/D, c/Subida al Castro 85, tel 985 852 005), **Albergue Juvenil El Furacu** (€20, 42 beds, open all year, must be reserved outside summer, includes breakfast, W/D, tel 985 856 661), **Hotel Monte y Mar** (doubles €35–45, @, tel 985 856 561).

STAGE 18

La Isla to Villaviciosa

Start	Iglesia de Santa María de Tona, La Isla
Finish	Parque Ballina, Villaviciosa
Distance	22km
% unpaved	19%
Total ascent	446m
Total descent	445m
Terrain	3
Route-finding	1
Pilgrim accommodation	Priesca, Sebrayo, Tornón, Villaviciosa

Today's walk is entirely inland (although an optional jaunt from La Isla might provide a short exception), following mostly minor, paved roads through tiny villages. It's peaceful, easy walking, and it brings you past one of the oldest churches along the Norte in Priesca. Facilities are very limited between Colunga and Villaviciosa, so plan ahead, but Villaviciosa offers a lively market town with plenty of options for food and drink to end your day!

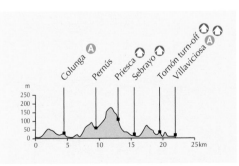

Backtrack to N-632, turn left and then turn right soon after onto a footpath. ▶

An alternative approach, roughly equivalent in length, passes behind La Isla's albergue to join a coastal trail: turn inland on a dirt road to pass through Huerres en route to Colunga.

Colunga, prepped for fiesta

COLUNGA (4.4KM)

All facilities. **Confiteria Las Palmeras** has rooms (singles €15, tel 985 856 560), **Hotel Las Vegas** (singles €28–35, doubles €35–55, Avda Asturias 11, tel 985 856 025), **Hotel Entreviñes** (€20 per pilgrim, meals available, @, tel 985 852 631).

The remains of the Romanesque **Iglesia de San Cristóbal** serve as the cemetery chapel.

A pedestrian-friendly, red-brick street leads through Colunga. At the end of town, turn left onto CL-1 to **Pernús**, then proceed through **La Llera** to

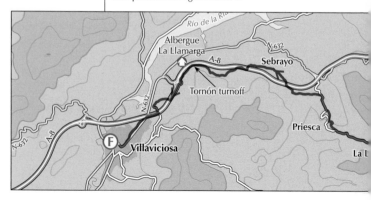

PRIESCA (8.4KM)

Albergue La Rectoral de Priesca (€12, 22 beds, open all year, breakfast available, kitchen, W/D, tel 636 056 520).

The Pre-Romanesque **Iglesia de San Salvador**, built in 921, is one of the oldest churches on the camino. Amazingly, some of the original painting is still visible in the apses and on the walls. A key is available at the albergue.

Descend an often-muddy trail, pass under A-8 expressway, and proceed into

SEBRAYO (2.9KM)

Albergue de Peregrinos (€4, 14 beds, open Feb–Nov, kitchen, tel 699 440 399), but no shops or bars, aside from a nightly food truck. Check with the hospitalero.

Folk art near Sebrayo

The next few kilometers on small roads and tracks are well marked, passing to the left of

TORNÓN TURN-OFF (3.3KM)

Albergue de Peregrinos La Llamarga (donativo, 8 beds, open Mar–Oct, communal meals, 500 meters off-route, tel 985 892 501)

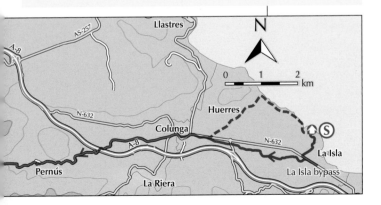

The walk to Villaviciosa is a bit wiggly, twice crossing A-8 before joining c/Cervantes and proceeding to the Parque Ballina in

VILLAVICIOSA (3KM)

All facilities. Stock up on food, as you may not encounter anything between here and Cabueñes. **Albergue Villaviciosa** (€11–15, 28 beds, kitchen, W/D, c/Marqués de Villaviciosa, tel 985 891 555), **Albergue El Congreso** (€10–15, 49 beds, open Mar–Nov, kitchen, W/D, Plaza del Ayuntamiento 25, tel 985 891 180). Shortly before town is **Albergue de Peregrinos la Payariega** (donativo, 6 beds, open all year, communal meals, kitchen, W/D, tel 651 068 840). **Hotel Carlos I** (singles €25, doubles €40, triples €52, open Apr–Oct, @, Plaza Carlos I, tel 985 890 121), **Hostal Café del Sol** (singles €25, doubles €35, pilgrim discounts, c/Sol 27, tel 985 891 130), **Hotel Casa España** (singles €38–53, doubles €48–66, Plaza Carlos I, tel 985 892 030).

Although its best years are past, Villaviciosa is a pleasant commercial town and the 'apple capital' of Spain. Many of those apples end up in the town's dozen cider distilleries. It was the first Spanish town to welcome Charles V when he arrived from Flanders in 1517. The 13th-century **Iglesia de Santa María de la Oliva** is worth a visit.

DETOUR: THE CAMINO COVADONGA

Amandi (Villaviciosa) to Covadonga

Start	Amandi
Finish	Santuario de Covadonga
Distance	51.9km
% unpaved	27.1%
Total ascent	1395m
Total descent	1154m
Terrain	3
Route-finding	2
Pilgrim accommodation	Miyares, Romillo, La Vega de los Caseros, La Riera

It could be said that Covadonga is where the Reconquista began, as a group of Iberian Christians, led by Pelayo (not the hermit, the soldier!), won their first victory over the conquering Umayyad forces. From there, the Kingdom of Asturias formed, and the resistance grew. Covadonga was a site well chosen to make a defensive stand, situated in the foothills with many caves. A statue of the Virgin Mary, ultimately known as Our Lady of Covadonga (the patron of Asturias), was hidden in one of those caves and ultimately credited for the victory.

Given that, it's no surprise that Covadonga is *the* major Asturian pilgrimage site, alongside of Oviedo, of course. A route to Covadonga is waymarked from Gijón and frequently overlaps with the Norte between Gijón and Amandi, before splitting off on its own. The waymarks – which include the Celtic-inspired Covadonga symbol, blue and orange arrows spray-painted on the road, and 'Camin a Cuadonga' signs – are dependable throughout. The route follows gently undulating hills; while the mountains grow in magnitude as you approach Covadonga, there are few ascents/descents of note. Food is limited, but several tourist albergues offer accommodation.

The route follows AS-255 from **Amandi**, before joining the Ruta de los Molinos to **Valbucar** (2km). Dirt tracks and minor paved roads lead through **Moratin** (1.9km) (fountain) to **Breceña** (2.1km) (bar). In this stretch, the route generally winds back and forth across AS-332, skirting **Sietes** (3.3km), but it then joins the highway to **Anayo** (4.7km) (bar). Following a stint on AS-258, an extended off-road section

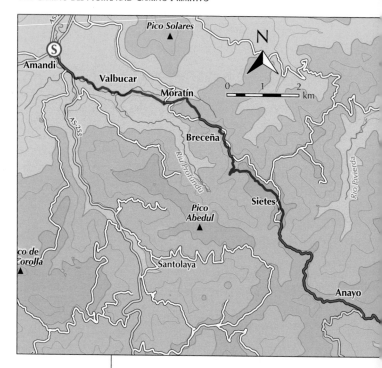

leads through **Vallobal** before joining AS-358 into **Miyares** (6.3km) (bar, Albergue de la Casona de Miyares – €25, includes breakfast, kitchen, @, tel 985 708 051).

After passing **El Cotal** (4.1km) (park/fountain), the route syncs up with GR-105/109 for a stretch, and also the Camin de la Reina, a former Roman road believed to be followed by Isabel II in the 19th century. After winding through **Villar de Huergo** (3km) and **Llames de Parres** (3.1km) (bars, fountain), the camino arrives in its second village with albergue accommodation, **Romillo** (3km) (Albergue El Puntual de Romillo – €18, kitchen, 'mini-zoo', tel 653 872 305). It then descends to the Río Deva, passing through neighboring villages **La Vega de los Caseros** (4.8km) (Albergue La Posada – €13–23, includes breakfast, @, tel 985 848 553) and **Villanueva** (0.2km).

The lone town of any size, **Cangas de Onís** (all facilities), is just southeast (2.5km), following the Deva, although most facilities are only accessible with a detour across the river. The last stretch of this short pilgrimage parallels AS-114 and then bears south alongside AS-262, passing through **La Riera** (7km) (Albergue Cangas de Onís – €20, 18 beds, kitchen, laundry, @, tel 669 350 843) and then continuing to **Covadonga** and its famous sanctuary (3.9km).

Covadonga is definitely accustomed to absorbing big crowds, but there is no special attention given to walking pilgrims. The two main components of the visit are: 1) the basilica, which is perched magnificently on a hill overlooking the valley below and 2) the holy cave, where 'Our Lady' is revered. Beyond that, there is a luxury hotel, a couple of cafes, and a souvenir shop. The small museum has a stamp available.

Buses depart from Covadonga periodically for Cangas de Onís and there are some direct buses for Oviedo. To return to Villaviciosa, to continue along the Norte, catch a bus to either Oviedo or Ribadesella, and then find a connection to Villaviciosa. The timing is not as convenient as one might like.

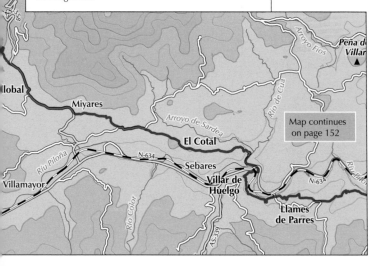

Map continues on page 152

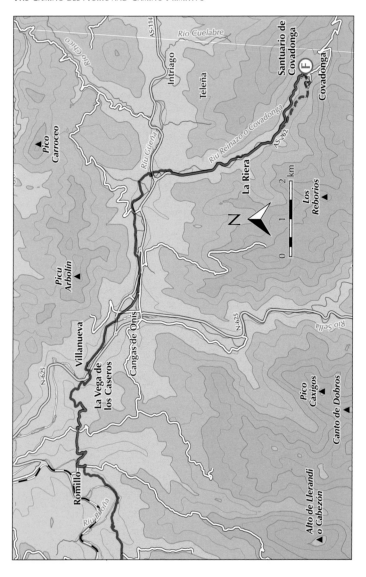

STAGE 19

Villaviciosa to Gijón

Start	Parque Ballina, Villaviciosa
Finish	Intersection of Calle Pedro Douro and the waterfront, Gijón
Distance	31.2km
% unpaved	36%
Total ascent	810m
Total descent	808m
Terrain	4
Route-finding	3
Pilgrim accommodation	Amandi, Niévares, Cabueñes, Gijón

Today brings great changes. First, the caminos split, with Primitivo-bound pilgrims saying their goodbyes and forking south. Second, the Norte hits its sharpest ascent in many days, with a 400m climb to the Alto de la Cruz. Finally, the stage ends in Gijón, the first big city in a week. With little traffic and few distractions, the route is surprisingly peaceful, making for a quiet day before the hustle and bustle of Gijón. Be prepared for no opportunities for food or drink along the way.

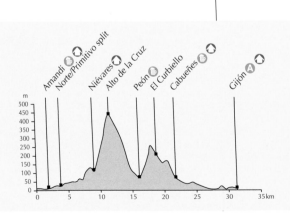

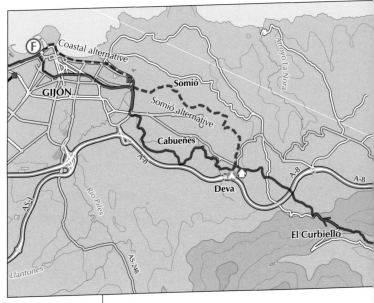

For pilgrims taking the Primitivo, today's route from Villaviciosa is described in the Camino Primitivo, Stage 1.

It is possible to follow the Primitivo to Oviedo and then return to the Norte in Avilés without backtracking. The route from Oviedo to Avilés is outlined at the end of the Camino Primitivo section (see Primitivo–Norte Link).

◄ Loop past the Iglesia de Santa María de la Oliva before bearing south on or parallel to AS-255. Fork right past Sidrería la Regatina in **Amandi** and then again soon after; alternatively, fork left for the pilgrimage to Covadonga (see Detour: The Camino Covadonga after Norte Stage 18) or Albergue La Ferrería (donativo, 12 beds, open mid Mar–Oct, communal meals, kitchen, @, tel 646 516 846). Minor roads and highways lead past Bar Caso and through **Casquita**. The Caminos del Norte and Primitivo split 3.7km from Villaviciosa. ◄

Keep straight on VV-10 for the Camino del Norte, forking left soon after onto a dirt road. The walk, which eventually loops back under the A-8 expressway and climbs uphill, is pleasant, but perhaps unnecessary. It is a significant detour (adding 2.4km) compared with simply remaining on the quiet VV-10.

Turn uphill on VV-9 towards **Niévares** (Casa Abierta La Xaldina Peregrina – donativo, 5 beds, open all year, communal meals, @, tel 636 921 287); a steep climb follows, bringing you to the **Alto de la Cruz**, where you join VV-8 and eventually descend into the next valley. ▶ Watch carefully for a sharp left turn 3km later. After a quick descent, turn right onto a minor paved road, arriving soon after at Casa Pepito in

PEÓN (15.6KM)

Bar Casa Pepito serves meals but doesn't open before midday.

Iglesia de Santiago was restored in 1929.

Be warned that there are many conflicting waymarks in this stretch, related to the Covadonga pilgrimage.

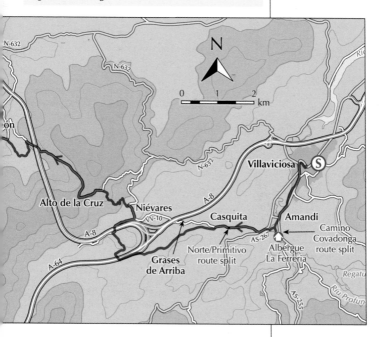

Continue straight along AS-331. Turn right at house 17, then follow a mix of footpaths and single-lane roads through peaceful countryside, eventually rejoining AS-331 in **El Curbiello**. Turn right at the km25 sign, enjoying a brilliant view. The descent follows mostly dirt tracks. Join N-632 just as you arrive in

The marker where the Norte and Primitivo split

CABUEÑES (6.3KM)

Bar/restaurant. Albergue de Peregrinos in Camping Deva (€6, 36 beds, open all year, W/D, tel 985 133 848).

From here, you have two options. We suggest turning left off N-632, passing the entrance to **Camping Deva** and turning right soon after. This route follows dirt tracks much of the way through shady terrain, arriving in Gijón 6km later. Alternatively, turn right off N-632, towards **Somió** (bars, supermarket). Waymarks are sparse, but the route primarily follows a single paved road as it winds through quiet suburbs. It is 900 meters shorter, but entirely roadbound.

The two routes rejoin just after a major roundabout at the entrance to Gijón. Once again, you have two options, this time roughly equivalent in length. The official route continues west along the highway, forking right 1km later onto Avda de la Costa and forking left soon after to remain on it. After 1.7km, turn right onto c/Palacio Valdés and then fork left at the **Iglesia de San José** onto c/Pedro Douro. Arrive at the waterfront soon after.

Alternatively, we suggest continuing along the riverside pedestrian/cyclist track to the coast. Fork left through an underpass and then emerge on the coastal promenade. At the end of Playa de San Lorenzo, turn left, passing through the **Plaza Mayor** and the **Cimadevilla**. Continue straight until you hit the ocean again, then turn left along the promenade. Rejoin the other route shortly after passing the turismo.

GIJÓN/XIXÓN (9.3KM)

All facilities and good transportation connections. Albergue El Peregrin (€10, 21 beds, open all year, @, located on Somió route prior to center, Plaza Pérez Pimentel 251, tel 652 767 601), Albergue Juvenil San Andrés de Cornellana is located 3km from the center (€15, 139 beds, meals available, @, tel 985 160 673). Hospedaje Don Pelayo (doubles €30–60, c/San Bernardo 22, tel 985 344 450), Hospedaje Cimavilla (doubles €38–80, c/Vicaria 29, tel 985 349 932), Hotel Costa Verde (singles €31–41, doubles €41–51, c/Fundición 5, tel 985 354 240), Hotel Begoña (singles €49–66, doubles €59–88, meals available, @, Avda de la Costa 44, tel 985 147 211).

Gijón is a major city with two lovely beaches. It has prehistoric origins, but it became far more organized and established under Roman rule. As the Via de la Plata's northern outpost, Gijón was a major economic link in the empire's Iberian operations. Dating from Augustan rule, the town still preserves its **Roman baths (Termas Romanas de Campo Valdés)** (€2.50, Tue–Fri 0900–1400 and 1700–1930, Sat–Sun 1000–1400 and 1700–1930, reduced hours in off-season). The city's most profound transformation occurred during the Industrial Revolution, when it became a major manufacturing center. Part of that development is documented in the **Railway Museum (Museo Ferrocarril)** (€2.50, Tue–Sun 1000–1900, reduced hours in off-season).

For something completely different, consider an attraction devoted to the inimitable bagpipe: the **Museo de la Gaita** (€2.35, open Tue–Sun 1000–1900). For nightlife and a historic feel, head for the **Cimadevilla**, the tiny peninsula dividing the town's beaches that was formerly the fishermen's quarter.

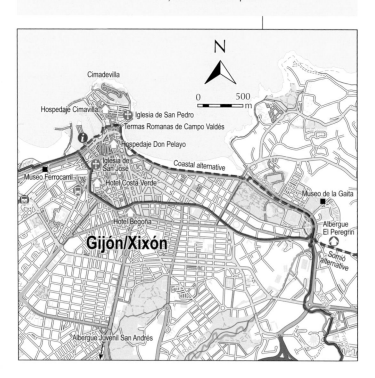

The Cimadevilla in Gijón

STAGE 20
Gijón to Avilés

Start	Intersection of Calle Pedro Douro and the waterfront, Gijón
Finish	Albergue de Peregrinos, Avilés
Distance	24.7km
% unpaved	16.7%
Total ascent	368m
Total descent	369m
Terrain	2
Route-finding	3
Pilgrim accommodation	Avilés

First, the bad news: this is probably the least enjoyable stage of walking on the Camino del Norte. The departure from Gijón passes through an ugly industrial district and a large portion of the stage's last third is highway-bound. But now, the good news: even on its worst day, the Norte still delivers some highlights. The ascent from Gijón brings you into the Monte Areo recreational area, which features a prehistoric dolmen. And Avilés, the day's final destination, is a lively, fashionable town with a wonderful park. Stock up before you leave because facilities are very limited after Gijón.

▸ Proceed westward along the waterfront. The route moves in a generally straight line, via c/Rodriguez San Pedro, Avda de Juan Carlos I, c/Mariano Pola (forking one block to the right), Avda de Galicia, and AS-19. Cross a railroad track and proceed through two roundabouts. Turn right out of the second, forking onto a footpath and then minor road. Join the highway in the next roundabout, turning right and then left before the railroad overpass. Cross the railroad then double back uphill, finally escaping the city's industrial outskirts 2km later. Those taking Bus 24 can disembark at this point.

Those not committed to walking every step might consider taking Bus 24 from the center of Gijón through the industrial district to Camin Rebesosu – ask for the 'Poago Alto' stop.

Turn right on Camin Rebesosu and follow a series of minor roads uphill, leading into **Monte Areo Park**; waymarks offer a possible detour to the prehistoric **Dolmen de San Pablo**. Continue through the park and descend the other side, arriving in **El Valle** 11.6km after leaving the center of Gijón where the 17th-century Iglesia de Santa Eulalia has a fountain.

Follow minor country roads for about 4km, passing under a tunnel at the entrance to **Tamón** (bars). Turn right at the church onto AS-326 and turn left shortly before the roundabout. Walk around the guard-rail and turn left on the highway. Soon after, cross the highway, climb the embankment, and then follow AS-19 into

TRASONA (20.2KM)

Bars/restaurants, supermarket.

Immediately after a sports field, turn right and climb a pedestrian bridge to cross the river, then proceed along a riverside track. As you enter Avilés, backtrack up steps to an overpass, turn right, and then right again onto AS-19. When the camino turns right on c/Rivero, look for the albergue on your left in

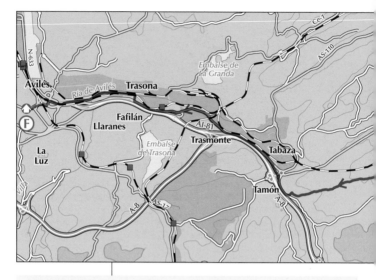

AVILÉS (4.5KM)

All facilities. **Albergue de Peregrinos** (€6, 56 beds, kitchen, credenciáles, W/D, c/Magdalena 1, tel 984 703 117), **Pensión La Fruta** (doubles €40, c/La Fruta 19, tel 985 512 288), **Hotel Don Pedro** (singles €50–70, doubles €60–80, triples €70–90, open all year, @, c/La Fruta 22, tel 985 512 288), **Hotel El Magistral** (doubles €43+, c/Llano Ponte 4, tel 985 561 100), **Hostal Puente Azud** (singles €25, doubles €35–45, open all year, @, c/Acero 5, tel 985 550 177).

A prominent naval town in the Middle Ages, with an economy built around ship-building and trade with France. Pedro Menéndez de Avilés, the founder of Saint Augustine, Florida (the first permanent European settlement in the US), was born here. Like Gijón, Avilés has become an industrial center, but its preserved pedestrian center feels more relaxed. Architecture buffs can anticipate a full range, from the 12th-century Romanesque **Iglesia de los Padres Franciscanos** to the stunning **Óscar Niemeyer International Cultural Center**. The **Plaza de España** is home to the monumental *ayuntamiento* (town hall) and Palacio de Llano Ponte, while the expansive **Parque de Ferrera** is just left of c/Rivero. The 17th-century **Fuente de los Caños de San Francisco**, located just southwest of the Plaza de España, is a masterpiece of civil engineering.

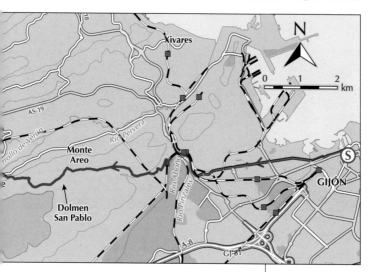

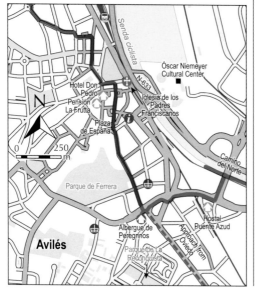

The pedestrian-friendly center of Avilés

STAGE 21
Avilés to Muros de Nalón

Start	Albergue de Peregrinos, Avilés
Finish	Iglesia de Santa María, Muros de Nalón
Distance	23.5km
% unpaved	22.9%
Total ascent	613m
Total descent	490m
Terrain	3
Route-finding	2
Pilgrim accommodation	San Martín de Laspra, Muros de Nalón

Today's walk generally holds to the interior, coming closest to the coast when it loops through Salinas. Instead, the focus is on the Río Nalón – the fortified village of El Castillo de San Martín is perched above its east bank, the camino juts southwest through Soto del Barco in order to reach the lone bridge crossing, and then Muros de Nalón sits nestled in the hills above the westside. While Muros was a small blip on the Norte a few years back, it now offers three albergues, making this (or El Pito, a few kilometers further) a good place to break up what used to be a very long stage.

▶ From the albergue, follow c/Rivero, a pedestrian-only road through the **Plaza de España**, then continue straight on c/la Ferraria, passing the Parque del Muelle and the Plaza de la Merced. Depart the city on Avda de Alemania and keep straight on.

In **San Cristóbal** (bar), 3km later, turn right at the bar. Turn left onto a dirt track and descend through woods. Cross N-632a and then follow a series of well-marked turns through the residential streets of

Waymarks in Avilés are a mix of arrows and blue/yellow scallop shells.

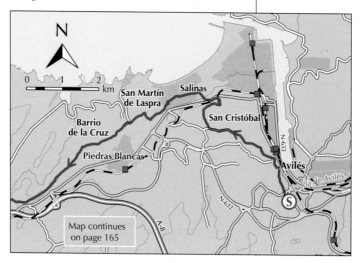

Map continues on page 165

SALINAS (6.3KM)

Bars/restaurants, supermarket, pharmacy. **Beach Hostel El Pez Escorpion** (€20, 16 beds, open all year, kitchen, W/D, Avda Marola 1, tel 985 500 859), **Las Dunas Hostel** (€15–20, c/Galán 1, tel 985 502 244), **Hotel Castillo de Gauzon** (singles €44–60, doubles €55–77 triples €66–99, breakfast available, Avda Campón 22, tel 985 502 634).

It is possible to follow the coast through this stretch – join Paseo de Cantábrico out of town and turn right after a zinc factory, following signs for the Senda Norte and La Mina. This leads to San Juan de la Arena (Albergue Los Novales – €12, 39 beds, open all year, kitchen, W/D, @, tel 985 586 119). Follow the highway onward to El Castiello. This roughly doubles the length of the camino.

Proceed uphill on Avda San Martín to leave Salinas. ◀ Minor roads lead through Barrio El Cueto and **San Martín de Laspra** (Albergue San Martín – donativo, 46 beds, open all year, kitchen, W/D, tel 659 803 290). After a long descent, cross the highway, and continue into **Barrio de la Cruz**. A beautiful walk follows, along a tree-lined dirt road through the hills, concluding with another descent into **La Ventaniella Santiago del Monte**. Fork left after the chapel, cross N-643 (Aeropuerto de Asturias is 1.7km to the right), and follow steps down and back up. After crossing A-8, join a dirt road and watch carefully for three waymarked right forks as you proceed. Complete a lengthy downhill stretch through a eucalyptus grove, then cross the medieval bridge into

EL CASTILLO DE SAN MARTÍN (11.9KM)

Built over ruins of a Roman fort, this medieval castle dates to Alfonso III's rule. This also used to be the embarkation point for pilgrims crossing the Río Nalón.

Proceed uphill through the old town. Turn left onto N-632, turning soon after into

SOTO DEL BARCO (1.1KM)

Bar, supermarket. **Hotel Palacio de la Magdalena** (doubles €80–150, includes breakfast, tel 985 588 899). The camino skirts the town and most facilities are just off-route.

A town shaped in many ways by trade and emigration to the Americas, as displayed in the many examples of Indianos architecture.

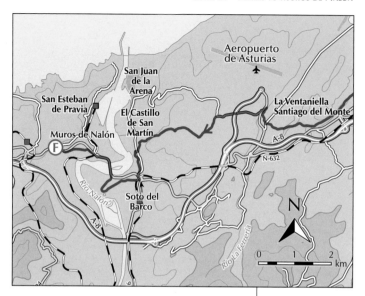

Follow the old N-632 as it swings widely out of town, joining the (current) N-632 as it crosses the Nalón. Fork left up a steep dirt road, passing through a small neighborhood (two of Muros's albergues are here). Re-cross the highway and proceed to the central plaza in

MUROS DE NALÓN (4.2KM)

Bars, supermarket. **Albergue Casa Carmina** (€14–15, singles €30, doubles €45, 20 beds, breakfast available, kitchen, W/D, Avda de Riego 21-23, tel 985 583 137), **Albergue La Naranja Peregrina** (donativo, 20 beds, open mid Mar–Nov, communal meals, W/D, @, c/Era 27, tel 685 245 111), **Albergue Camino de la Costa** (€10, singles €15, doubles €30, open all year, breakfast available, kitchen, Plaza del Marqués 12, tel 636 580 365), **Apartamentos Turísticos La Flor** (doubles €40–60, kitchen, pilgrim discount, c/Arango 28, tel 985 583 106).

The 16th-century **Plaza del Marqués de Muros** includes the Iglesia de Santa María.

The mouth of the Río Nalón

STAGE 22
Muros de Nalón to Cadavedo

Start	Iglesia de Santa María, Muros de Nalón
Finish	Albergue de Peregrinos, Cadavedo
Distance	35.2km
% unpaved	44.6%
Total ascent	997m
Total descent	1039m
Terrain	4
Route-finding	3
Pilgrim accommodation	El Pito, Soto de Luiña, Cadavedo

The first portion of this stage is familiar walking, with the mix of quiet paved roads and dirt tracks typical in recent days, accented with highlights in El Pito's Renaissance gardens and the Concha de Artedo beach. After Soto de Luiña, however, you have a big choice. The widely recommended 'Ballotas' approach passes through a series of small towns and mixes short highway jaunts with enjoyable footpaths through wooded hills and gullies. Fit and motivated pilgrims may prefer the high-level 'Camino' route, which climbs dirt roads and footpaths high into the coastal hills, offering some of the finest views of the entire Norte. Be prepared if you take the latter – there are no facilities anywhere along the walk.

A series of minor roads leads out of Muros, passing the rail station before transitioning to a picturesque footpath that winds through densely forested hills into

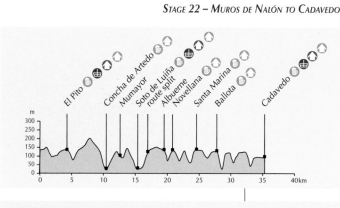

EL PITO (4.1KM)

Bar, grocery. **Albergue Cudillero** (€12.5+, 8 beds, open all year, kitchen, Avda Selgas, tel 985 590 204), **Hotel Álvaro** (doubles €40–55, pilgrim discounts, tel 985 590 204), **Hotel Aguilar** (singles €36–52, doubles €45–65, tel 685 162 882), **Hotel Casa Vitorio** (singles €35–66, doubles €45–88, breakfast available, tel 985 591 377).

A small town shaped by the powerful Selgas family. The 19th-century **Quinta de Selgas** palace and its adjoining gardens are styled after the Italian Renaissance, and the palace is home to an art collection that includes works by Goya and El Greco. It may be possible to arrange a tour (tel 985 590 120). Nearby, the **Escuelas Selgas**, one of the family's many gifts to the town, remains open as a museum.

The Selgas Renaissance Gardens in El Pito

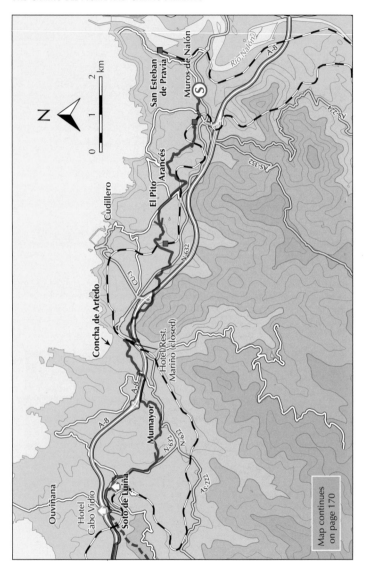

Map continues
on page 170

Fork left after El Pito's church onto a road that quickly becomes a dirt track, and then a footpath. Minor roads lead past Hotel Lupa (singles €35–45, doubles €55–65, includes breakfast, tel 985 590 973), eventually crossing N-632. Three crossings of A-8 follow, ultimately passing the old Hotel/Restaurant Mariño (now closed) and making a sharp left downhill. After a steep descent, arrive at a T-junction with a footpath.

Turn left to continue along the camino. ▸ Pass under the expressway again and then continue on a dirt road through the woods to **Mumayor**. Return to N-634a later for the final stretch into

Alternatively, turn right for the Concha de Artedo beach (Restaurante/Pension Casa Miguel – doubles €45–55, includes breakfast, tel 985 596 350).

SOTO DE LUIÑA (11.7KM)

Bars, restaurants, grocery. Albergue de Peregrinos (€5, 24 beds, 20+ in high season, open all year, W/D, key from Café Bar Ecu, tel 985 597 257), Hostal Paulino (singles €15–20, doubles €25–30, extra bed €12.5, open Mar–Oct, @, c/Los Quintos, tel 985 596 038), Hotel Casa Vieja del Sastre (singles €35–47, doubles €57–82, 15% pilgrim discount, open Mar–Oct, pilgrim menu, @, tel 985 596 190), Hotel Valle de las Luiñas (singles €44–66, doubles €55–114, includes breakfast, tel 985 596 283).

A pleasant town where a former pilgrim's hospital is now used as a cultural center. The 18th-century **Iglesia de Santa María** contains a baroque altarpiece dedicated to Nuestra Señora de la Humilidad.

From Soto de Luiña to Albuerne, the route generally follows N-634a, although it frequently veers onto parallel tracks. After passing **Hotel Cabo Vidio** (singles €40–50, doubles €50–60, includes breakfast, tel 985 596 112), the camino splits. ▸ Continue straight along N-634a for the 'Ballotas' approach, recommended for most pilgrims. Fork into **Albuerne** and then transition onto a dirt track through the woods, returning to N-634a in

The high-level variant is described at the end of this stage.

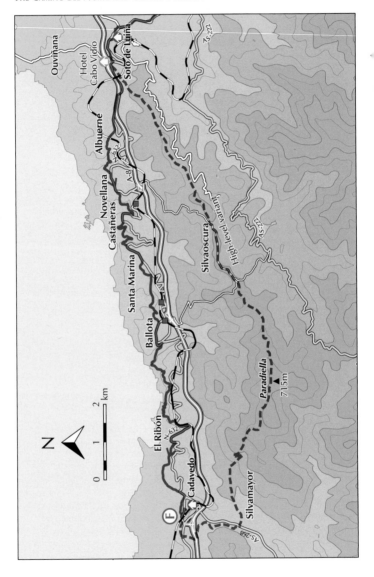

NOVELLANA (5.1KM)

Bar. **Hotel El Fernón** (doubles €40–60, pilgrim discounts, breakfast available, tel 985 598 082).

Fork right off the highway and then left, off-road. The footpath proceeds across the wooded hillside and into **Castañeras**. Following another short highway jaunt, once again fork right and return soon after to a footpath leading towards

SANTA MARINA (3.8KM)

Bar. **Pensión Prada** (doubles €30–40, pilgrim discounts, tel 985 598 184).

Fork right at the town entrance, then fork right before Pensión Prada, immediately after the bar. The pattern continues, as you transition to an off-road stretch, only to re-emerge on N-634a as you enter

BALLOTA (2.8KM)

Hotel/Restaurant Casa Fernando (singles €25–30, doubles €45–50, tel 985 598 291).

Take a sharp right onto a dirt road, the longest off-road stretch of this stage. Turn left before the coast, passing the site of the former **Puente que Tiembla** ('the bridge that trembles'). The old wooden bridge was a well-known pilgrim hazard; today, a stone structure has taken its place. Join a minor paved road in **El Ribón**, then rejoin N-634a. Turn right before the km153 sign, then rejoin the highway as you enter **Cadavedo**. The albergue is at the town's end, 1.8km further on, just off the highway.

High-level variant
Alternatively, turn left at the route split to follow the 'Camino' approach. Discouraged for many years due to disuse and poor maintenance, this route has experienced a resurgence in popularity and care over the last few years. In

A waymark on the high-level variant towards Cadavedo

good weather, it is spectacular, offering sweeping views of the coastline and interior. Pilgrims should be prepared, however, for multiple strenuous ascents, an extended descent (generally on good footing, although with a couple of trickier stretches), and a complete lack of facilities, and they should also take care at trail intersections to confirm waymarking, as some may be overgrown.

The route begins with a lengthy, sustained climb, passing through the village of **Silvaoscura** (and crossing the road to Novellana) 5.4km from the split. Cross the Ballota road 2km later. ◀ The high point of the walk, along the side of the **Pico de Paradiella**, comes 3.2km further on. The village of **Silvamayor** is 4.5km ahead, following a long downhill stretch; it may be possible to refill water here. While the waymarks call for you to cross AS-268 and continue along a footpath, this is often quite muddy and swings past Cadavedo, forcing you to backtrack into town. Instead, it may be preferable to turn right on the highway and follow it directly into **Cadavedo**, shaving a kilometer from the walk. Overall (not including the final shortcut), this route is 800 meters longer than the 'Ballotas' approach, spanning 18.9km total.

This is your last bailout point, if you're having any second thoughts.

CADAVEDO (7.7KM)

Bars/restaurants, grocery. Albergue de Peregrinos (€5, 13 beds, tel 985 645 320), Casa de Peregrinos Covi y Peter (donativo, 10 beds, tel 660 147 482, Barrio Las Corradas 7), Hotel Astur Regal (doubles €45–70, includes breakfast, c/Millares, tel 985 645 777), Apartamentos Casa Carin (beds €15, tel 615 898 185), Casa Family Astour (singles €30, doubles €37, breakfast available, W/D, @, tel 622 898 387).

A prominent medieval whaling port, Cadavedo is today focused more on agriculture and livestock. A thoroughly decentralized town, with some 300 structures scattered across 10km², one-third of which predate the 20th century.

STAGE 23
Cadavedo to Luarca

Start	Albergue de Peregrinos, Cadavedo
Finish	Albergue Villa de Luarca, Luarca
Distance	15.7km
% unpaved	39.5%
Total ascent	233m
Total descent	313m
Terrain	2
Route-finding	2
Pilgrim accommodation	Almuña, Luarca

Today's walk is a quick foray through the Asturian countryside. Unfortunately, it is a day spent too close to the highway and too far from the coast, although the newer expressway has eliminated most of the auto traffic and significant efforts have been made to get more of the walk off the pavement. On the plus side, you can maintain a leisurely pace and still finish before lunch, with plenty of time to enjoy the cozy port town of Luarca.

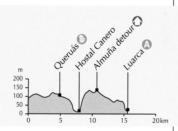

The opening leg of the stage begins and ends on N-634a. Follow for 5km, swinging just north of it in between, en route to **Queruás** (bar). Cross A-8 and join N-634a, leaving it briefly to visit the Iglesia de San Miguel. Later, when the highway curves right, fork right onto a footpath. Arrive at **Hostal/Restaurante Canero** soon after (beds €10–12, singles €20–30, doubles €30–50, open Feb–Nov, meals available, W/D, @, tel 985 475 036), which is very pilgrim-friendly. Continue on the dirt road through the woods. Climb to a track paralleling

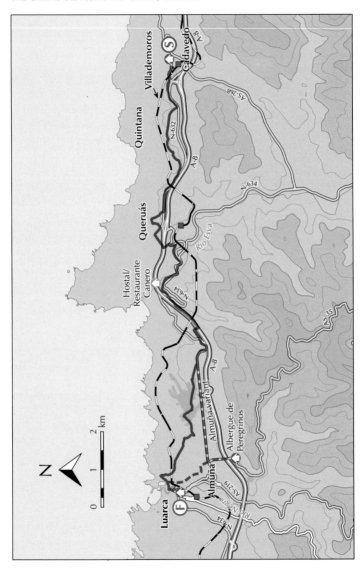

A-8, crossing it at the next opportunity. The route then rejoins N-634a.

The camino splits soon after, near the turn for La Rampla. For the albergue, continue straight along the highway. It is 3.3km away in **Almuña** (bar, Albergue de Peregrinos – €5, 22 beds, open all year, located on AS-351, tel 650 218 326, Hotel Zabala – doubles €40–60, open May–Sep, @, tel 985 640 208). ▸ To continue along the camino, fork right. The approach to Luarca is deceptively long, spanning 4.5km, briefly joining Crta Lugar 1 before forking left onto unpaved tracks. The steep, final descent, involving many steps, leads to the bridge over the Río Negro in

Those who stay at the albergue will rejoin the camino tomorrow by walking 1.7km to Luarca via a waymarked series of roads.

LUARCA (15.7KM)

All facilities. Albergue Villa de Luarca (€11–12, 22 beds, open all year, kitchen, W/D, @, c/Álvaro de Albornoz 3, tel 660 819 434), Hotel Villa de Luarca (doubles €50–96, pilgrim discounts, tel 985 470 703), Hotel Báltico (doubles €45–75, Paseo del Muelle 1, tel 985 640 991), Hotel La Colmena (singles €35–45, doubles €50–60, @, c/Uría 2, tel 985 640 278), Hotel Dabeleira (single €35–45, doubles €40–65, @, c/Nicanor del Campo 12, tel 684 630 098), Hostal Oria (singles €25, doubles €35, c/Crucero 7, tel 984 081 309).

A small fishing town that packs its white and gray buildings tightly around the rectangular harbor. Luarca was founded in the 13th century as an administrative center. Threats from the English and French in the 16th century necessitated the establishment of fortifications, some of which are still visible. Emigration to Cuba and Argentina reshaped the town once again in the 19th and early 20th centuries.

The port of Luarca

STAGE 24
Luarca to La Caridad

Start	Albergue Villa de Luarca, Luarca
Finish	Albergue de Peregrinos, La Caridad
Distance	30km
% unpaved	29.1%
Total ascent	587m
Total descent	540m
Terrain	2
Route-finding	2
Pilgrim accommodation	Piñera, Navia, La Caridad

As has been true for the last several stages, the walk from Luarca to La Caridad is generally level (although the climb out of Luarca will break a sweat), passes primarily through quiet countryside, and offers few notable sights. It has one energetic market town along the way, Navia, and several minor possible stopping points. Near the midway point, Piñera offers an Albergue de Peregrinos, which can be particularly useful for those hoping to go farther than Luarca in one day. La Caridad is a pilgrim-friendly place to end your walk, with a well-situated albergue.

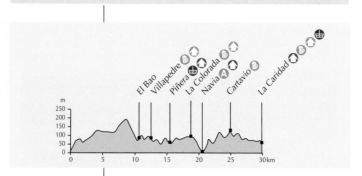

Those who stayed at the albergue in Almuña will start their day by walking 1.7km to Luarca.

◀ Proceed uphill on c/La Peña. Pass the 10th-century **Antigua Iglesia y Cementerio de Santiago**, then cross the railroad and N-634, with a bar and restaurant nearby. The route proceeds between N-634 and A-8, where it will remain for most of the day, with brief exceptions. ▶ After a short up-and-down across a modest ridge and a crossing of the Río Barajo, the camino passes through **El Bao** and **El Carreion** before arriving in

A coastal variant is possible from El Bao, much more scenic and also significantly longer, reconnecting with the camino in Navia.

VILLAPEDRE (12.7KM)

Two bars. Hotel El Pinar (singles €25–28, doubles €36–45, W/D, @, tel 985 472 221), Villa Auristela (singles €35–40, doubles €50–70, includes breakfast, tel 655 846 206).

The 13th-century **Iglesia de Santiago** features Santiago Matamoros in its altarpiece.

Pass the church, loop under the railroad, and cross the highway. Follow minor roads to Piñera, then cross the railroad twice, curve around the church, and return to N-634. The albergue is located here, on the outskirts of

PIÑERA (2.6KM)

Grocery. Albergue de Peregrinos (€5, 20 beds, meals available, W/D, tel 611 040 517).

Turn right onto a footpath, then right again at a T-junction towards **Villaoril**. Continue along the road into

LA COLORADA (3.4KM)

Bar. Hotel Blanca (doubles €65–70, tel 985 630 775).

Turn left after Hotel Blanca and then right onto a footpath. Keep straight on past the cemetery, proceeding downhill into

NAVIA (1.8KM)

All facilities. Albergue San Roque (€10, 24 beds, open Mar-Nov, W/D, Avda

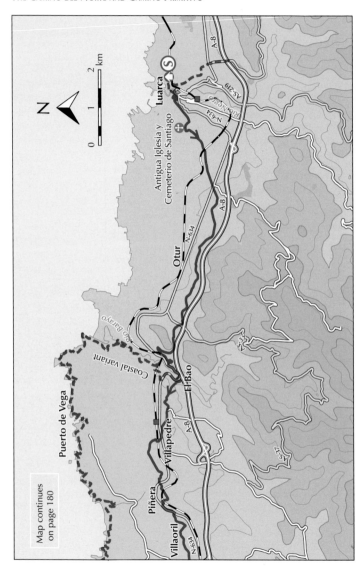

Map continues
on page 180

Manuel Suarez 3, tel 691 904 242), **Hotel Palacio Arias** (singles €36–46, doubles €50–71, @, breakfast available, Avda de los Emigrantes 11, tel 985 473 671), **Pensión Cantabrico** (singles €20, doubles €30, triples €45, microwave/refrigerator, @, tel 985 474 177).

Navia was first documented in the 10th century, although Celtic remains have been found in the area. Alfonso X ordered the construction of walls in the 13th century, and parts of these remain. The town's architectural highlights are more recent, including the baroque **Iglesia de Santa Marina de Vega** and the neo-Gothic parish church.

Cross the river on N-634, then take the second left towards **Jarrio**. After the village, the route generally moves in a westwardly direction, first paralleling A-8, and then crossing it and moving closer to N-634 near **Cartavio** (bar). La Caridad's old albergue, which now serves as overflow space in the summer, is located 1.5km before town, left off the highway. Continue on, forking to the right of N-634 and descending into a wooded patch with the newer albergue at the entrance to

A pilgrimage cross near La Caridad

LA CARIDAD/A CARIDÁ (9.5KM)

Bars/restaurants, grocery. **Albergue de Peregrinos** (€5, 18 beds, open all year, tel 685 154 405), **Albergue La Xana** (€11–17, 14 beds, kitchen, W/D, Avda de Asturias 18, tel 984 196 830), **Pensión Sayane** (doubles €45–55, Avda de Asturias 6, tel 985 478 229), **Hotel Casa Xusto** (doubles €50+, tel 985 154 405).

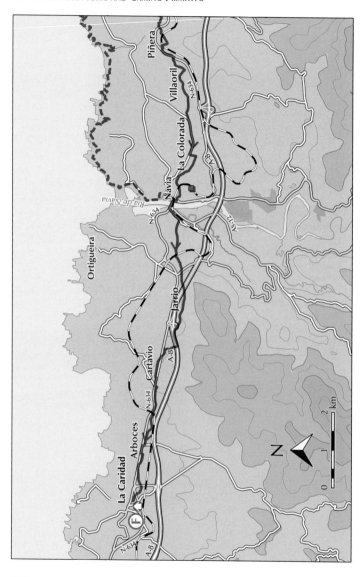

STAGE 25

La Caridad to Ribadeo

Start	Albergue de Peregrinos, La Caridad
Finish	Albergue de Peregrinos, Ribadeo
Distance	24.1km
% unpaved	22.3%
Total ascent	301m
Total descent	338m
Terrain	1
Route-finding	4
Pilgrim accommodation	Tapia de Casariego, Tol, Figueras, Ribadeo

Today is your last day on the coast. While the 'official' camino hews to the interior, we suggest an alternative route, via Tapia de Casariego, that offers extra time near the water. Ribadeo represents a major landmark along the pilgrimage. On crossing the river into town, with the wind whipping your face and ripping into your pack, you enter Galicia, the final region of the trip. And you can plan on sleeping well, with an albergue offering million-dollar views.

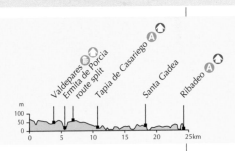

Proceed straight through La Caridad, following sidewalk waymarks. At the town's end, fork right downhill onto a footpath. The route ultimately returns to N-634, leading into

VALDEPARES (3.8KM)

Two bars. **Casa Rego** (doubles €35–40, tel 985 637 334).

Nearby is the **Castro del Cabo Blanco**, an excavated Celtic settlement from the fourth century BC.

For a pleasant detour, turn right immediately after the bridge and follow the waymarked track 1km to the Playa de Porcia; the GR later loops back to the camino.

A series of minor roads leads through the village of **El Franco**, followed by a more enjoyable off-road stretch to the **Ermita de Porcia** and its impressive Romanesque bridge. ◄

Soon after a fountain, arrive at a route split: continue straight for the coastal approach to Tapia de Casariego or fork left for the 'official' camino via Tol. We recommend the coastal approach, which leads straight ahead for several kilometers. Pass Tapia's albergue, which is situated in an incredible position overlooking the Atlantic, as you enter town.

TAPIA DE CASARIEGO (7.2KM)

All facilities. **Albergue de Peregrinos** (donativo, 30 beds, key from Turismo, open 1000–1400 and 1700–2000 in the summer or call tel 660 689 228 when closed). **Hotel Casa del Abuelo** (singles €35–55, doubles €55–95, includes breakfast, 1km before Tapia, tel 686 481 555), **Hotel La Ruta** (singles €35+, doubles

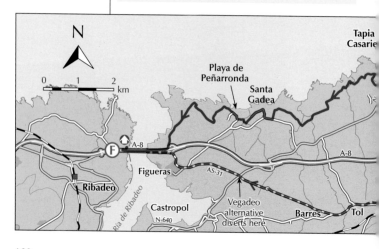

€45+, Avda de Galicia 4, tel 985 628 138), **Hotel Puente de los Santos** (singles €33, doubles €50, c/Primo de Rivera 31, tel 985 628 155).

While the modern town wasn't established until the 19th century, the region has been inhabited since the Paleolithic era, and was a prominent fishing center in the Middle Ages.

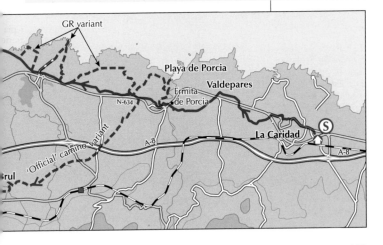

Continue straight into the center of Tapia. At a T-junction, turn left and then take the next right through a small parking lot. Turn left at a T-junction, then right onto the main road through Tapia, the Avda de Galicia. Towards the end of town, fork right onto a pedestrian track skirting the coastline. After looping around the inlet, turn left on a minor road. The route zigzags through fields, arriving in the village of **Santa Gadea** and then the **Playa de Peñarronda** (Hostal Parajes – doubles €40+, meals available, @, tel 985 979 050). Continue along the coast to another beach, the **Playa de Arnao**, and then veer inland, turning right and proceeding alongside the A-8. Cross the Ría de Ribadeo, descend from the bridge back towards the river, and then turn left. The albergue in **Ribadeo** is on your right, 1km from the center of town. This route spans 13.2km total.

'Official' camino variant

The inland option forks left, across N-634. On the other side, follow the middle of three roads, which quickly becomes a dirt track, leading to **Brul**. Leaving the village, join a paved road soon after passing sports fields. Turn left at the intersection, joining AS-31 soon after. Follow this to the albergue in

TOL (10KM)

Bar, grocery. Albergue de Peregrinos (€6, 16 beds, tel 982 128 689).

An alternative route, forking left, follows the historic route through Vegadeo (26km, Albergue de Peregrinos Mar y Montaña – tel 698 400 416), A Trapa (23km, Albergue Casa Xica – tel 628 457 427), and then connects with the 'official' Norte in Mondoñedo (16km).

Keep straight on AS-31, crossing the Río Tol. The camino splits again soon after, near signs for Castropol/Barres. ◀ The 'official' route towards Ribadeo, described here, continues straight, passing through **Barres** (bar), crossing N-640, and then proceeding into

FIGUERAS (5.4KM)

Bars/restaurants, supermarket. Albergue Turístico Camino Norte (€15, 20 beds, meals available, W/D, tel 985 636 207), Hostal Casa Venancio (Crta de Figueras, tel 985 623 072).

The 16th-century **Palacio de los Pardo de Donlebún** has been declared a national monument.

▶ Fork right as you enter. Turn right at T-junction soon after. Pass through a roundabout and under N-634, and then turn left at the next roundabout. Join N-634 across the Ría de Ribadeo, merging with the coastal route here. This route is 2.8km shorter than the coastal approach.

Waymarks in town are white stickers with red Xacobeo 2010 logos (mostly faded) on traffic poles.

RIBADEO (13.1KM)

All facilities. **Albergue de Peregrinos** (€6, 12 beds, kitchen, tel 659 942 159), **Albergue Ribadeo a Ponte** (€13-15, 28 beds, open all year, kitchen, W/D, @, c/ Barreiro 7, tel 686 794 389), **Hotel Santa Cruz** (singles €25, doubles €40, triples €60, c/Diputación 22, tel 982 130 549), **Pensión Linares** (doubles €36+, Plaza España 13, tel 982 129 633), **Hotel Rosmary Ribadeo** (doubles €33–49, pilgrim discount, c/San Francisco 3, tel 982 128 678), **Hotel Rolle** (doubles €60–98, includes breakfast, c/Enxeñeiro Schulz 6, tel 982 120 670).

The camino's primary routing through Ribadeo is a modern development, thanks to the construction of the highway bridge. Many medieval pilgrims would have cut south, through Vegadeo. Although Ribadeo was founded by Fernando II in 1183, it was taken by the French knight Pierre de Vaillanes and not fully integrated into the larger region until the 19th century. The nearby

Ribadeo's Albergue de Peregrinos

beach of **As Catedrais** is a major tourist stop and worth an afternoon train or taxi ride. Within the city, the **Plaza de España** features many interesting buildings, including the *ayuntamiento* and the **Torre de los Moreno**. The tower is a modern structure in the Indianos-style, but it has fallen into a state of disrepair.

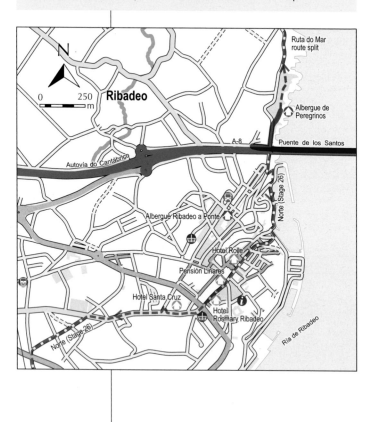

STAGE 26
Ribadeo to Lourenzá

Start	Albergue de Peregrinos, Ribadeo
Finish	Albergue de Peregrinos, Lourenzá
Distance	28.7km
% unpaved	31%
Total ascent	803m
Total descent	751m
Terrain	4
Route-finding	2
Pilgrim accommodation	Vilela, Gondán, San Xusto, Lourenzá

The route from Ribadeo leaves the coast behind, climbing into the Galician hills. Dense eucalyptus groves line much of the camino, filling the air with their unmistakable fragrance. Throughout Galicia, anticipate smaller, decentralized villages and many little-used roads. Road signs are now in Gallego, although changes are modest. Conditions today are particularly rural, with few opportunities to refuel – be sure to pick up extra provisions in Ribadeo. Fortunately, arrival in Lourenzá brings all necessary facilities and a beautiful monastery.

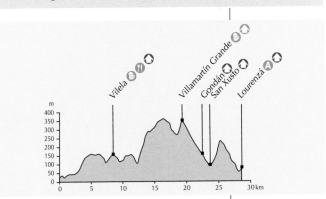

The route through **Ribadeo** is poorly marked. Turn left out of the albergue and proceed straight, passing under the expressway. Turn right on Avda Leopoldo Calvo Sotelo. At

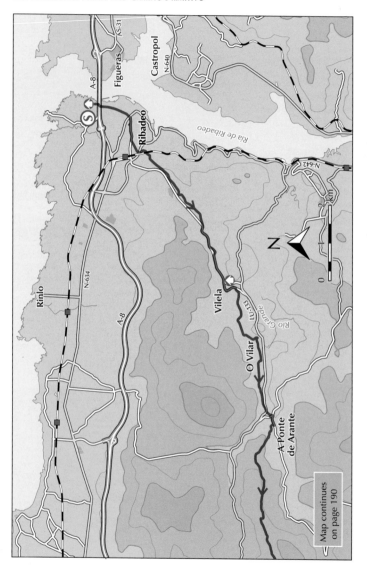

Map continues
on page 190

the T-junction, turn right on Rúa San Roque and then left on Rúa de Ramón González. Turn right on Rúa San Lázaro. As you pass the soccer pitch, turn left to leave town. From this point, waymarks are very reliable. Follow a mix of paved and unpaved roads, including a long stretch along LU-5207. Continue uphill past the cluster of houses on your right to reach the turn-off for

VILELA (7.9KM)

Bar/restaurant. Albergue A Pena (€10, 12 beds, kitchen, W/D, @, tel 649 075 449).

Turn right at the intersection with the bar/albergue. Continue along a forested road to **O Vilar**. Turn right onto a dirt road and proceed 3km to **A Ponte de Arante**. Descend to the small bridge and past the church. Turn right at the end of town, proceeding uphill on a mix of minor paved and dirt roads, ascending a steep 5.4km to first **Villamartín Pequeño**, and then the slightly larger

VILLAMARTÍN GRANDE (11.7KM)

Bar/restaurant. Habitaciones Tentempé Peregrino (doubles €30–35, open Easter–Oct, meals and basic provisions available, @, tel 610 451 518, tel 647 823 378).

Head downhill on a minor road, passing the **Capela do Carme** on the way out. Continue through

GONDÁN (2.3KM)

Albergue de Peregrinos (donativo, 30 beds, kitchen, tel 630 329 028). This albergue may be closed – check before you rely on it.

Follow minor roads into

SAN XUSTO (1.8KM)

Bar/restaurant. Albergue de Peregrinos (€5, 12 beds, kitchen, W/D, keys from bar A Curva, @, tel 982 144 072).

Galician waymarks need to be read differently from those in Asturias. Up to now, the direction of the route was indicated by following the lines of the scallop shell as they converged. But in Galicia, the opposite is true. Turn in the direction that the lines diverge. Cement waymarks indicate the distance remaining to Santiago.

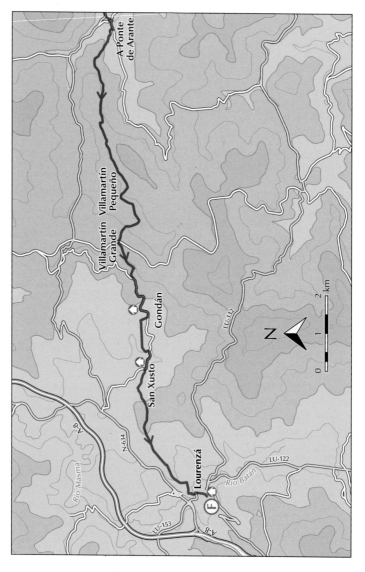

Continue along the road over a brief climb, followed by a longer descent into

LOURENZÁ (5KM)

Bars, supermarkets. Albergue de Peregrinos (€6, 20 beds, kitchen, c/Campo de la Gracia, tel 652 18 67 31), Albergue O Camiño (€11, 8 beds, kitchen, @, c/Calvo Sotelo 3, tel 696 570 192), Albergue Savior (€13, 24 beds, doubles €32, kitchen, breakfast available, W/D, @, Rúa Calvo Sotelo 15, tel 649 837 421), Albergue Castelos Lourenzá (€12, €30 doubles, 40 beds, kitchen, breakfast available, W/D, @, Avda de Mondoñedo 26, tel 982 100 887), Casa Gloria (doubles €35–48, includes breakfast, c/Peregrín Otero 3, tel 982 121 119), Hostal La Unión (singles €25–30, doubles €30–40, Avda do Val 16, tel 982 121 028), Hostelería Rego (c/Isla Nova 17, tel 982 141 819).

The town's undisputed highlight is the 10th-century Benedictine **Monasterio de San Salvador**, a national historical monument. The baroque façade, made by the architect Casas y Novoa (also responsible for the Santiago cathedral's façade), is highly regarded, as is the sarcophagus of the cathedral's founder, Don Osorio Gutiérrez. Today, it also houses a museum of religious art.

Monasterio de San Salvador, Lourenzá

STAGE 27
Lourenzá to Gontán/Abadín

Start	Albergue de Peregrinos, Lourenzá
Finish	Albergue de Peregrinos, Gontán
Distance	24.3km
% unpaved	31%
Total ascent	853m
Total descent	449m
Terrain	4
Route-finding	2
Pilgrim accommodation	Mondoñedo, Maaríz, Gontán

Today's walk rewards its steep ascents with expansive views. The route first climbs through the hills and into Mondoñedo. Once one of the seven capitals of the Kingdom of Galicia, its old town is a national cultural-historical site. From Mondoñedo, the route climbs 11km uphill, passing through tiny villages, while the valley unfolds below. A short and welcome descent leads into Gontán.

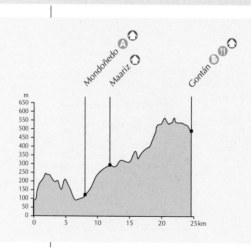

From the albergue, turn right, heading uphill on a small footpath. After a short climb, cross under A-8 and continue on a brick path through **Arroxo**. Turn right on a minor road through **Grove** (restaurant). At the cemetery, turn left onto a footpath, joining a series of tracks and small roads passing the Capela da Virgen de Guadalupe in **Carballal** and continuing through **San Pedro da Torre**. Continue past the church, then turn right onto a paved lane through town. Continue weaving through the outskirts of Mondoñedo, finally joining LU-124 and proceeding into the main plaza of

MONDOÑEDO (8.5KM)

All facilities. Stock up here: it's your only opportunity to purchase supplies during this stage. Albergue de Peregrinos (€6, 28 beds, kitchen, c/Alcántara, tel 982 507 040, tel 982 507 177), Albergue del Montero (€15, 38 beds, kitchen, W/D, Avda Eladio Lorenzo 7, tel 982 521 751), Hospedería del Seminario de Santa Catalina (singles €20–25, doubles €28–42, located inside 18th-century seminary, tel 982 521 000), Pensión Casa Bracamonte (singles €30–45, doubles €40–55, c/Jose María Pardo 23, tel 629 165 342), Hostal Padornelo (doubles €50, pilgrim discount, meals available, Avda Buenos Aires 1, tel 982 521 892).

Nestled in mountains and full of historical charm, Mondoñedo is one of the highlights of this stage. Bronze Age remains have been found in the vicinity, including an altar once used for human sacrifices. Bronze busts of Marcus Aurelius and Hadrian bear witness to the former Roman presence as well. The 13th-century **cathedral** was declared a national monument in 1902 and is known as the *catedral arrodillada* ('kneeling cathedral') for its perfect proportions and short stature. Its frescos are among Galicia's oldest, the walnut choir stalls are Gothic masterpieces, and the 5-meter rose window is especially stunning on a sunny day.

Mondoñedo cathedral

Cross the main plaza and turn right onto c/Fonte Vella. Fork left uphill onto Rúa Rigueira. Ascend through **Barbeitas**, and then to

MAARÍZ (2.6KM)

O Bisonte de Maaríz is run by Katova, a hospitable artist who opened her home to pilgrims (donativo, 6 beds, communal homegrown dinner/breakfast, cannot leave before 7am, @, phoning ahead is appreciated, tel 626 766 235)

Continue winding uphill past **Paadín**, and **Lousada**. After Lousada, turn left onto a gravel track, climbing a steep 2km. Proceed across N-634 and follow a series of gravel tracks and minor roads to

GONTÁN (13.2KM)

Bar, restaurant. Albergue de Peregrinos (€6, 26 beds, kitchen, tel 616 251 462), Pensión da Feira (doubles €25, Campo da Feira, tel 982 508 046).

A small community dwarfed by neighboring Abadín, located 500 meters further along the camino (and offering a wider array of facilities). Gontán is home to many fiestas and special markets, including the annual **Feria de Santos**.

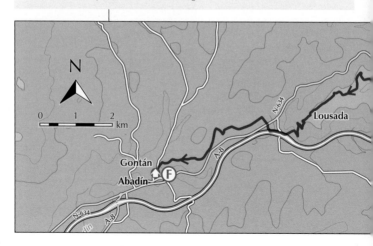

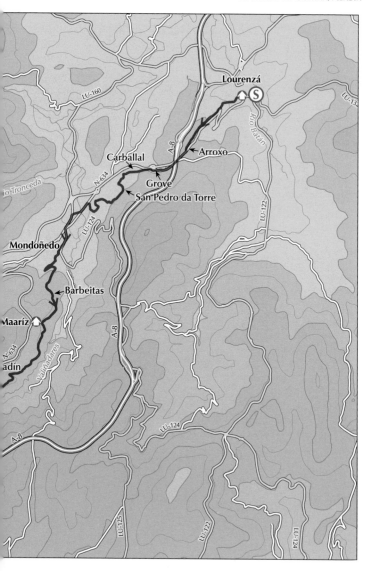

STAGE 28

Gontán/Abadín to Vilalba

Start	Albergue de Peregrinos, Gontán
Finish	Plaza Santa María, Vilalba
Distance	21.2km
% unpaved	48%
Total ascent	261m
Total descent	263m
Terrain	1
Route-finding	1
Pilgrim accommodation	Abadín, As Paredes, Vilalba

Today's walk meanders easily along rural roads, through forests and farming villages. The destination, Vilalba, is a bustling city that provides pilgrims an opportunity to recover from yesterday's hills and resupply for the next few days.

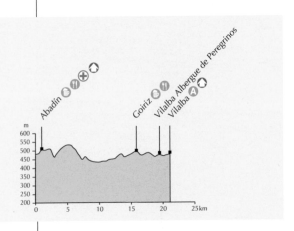

Keep straight on through **Gontán**, passing a fountain on the left before forking right uphill. Join N-634 and proceed into

ABADÍN (0.5KM)

Bars, restaurant, grocery store, pharmacy. Albergue Xabarín (€15, 25 beds, kitchen, W/D, @, tel 690 181 811, tel 982 508 025), Albergue Goás (€12, 46 beds, kitchen, W/D, @, tel 982 508 005), Casa Goás (singles €32, doubles €45, triples €57, meals available, tel 982 508 005), Pensión Niza (doubles €15–28, tel 982 508 032).

Follow the main road through town. Turn right towards the Correos and then left in front of it. Follow a minor road out of town. Fork right onto a footpath downhill. Keep straight on, crossing the Río Abadín. Turn left onto a paved road through **Ponterroxal**.

Proceed along the dirt/gravel track, eventually crossing A-8 and passing through **As Paredes (Castromaior)**, then past **Albergue O Xistral** (€12, 19 beds, kitchen, breakfast available, W/D, tel 673 524 257). Cross back under A-8, continuing along the minor road before crossing once more under A-8. Keep straight on through **Martiñán**, crossing over N-634, and follow a mix of minor roads before reaching the highway town of

GOIRIZ (15.3KM)

Bar/restaurant. Pensión H. O Cristo (singles €20, doubles €35, tel 982 527 322).

Fruit stand outside of Goiriz

Cross N-634 onto a footpath. Continue as the path transitions to pavement and then a dirt track. Turn left onto a road through **As Casanovas**. Continue through **A Casilla** and then onto the highway. Keep straight on to

VILALBA ALBERGUE (3.4KM)

Bar/restaurant. Albergue de Peregrinos (€6, 48 beds, kitchen, @, tel 982 523 911).

Continue along the highway, passing through a roundabout-overpass into Vilalba. The route through Vilalba is marked by signs on lampposts and bronze scallop shells in the sidewalks. Fork right onto Rúa Porta de Cima, which leads to Plaza Santa María in

VILALBA (2KM)

All facilities. Albergue As Pedreiras (€10, 28 beds, kitchen, W/D, @, Rúa Pita da Veiga 4, tel 620 137 711), Albergue Turístico Castelos (€12, 38 beds, kitchen, W/D, @, Rúa das Pedreiras 16, tel 982 100 887), Hotel Venezuela (singles €20, doubles €35, Plaza Suso Gayoso 10, tel 982 510 659), Hotel Vila do Alba (singles €35, doubles €45, discounted breakfast, c/Campo del Puente 27, tel 982 510

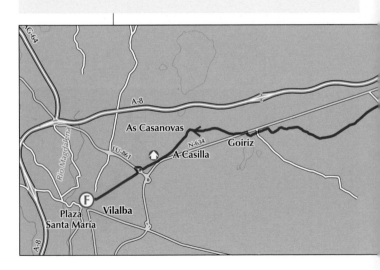

245), **Hostal Terra Chá** (singles €25, doubles €40, c/Domingo Goás 10, tel 982 511 702), **Casa Seijo** (doubles €35, c/Plácido Peña, tel 982 510 719), **Parador Vilalba** (singles from €65, doubles from €75, pilgrim discount, meals available, Rúa Valeriano Valdesuso, tel 982 520 011).

Vilalba's medieval emergence was closely linked to the Andrade family. A tower from the family castle, the 15th-century **Torre de los Andrade**, has since been converted to use as a Parador hotel. In the 20th century, the town experienced a cultural boom, emerging as a surprising hotbed of intellectual and literary activity.

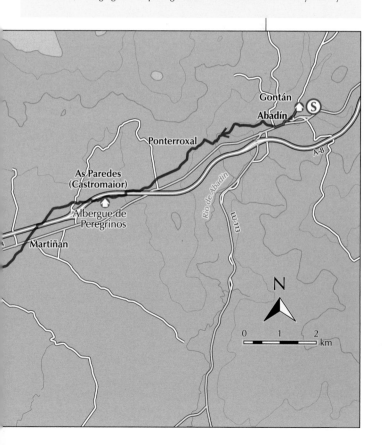

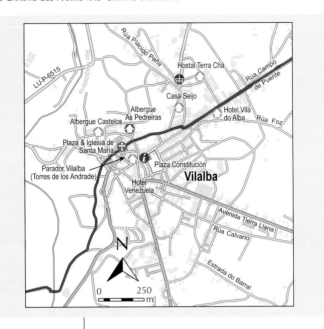

STAGE 29

Vilalba to Miraz

Start	Plaza Santa María, Vilalba
Finish	Albergue de Peregrinos, Miraz
Distance	34.5km
% unpaved	38%
Total ascent	408m
Total descent	352m
Terrain	1
Route-finding	2
Pilgrim accommodation	Carballedo, A Lagoa, Miraz

Today's walk to the village of Miraz is a pleasant stroll through the small villages dotting the Galician countryside. Look forward to an afternoon spent in the albergue in Miraz – relaxing in the garden, drinking tea, and speaking English with the hospitaleros. This albergue is run by volunteers from the British Confraternity of Saint James.

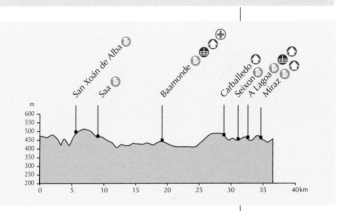

From the plaza, follow bronze shells out of town, first along Rúa Concepción Arenal and then on Travesía del Matadero. Follow a series of minor roads, eventually passing under A-8, and then over Río Ladra. Fork right onto a footpath. Continue along a series of minor roads and tracks through **Gabín** and **As Turbelas**. Shortly after, turn left to cross back over A-8. Turn right onto N-634, heading into

SAN XOÁN DE ALBA (6.2KM)

Bar with provisions just off-route.

San Xoán de Alba is home to the 14th-century **Iglesia de San Xoán**.

Shortly after the church, fork right onto a footpath. Continue onto a series of minor roads, cross over N-634 and keep straight on a dirt track, before turning right onto a footpath, leading into

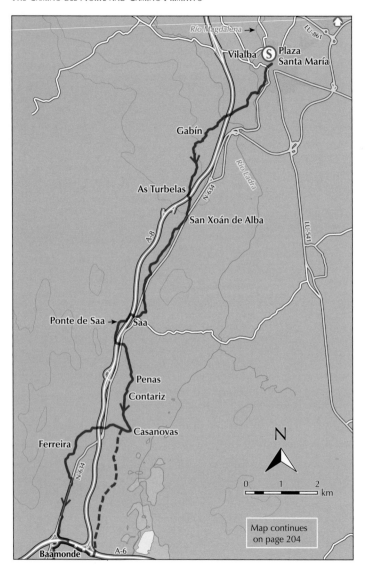

Map continues
on page 204

SAA (3.4KM)

Bar with provisions.

Ponte de Saa dates from the medieval period.

Ponte de Saa

Cross N-634, pass under A-8, and walk across the beautifully restored medieval bridge over the Río Labrada. Soon, join a gravel track, then follow another minor road back under A-8. Continue back across N-634, onto a footpath. If you'd rather skip the circuitous crossing of the Ponte de Saa, turn left onto N-634 instead of crossing it when leaving Saa. You will rejoin the camino after 1km on N-634, turning left.

Proceed straight as the path becomes a minor road and passes through **Penas**, **Contariz**, and **Casanovas**. Reports indicate that a waymarked route now follows minor roads just after Casanovas, rather than crossing back under the A-8, but we can't confirm this: the option is marked on the corresponding map. After 3.5km cross back over N-634, then under A-8.

Follow rural dirt and paved roads through **Ferreira** and back to N-634. Continue as the dirt track winds under A-6. Follow the waymarks through a neighborhood, then turn right onto the highway. Continue into

BAAMONDE (10.1KM)

Bars, restaurant, grocery, pharmacy. **Albergue de Peregrinos** (€6, 94 beds, kitchen, tel 628 250 323), **Hostal Ruta Esmeralda** (doubles €32–40, on the N-VI, tel 982 398 138).

▸ Follow the highway out of town; after 3km, turn left onto a dirt track and cross the railroad and the Río Parga. Pass the 14th-century **Santuario de San Alberte**, and continue through the woods, before reaching the hamlet **Toar**. From here, the route follows well-marked paved and gravel roads to Miraz. Proceed through the villages of **Bandoncel**, **Deva**,

Baamonde is the only large town you'll visit today, so purchase any needed provisions before leaving.

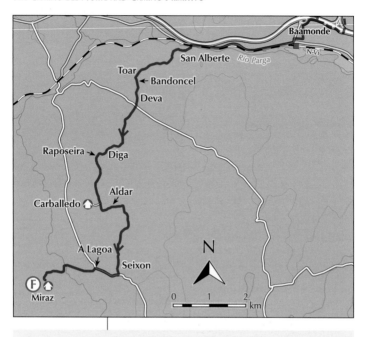

The Romanesque **Iglesia de Santiago** dates to the 14th century. Baamonde was the birthplace of acclaimed sculptor Victor Corral. His home has been turned into a museum, documenting his life and containing his works.

Diga, and **Raposeira** and past the turn-off for the hospitable Albergue Witericus in **Carballedo** (€12, 9 beds, café, closed late-Dec and Jan, @, located 150 meters off camino, tel 678 415 728).

Proceed through **Aldar**, following minor roads to Seixon (bar and 12th-century church) and

A LAGOA (12.9KM)

Bar/restaurant, small grocery. Albergue A Lagoa (€10, 16 beds, kitchen, meals available, @, tel 646 190 292).

Turn left after Bar Laguna, then fork right on the high-way. Turn right onto a dirt track, which soon becomes a paved road, leading into

MIRAZ (1.9KM)

Bar with provisions. Albergue de Peregrinos (donativo, 26 beds, open 1430, Easter–Nov, includes breakfast, kitchen, @, tel 982 830 700), Albergue Ó Abrigo (€10, 40 beds, open 1100, Easter–Oct, W/D, @, tel 982 194 850).

STAGE 30
Miraz to Sobrado dos Monxes

Start	Albergue de Peregrinos, Miraz
Finish	Albergue de Peregrinos, Sobrado dos Monxes
Distance	25.5km
% unpaved	33%
Total ascent	408m
Total descent	352m
Terrain	2
Route-finding	2
Pilgrim accommodation	A Roxica, A Cabana, Sobrado dos Monxes

Savor the first 4km of the day – some of the last scenic, off-pavement walking on the Norte. Today you'll reach the route's high point at 710m in Marcela, before continuing onto the destination and highlight, the monastery in Sobrado dos Monxes. The monastery is a spectacular work of architecture, and the albergue housed inside provides pilgrims with an excellent chance to explore the monastery's cloisters, chapels, and surrounding grounds.

Turn left out of the albergue and follow the road out of town. Soon fork left onto a gravel track, leading gently uphill through rocky terrain and onto a forested path. After emerging on a minor road, turn left. Follow rural roads through a series of small villages: 6km to **A Roxica** (Albergue Casa Roxica – €10, 10 beds, meals available, W/D, tel 630 487 008), soon followed by A Cabana (Albergue de Peregrinos – €6, 30 beds, Jun–Sep, kitchen, tel 616 251 462), 2km to

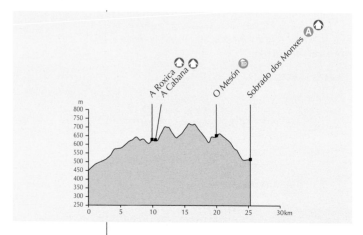

A Travesa de Ledro, and 500m up to **A Marcela**, the highest point on the Norte. Arrive in the province of A Coruña, then turn right on AC-934, and proceed into

O MESÓN (20KM)

Bars, some provisions.

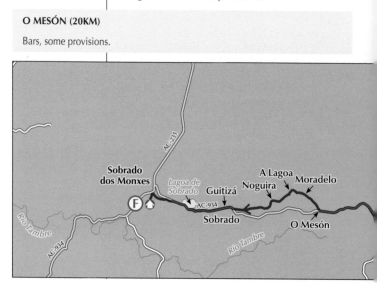

Minor roads and foothpaths lead through three villages: **Moradelo**, **A Lagoa**, and **Noguira**. Join AC-934 and keep straight on through **Guitizá**. Fork right onto a gravel track downhill, skirting the lake below. Rejoin the highway and proceed across the bridge. Continue into

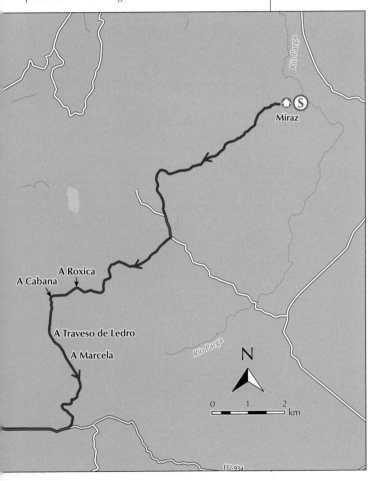

The spectacular Sobrado dos Monxes Monastery

SOBRADO DOS MONXES (5.5KM)

Bars, restaurants, grocery stores, pharmacy. Albergue de Peregrinos in monastery (€6, 120 beds, open 1000, closed 1300–1630, kitchen, W/D, tel 628 838 965), Albergue Lecer (€10, 28 beds, kitchen, W/D, @, tel 699 372 684), Hotel San Marcus (singles €35, doubles €50–55, tel 981 787 527).

The **Monasterio de Santa María de Sobrado dos Monxes** was founded in 952 and soon rose to prosperity in the late-10th century when the then-abbot of Sobrado became a bishop in Santiago. In 1142 it became the first Spanish monastery to join the Cistercian order – a good thing for pilgrims, as the Cistercians established a pilgrim hospital within the monastery. The monastery features an impressive baroque main church with a dominating façade, as well as two 17th-century cloisters, a 12th-century chapter house, a Renaissance sacristy, and multiple chapels, including the early Romanesque Chapel of John the Baptist, built in the monastery's pre-Cistercian history.

STAGE 31
Sobrado dos Monxes to Arzúa

Start	Albergue de Peregrinos, Sobrado dos Monxes
Finish	Albergue de Peregrinos, Arzúa
Distance	22km
% unpaved	19%
Total ascent	230m

Total descent	344m
Terrain	1
Route-finding	2
Pilgrim accommodation	Boimorto, Arzúa

Today, the Camino del Norte joins the densely populated Camino Francés. Prepare yourself for pilgrim culture shock when you arrive in Arzúa; it can be jarring to suddenly find yourself among not 50, but 500 fellow pilgrims. Enjoy the relative solitude of the morning before reaching Arzúa.

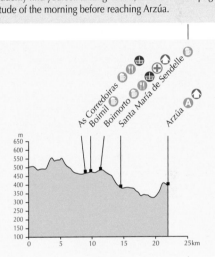

Leave **Sobrado** on the main street. Fork left onto a small paved road. Continue on a mix of minor roads, passing through **Vilarchao** and **O Peruxil**, then rejoin the highway and continue through **Castro**. Follow rural roads through **Froxa** and **Casanova**, then join the highway into

AS CORREDOIRAS (8.5KM)

Bar, restaurant, small grocery. **Turismo Rural Casa Boada** (doubles €36–45, located on AC-540, tel 981 516 187).

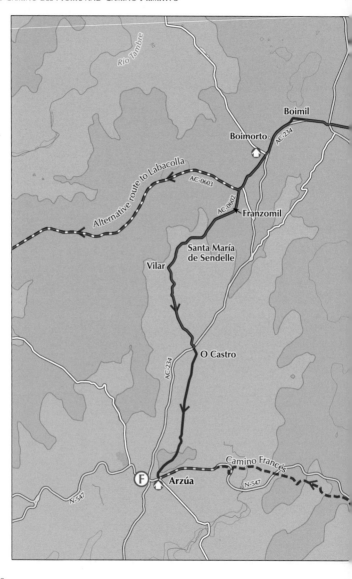

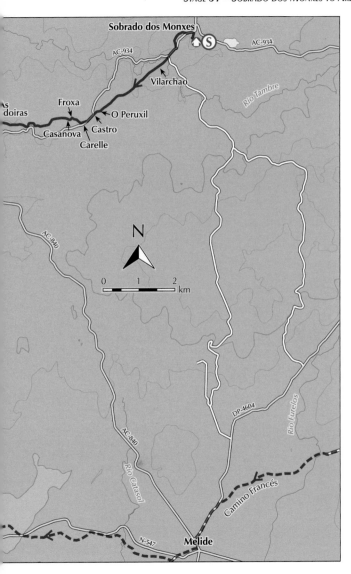

A cow near Sendelle

Leave town along the main road, then fork right onto a paved road. Pass a church on your left, rejoin the highway, and proceed to **Boimil** (bar, Pensión O Real – singles €45, doubles €60, tel 659 852 121). Continue into

BOIMORTO (3.2KM)

Bar, restaurant, grocery, pharmacy. Albergue de Peregrinos (€6, 32 beds, kitchen, tel 638 392 024), Casa da Gándara (€14, private rooms €45, Rúa Gándara 49, tel 981 516 114).

Proceed along the main road, then fork left onto AC-0602.

Route to Labacolla
An alternative route makes it possible to join the Camino Francés just before Labacolla, roughly 25km after Arzúa. To do this, follow **AC-0603** out of Boimorto, and then continue, following camino markers along a series of minor roads, eventually walking alongside N-634 before joining up with the Camino Francés near the airport, before heading into **Labacolla** (Stage 32). This route covers 27km.

Continue through **Franzomil** to **Santa María de Sendelle** (bar and 12th-century church), and then **Vilar**. After crossing the highway, continue on a small road towards **Castro**. Follow a series of minor roads into

ARZÚA (10.4KM)

All facilities. **Albergue de Peregrinos** (€6, 48 beds, kitchen, W/D, Cima de Lugar 6, tel 660 396 824). Arzúa has an overwhelming assortment of private albergues, many clustered near the entrance, including **Ultreia** (tel 981 500 471), **Da Fonte** (tel 659 999 496), **Via Lactea** (tel 981 500 581), **Los Caminantes II** (tel 647 020 600), **Don Quixote** (tel 981 500 139), and **Santiago Apostól** (tel 981 508 132). **Albergue-Pensión Arzúa** (€10, doubles €30–40, 981 508 233). **Hotel Suiza** (singles €30–43, doubles €48–58, meals available, situated on the N-547, tel 981 500 908).

A mostly modern market town, offering all facilities and specializing in cheese. The **Iglesia de Santiago** contains a 19th-century medallion depicting Santiago's intervention in Clavijo.

STAGE 32
Arzúa to Santiago de Compostela

Start	Albergue de Peregrinos, Arzúa
Finish	Praza do Obradoiro, Santiago
Distance	38.8km
% unpaved	58%
Total ascent	685m
Total descent	790m
Terrain	2
Route-finding	1
Pilgrim accommodation	A Calle, Salceda, A Brea, Santa Irene, Pedrouzo, Monte de Gozo, Santiago

The reality of arrival strikes pilgrims in different ways. For some, it is a moment of unbridled euphoria, a culmination of weeks of exhaustion and joy, self-doubt and discovery. Walking into Santiago represents a victory, even an epiphany. For others, it can feel anti-climactic, an end to the great adventure and a return to the mundane. Where is the great lesson, the heightened sense of self promised by the walk? Where is the life-changing moment? Many of us jump manically between each of these lines of thinking, uncertain one second and excited the next. Regardless of whatever doubts may linger, allow yourself to be happy with, and proud of, what you have accomplished. Besides, with the completion of one pilgrimage comes the planning of the next!

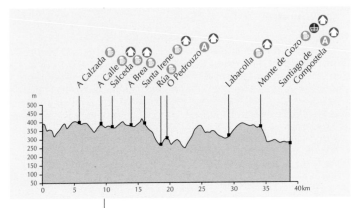

From Arzúa, the pleasant route proceeds through tiny hamlets and quiet forests. Follow a series of footpaths and minor roads through **A Calzada** (bar), **A Calle** (bar, Albergue A Ponte de Ferreiros – €13, 30 beds, W/D, tel 665 641 877), and onto

SALCEDA (11.3KM)

Bar. Albergue Pousada de Salceda (€10–12, 14 beds, W/D, tel 981 502 767), Albergue de Boni (€12, 20 beds, W/D, tel 618 965 907), and Albergue Alborada (€12, 10 beds, rooms €50, kitchen, W/D, tel 981 502 956).

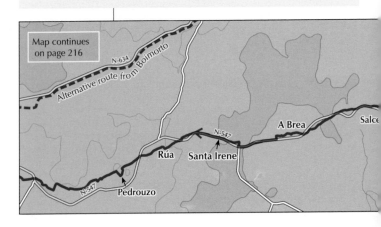

Map continues on page 216

Continue ahead, weaving around N-547 (the route generally stays off the highway), passing through **A Brea** (bars, Pensión The Way – beds €17, doubles €42, tel 628 120 202; Pensión O' Mesón – singles €28, doubles €38, tel 981 511 040), then turning right immediately after the last bar. Proceed to

SANTA IRENE (5.2KM)

Bar/restaurant. Albergue de Peregrinos (€6, 36 beds, kitchen, W/D, tel 660 396 825), Albergue de Santa Irene (€13, 15 beds, meals available, W/D, tel 981 511 000).

Keep straight on, passing the albergue municipal on your right, then cross the highway, and curve back to the left. Proceed into

RÚA (O PINO) (1.8KM)

Bar. Hotel O Pino (singles €27–36, doubles €40–48, tel 981 511 035), Casa Rural O Acivro (singles €35, doubles €45, meals available, tel 981 511 316), Pensión Casa da Gallega (€30, tel 981 511 463), Pensión Casa da Fonte (singles €35, doubles €50, triples €65+, tel 684 312 390).

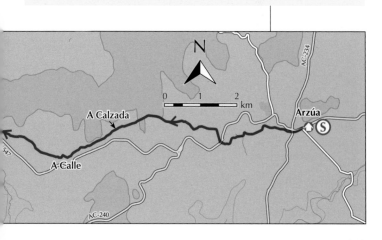

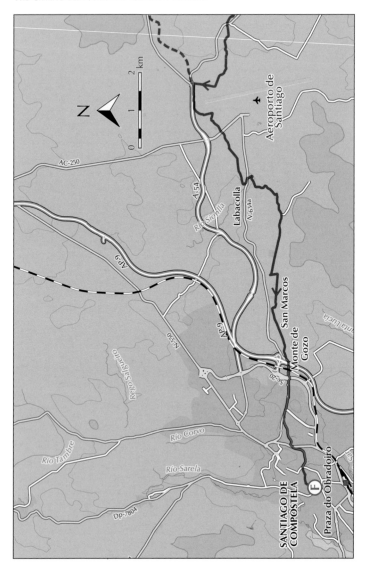

Keep straight on until the turn-off for

O PEDROUZO (1.4KM)

All facilities. To reach town, turn left on N-547 and proceed 500 meters. Waymarks allow you to reconnect with the camino without backtracking. Albergue de Peregrinos (€6, 120 beds, kitchen, W/D, @, tel 660 396 826) and many private albergues, including: Albergue Porta de Santiago (€10, 54 beds, W/D, @, tel 981 511 103), Albergue Edreira (€10, 52 beds, W/D, @, tel 981 511 365), and Albergue O Burgo (€10, 14 beds, singles €26, doubles €38, W/D, @, tel 630 404 138). Pensión Compás (singles €20–25, doubles €25–35, tel 981 511 309), Pensión Arca (singles €30, doubles €40, tel 657 888 594).

Continue across N-547 and proceed on a footpath. Transition to minor roads along the outskirts of O Pedrouzo. At the far edge of town, turn left onto a broad, heavily shaded trail. Far removed from the highway, this is the last best stretch of Galician walking – unpaved footpaths, tall trees, stone bridges, and gurgling creeks. Continue ahead, eventually passing to the right of Santiago's Labacolla airport before arriving in Labacolla. ▸

Those taking the alternative route from Boimorto will join the Francés here.

LABACOLLA (9.2KM)

Bars. Albergue Lavacolla (€12, 34 beds, kitchen, W/D, @, tel 981 897 274, tel 653 630 300), Hotel Ruta Jacobea (doubles €59, c/Lavacolla 41, tel 981 888 211), Hotel Garcas (singles €35, doubles €50, C/ Naval 2, tel 981 888 225).

In the Middle Ages, pilgrims paused here to clean themselves in the river, prior to arrival in Santiago. The translation of the name Labacolla highlights a particular concern: 'wash scrotum'.

Keep straight on, cross under N-634, passing a bar and supermarket. Soon after, cross the Labacolla river, washing as needed. Join a road leading steeply uphill and continue through open countryside, making occasional well-marked turns and eventually passing the local television station's headquarters. Pass through **San Marcos** (bars, grocery) making a final, gentle ascent into

MONTE DE GOZO (5.5KM)

Bars, restaurants, grocery. Massive **Albergue de Peregrinos** (€6, 370 beds, kitchen, W/D, @, tel 981 558 942). An unfortunate cross between an army bunker and summer camp, this is the last possible stopping point before Santiago.

Proceed downhill, cross A-8, and let loose a cheer when you see the road sign announcing your arrival in Santiago! But, there's still a bit to go before reaching the cathedral. The route follows busy streets through modern Santiago for 3km before crossing into the old town. Only 1.4km now separates you from the Praza do Obradoiro and the end of your pilgrimage in

SANTIAGO DE COMPOSTELA (4.4KM)

Santiago has a wide range of accommodation. Albergue options include **San Lázaro** (€10, 80 beds, kitchen, W/D, Rúa San Lázaro, tel 981 571 488), **Seminario Menor** (€10–15, 199 beds, W/D, Rúa de Belvís, tel 881 031 768), **The Last Stamp** (€15, 62 beds, kitchen, W/D, @, Rúa do Preguntoiro 10, 981 563 525), **Porta Real** (€10–20, 24 beds, W/D, @, c/Concheiros 10, tel 633 610 114), **Mundoalbergue** (€16–18, 34 beds, kitchen, W/D, c/San Clemente 26, tel 981 588 625), **Roots & Boots** (€16–20, kitchen, W/D, c/del Campo del Crucero del Gallo 7, tel 699 631 594). In most cases, reservations are accepted and pilgrims can stay multiple nights. **Hostal Suso** (doubles €40–49, Rúa do Vilar 65, tel 981 586 611), **Hostal Costa Azul** (singles €30, doubles €37+, Rúa das Galeras 18, tel 602 451 906), **Hostal Alfonso** (singles €35–50, doubles €45–70, Rúa do Pombal 40, tel 981 585 685), **Hospedería San Martín Pinario** (singles €50+, doubles €57+, Plaza Inmaculada 3, tel 981 560 282), For a splurge, consider Santiago's Parador, the **Hostal de los Reyes Católicos** (doubles €155+, Praza do Obradoiro, tel 981 582 200). Once upon a time, this was a pilgrim hospital, founded by Ferdinand and Isabel.

Buses to Labacolla airport run daily every 30min between 0610 and 0010. The trip takes 25min. The central bus station is located roughly 2km from the cathedral in Praza Camilo Díaz Baliño. The RENFE station is a similar distance in the opposite direction. Those hoping to visit Finisterre as a daytrip may find it more convenient to arrange this through their albergue, as minibus tours lessen the drive time significantly and offer a competitive price.

Cathedral de Santiago

Head south of the cathedral for Santiago's most lively areas: Rúa do Franco, Rúa do Vilar, and Rúa Nova offer popular restaurants, bars packed full of celebrating pilgrims, souvenir shops, and bookstores. The Correos is just off Franco on Travesa de Fonseca. If city life is too much after so many peaceful days, keep straight on along Franco, cross out of the old town, and proceed into the Alameda, a large, green park with many quiet corners.

Congratulations! Upon arrival in Santiago, you have two main pilgrim destinations remaining. First and foremost is the **cathedral** (open 0700–2000). Access to a statue of the apostle Saint James (for hugging purposes) is limited to 0930–1320 and 1600–1900. Pilgrims may visit the apostle's relics all day. Confessions (in multiple languages) are heard 0800–1300 and 1700–2100. Pilgrim mass takes place 1200–1300 and 1930–2030 daily; arrive early. Second is the **Pilgrim's Office** (Rúa Carretas 33), which issues Compostelas (0800–2000, shorter winter hours). You are not required to pick this up on the day of arrival; pilgrims continuing to Finisterre may prefer to obtain their Compostela upon return.Although there is much to see and do in Santiago, many pilgrims are drawn back to the Praza do Obradoiro many times, reliving the moment of arrival as new waves of pilgrims surge in front of the cathedral and reuniting with friends from the walk. For those having walked the Northern Caminos, it can be more than a little overwhelming, encountering so many new pilgrims. But, it is a powerful reminder of the larger community to which you all now belong, pilgrims on the Camino de Santiago, owners of the Compostela.

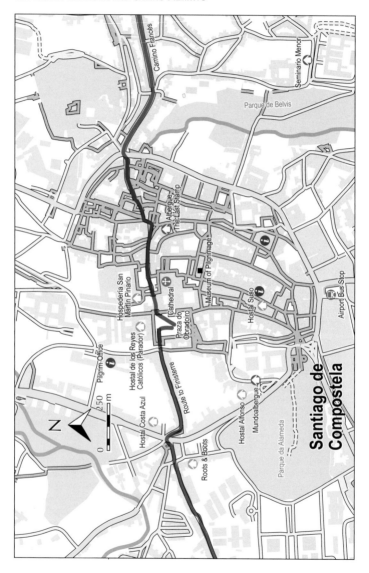

THE CAMINO PRIMITIVO

Pilgrims on Hospitales Route (Stage 6)

INTRODUCTION

The Camino Primitivo is where it all began. This first major pilgrimage route to Santiago originated in Oviedo; even after the Camino Francés emerged, many pilgrims viewed Oviedo to be a mandatory stop along the way. Today, the Primitivo feels largely untouched, enjoying long stretches of rugged countryside dotted with occasional small villages and towns. While the route traditionally begins in Oviedo, this guide picks up the trail near Villaviciosa, where the Primitivo splits from the Camino del Norte. All told, the Primitivo spans roughly 300km between Villaviciosa and Melide, where it joins the Camino Francés for the final 50km to Santiago. Along the way, the Camino Primitivo enjoys two striking cities – Oviedo and Lugo – numerous medieval villages, and some of the most dramatic mountain views of any camino.

STAGE 1
Villaviciosa to Pola de Siero

Start	Parque Ballina, Villaviciosa
Finish	Albergue de Peregrinos, Pola de Siero
Distance	27.6km
% unpaved	24%
Total ascent	592m
Total descent	381m
Terrain	2
Route-finding	3
Pilgrim accommodation	Amandi, San Salvador de Valdediós, Vega de Sariego, Pola de Siero

The Camino Primitivo forks off from the Norte, pushing into the heart of Asturias. As the Primitivo climbs into the hills, the route splits again. One route descends to the Monastery of San Salvador, while a high-level option continues uphill through the village of Arbazal. The monastery is stunningly situated in a narrow valley and easy to appreciate, regardless of which route you choose. From San Salvador, a steep ascent brings you through hillside villages before the two routes rejoin and, eventually, descend suburban streets into Pola de Siero.

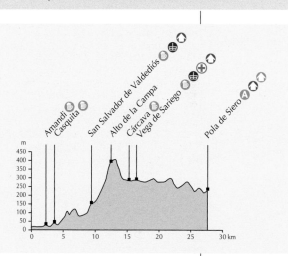

Loop past the Iglesia de Santa María de la Oliva before bearing south on or parallel to AS-255. Fork right past Sidreria la Regatina in **Amandi** and then again soon after; alternatively, fork left for the pilgrimage to Covadonga or **Albergue La Ferreria** (donativo, 12 beds, open mid Mar–Oct, communal meals, kitchen, @, tel 646 516 846). Minor roads and highways lead past Bar Caso and through **Casquita**. The Caminos del Norte and Primitivo split 3.7km from Villaviciosa. ▸

Turn left to follow the Primitivo. Continue on a series of minor roads and dirt tracks through **El Ronzón** and **Camoca**. In 2km, the route splits, with spray-painted signs marked for both 'Valdediós' and for 'Arbazal.' Wooden directional plaques, painted in red with 'R-V,' also mark the way to San Salvador de Valdediós. ▸

We recommend turning right, heading down a long, paved road into

It is possible to follow the Primitivo to Oviedo and then return to the Norte at Avilés without backtracking: the route is outlined at the end of the Camino Primitivo section (see Primitivo–Norte Link).

The high-level variant to Arbazal is described below.

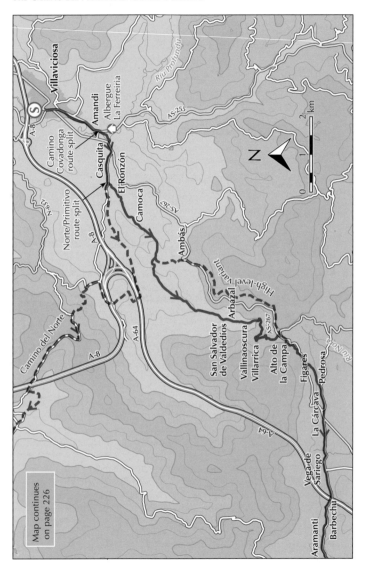

Villaviciosa

Amandi
Albergue
La Ferreiria

Camino
Covadonga
route split

Casquita

El Ronzón

Norte/Primitivo
route split

Camoca

Ambás

High-level variant

Arbazal

San Salvador
de Valdedios

Vallinaoscura
Villarrica

Alto de
la Campa

Figares

Pedrosa

La Cárcava

Vega de
Sariego

Camino del Norte

Aramanti

Barbechu

Riu Profundu

AS-255

AS-267

SV-267

Río Norte

A-8

N-632

A-64

A-64

A-8

Map continues
on page 226

N

0 1 2 km

SAN SALVADOR DE VALDEDIÓS (9.6KM)

Bar/grocery. Albergue de Peregrinos (€6, 22 beds, open 1430, small kitchen, tel 681 676 335, 693 701 173), Posada Samaritana de Valdediós (singles €45, doubles €60, tel 681 676 335).

This is a religious center of Asturias and has been an important spiritual destination for millennia. The pre-Romanesque **Templo de San Salvador** dates to 893, when Alfonso III ordered its construction. The 13th-century Cistercian **Monasterio de Santa María** was originally built around the **Basilica de Santa María**. Only the Romanesque portal and apse survive from the original; the interior, including a Santiago Matamoros, is newer and in baroque style. Tours of San Salvador and the monastery are offered Apr–Sep 1100–1330 and 1630–1930; Oct–Mar, 1100–1330.

Follow the main road out of town. Head steeply uphill, through **Vallinaoscura** and neighboring Villarrica, with striking views of the monastery below. Once on the hilltop, join the road leading to **Alto de la Campa**.

High-level variant
This route bypasses the monastery, instead heading into the hills. Turn left at the fork, and follow a series of minor roads across AS-267 and through **San Pedro de Ambás**. Join a forested footpath, which can be quite overgrown in the off-season, heading steeply uphill towards **Arbazal**. From there, minor roads lead to **Alto de la Campa**, where the routes rejoin. This route is 500 meters shorter than the San Salvador option.

ALTO DE LA CAMPA (2.7KM)

The next section follows minor roads through the countryside, passing back and forth across AS-267. Follow well-marked roads and tracks through **Figares**, **Pedrosa**, and **La Cárcava** (bar), and then into

VEGA DE SARIEGO (4.5KM)

Bars, grocery, pharmacy. Albergue de Peregrinos (€5, 16 beds, keys from Taberna la Casuca, tel 985 748 290, 985 748 120).

Follow SR-1 out of town, under A-64, and through the villages of **Barbechu**, **Aramanti**, and **El Castru**. Fork right on a dirt track, curving alongside pastures, with the Peña Careses mountains forming a striking background behind them. Continue through Aveno, eventually joining and crossing AS-331. Bear left onto a gravel track, which soons turns into a footpath. Cross the Río Seco and follow the forested path to the **Ermita de La Bienvenida**. Continue onto a paved road through **Curuxeo**, crossing the medieval bridge over the Río Recuna.

Join AS-331, following this into town. Fork right on c/ Rebollar, which soon turns into c/Ángel Embil, and then c/ San Antonio. Turn left at the T-junction, then right onto c/ Celleruelo, continuing to the albergue on the far side of

POLA DE SIERO (10.8KM)

All facilities. **Albergue de Peregrinos** (€6, 18 beds, @, tel 985 726 422), **Hotel Loriga** (singles €35–50, doubles €45–60, tel 985 720 026).

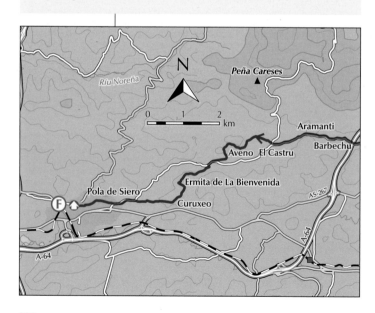

STAGE 2
Pola de Siero to Oviedo

Start	Albergue de Peregrinos, Pola de Siero
Finish	Plaza de Alfonso II el Casto, Oviedo
Distance	16.9km
% unpaved	4%
Total ascent	164m
Total descent	155m
Terrain	1
Route-finding	3
Pilgrim accommodation	Oviedo

Today's short walk allows you to make the most of your time in Oviedo – a major pilgrimage site in its own right and the 'official' starting point of the Camino Primitivo. Unsurprisingly, the approach to the city brings long stretches of highway walking and little of interest to see. However, arrival in Oviedo is well worth it. With its amazing architecture, historical sights, and modern conveniences, the city has something to offer every pilgrim.

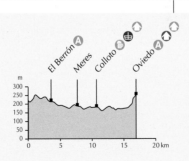

Continue on the main road away from town. Fork right onto a minor road, eventually crossing AS-1. Proceed along minor roads, turning onto AS-246, and then right on Avda de Oviedo into

227

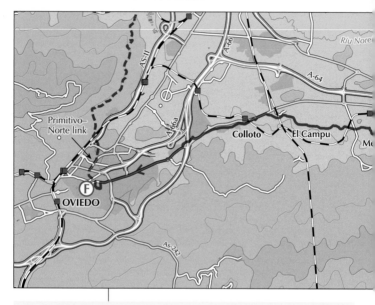

EL BERRÓN (3.4KM)

All facilities.

A crossroads town, where major highways and railroad lines converge.

Follow Avda de los Campones out of town. Proceed over A-64 and then AS-III. Follow a series of minor roads into

MERES (4.5KM)

The 15th-century Palacio de Meres has a beautiful chapel, **La Capilla de Santa Ana** (Mon–Fri 1000–1400, 1600–1900).

Continue across the highway and railroad, and through **El Campo**. Turn left onto N-634, then fork left soon after. Cross a medieval bridge and proceed to

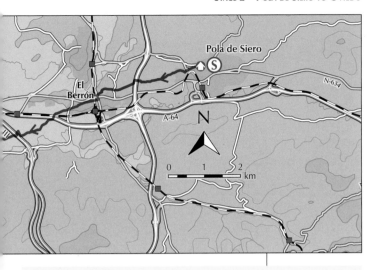

COLLOTO (3.7KM)

Bars, supermarket. Hotel Palacio de la Viñona (singles €50–94, doubles €60–120, tel 985 793 399).

There is a notable Romanesque bridge here.

Rejoin N-634. Waymarks virtually disappear from this point until Oviedo's cathedral. Keep straight on, passing under A-66 and through a roundabout. Continue on c/ Tenderina Baja. At the next major intersection, continue straight ahead, bearing slightly right upon entering the old town, on c/Azcárraga. Turn left onto c/de San Vicente, turn right in Plaza Corrada del Obispo and right again taking Travesía de Santa Barbara to the edge of Plaza de Alfonso II and the front of the cathedral in

OVIEDO (5.3KM)

All facilities. Albergue de Peregrinos El Salvador de Oviedo (€6, 51 beds, kitchen, open 1300 May–Sep, at other times call to check, credenciáles available, c/Leopoldo Alás 20, tel 985 228 525), Albergue La Peregrina (€12–15,

26 beds, @, c/Gascona 18, tel 687 133 932), **Hostal San Juan** (singles €20+, doubles €30+, c/Palacio Valdes 4–3, tel 985 215 422), **Hostal Arcos** (singles €30, doubles €45, c/Magdalena 3, tel 985 214 773), **Hostal Fidalgo** (doubles €40, c/Jovellanos 5, tel 985 213 287), **Hotel Ovetense** (singles €30–35, doubles €40–50, triples €57–63, c/San Juan 6, tel 985 220 840), **Hotel Vetusta** (singles €48, doubles €55, c/Covadonga 2, tel 985 222 229). Internet available in Biblioteca Municipal. Credenciáles available in cathedral.

Founded in 757 by Fruela I as a fortress to guard the central road linking the coast and interior, Oviedo became the capital of Christian Spain a half-century later when Alfonso II 'The Chaste' built his palace here.

The construction and expansion of Oviedo's **cathedral** spanned eight centuries, consequentially combining a broad range of architectural styles. The original ninth-century church – oddly designed, with fine carvings of the apostles on the capitals and disembodied heads on the walls – survives as the **Cámara Santa**, accessed by a door in the right transept. The **Capilla de San Miguel**, situated within, houses the cathedral's greatest treasures, including the Cruz de la Victoria (carried by Pelayo at Covadonga), the Cruz de Los Angeles (a gem-studded cross said to have been created by angels), and a silver reliquary chest (contains a vial of the Virgin Mary's milk and one of Judas's 30 pieces of silver). The new cathedral was started in 1388, and its 10 chapels range in style from early Gothic to baroque. The **Capilla Mayor** has an acclaimed, enormous retablo on the Life of Christ.

Oviedo is also home to three pre-Romanesque churches, identified by UNESCO as the finest examples of ninth-century Christian European architecture. **San Julián de los Prados** is the largest and most central, built during Alfonso II's reign. It has two long porches, a wide transept which is also the highest part of the building, and tunnel-vaulted chapels. The interior is filled with frescoes that, while faded, speak to its original beauty. The other two churches are roughly 3km from Oviedo's center. **Santa María de Naranco**, started shortly after the completion of San Julián, is nearly perfectly preserved. Only one-third of **San Miguel de Lillo** survives, but the Visigothic influence remains starkly apparent. The original plan called for a 21-meter-long basilica, a three-bay nave with tall, circular columns, and impressive stone latticework in the windows and doors. The use of buttresses around the exterior is particularly advanced for the time.

Romanesque capitals in the Cámera Santa

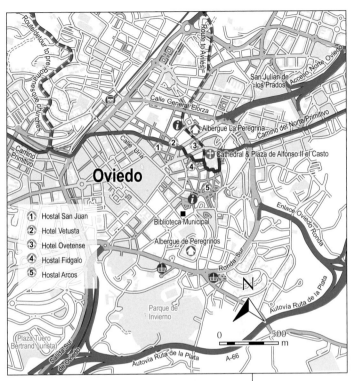

Oviedo

San Julian de los Prados
Calle General Elorza
Albergue La Peregrina
Cathedral & Plaza de Alfonso II el Casto
Calle Uría
Camino Primitivo
Camino del Norte/Primitivo
Acceso Norte Oviedo
Route to Avilés
Route detour to pre-romanesque churches

1. Hostal San Juan
2. Hotel Vetusta
3. Hotel Ovetense
4. Hostal Fidgalo
5. Hostal Arcos

Biblioteca Municipal
Albergue de Peregrinos
Enlace Oviedo Ronda
Ronda Sur
Autovía Ruta de la Plata

Parque de Invierno

N

0   500
m

Plaza Tuero Bertrand (jurista)
Salida Sur de Oviedo
Autovía Ruta de la Plata
A-66

Calle Cimadevilla, Oviedo

STAGE 3
Oviedo to Grado

Start	Plaza de Alfonso II el Casto, Oviedo
Finish	Albergue de Peregrinos, Grado
Distance	25.8km
% unpaved	50%
Total ascent	469m
Total descent	621m
Terrain	3
Route-finding	3
Pilgrim accommodation	Venta del Escamplero, Grado

Oviedo marks the 'official' start of the Camino Primitivo. Many new pilgrims will begin their caminos here and the route, leading into quiet countryside, offers a promising beginning and a glimpse of what's ahead. Once beyond the city limits, the route follows rural roads, gently climbing over hills and offering frequent, expansive views. Grado is a bustling market town – an excellent place to enjoy a well-earned meal and a good night's rest.

Consider making the optional detour to the remarkably well-preserved pre-Romanesque churches Santa María del Naranco and San Miguel de Lillo, described below.

◄ Small bronze shells in the sidewalk mark the camino out of Oviedo. From the front of the cathedral, head north on c/Águila. Turn left onto c/Schultz, then right onto c/San Juan. Turn left briefly on c/Argüelles, then right onto c/La Luna, forking left through the busy intersection onto c/Covadonga. This becomes c/Melquiades Álvarez and then c/Independencia. Yellow arrows reappear at this point. When the road merges with N-634, cross it and continue through Plaza de la Liberación. Fork left at the roundabout onto c/Argañosa. Continue through one more roundabout before crossing the metal footbridge over the railroad.

Turn right on c/Burmudo I El Diácono, then left through an intersection and onto c/Illas. Turn left on Paseo de la Florida, right at the roundabout, and then left, following the edge of a park until turning right onto a minor road heading uphill. Follow a series of minor roads into

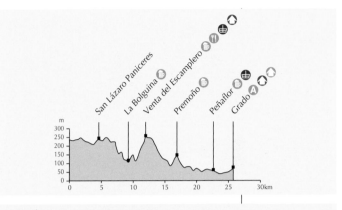

SAN LÁZARO PANICERES (4.5KM)

A *malatería* is documented here in 1331, providing care for sick pilgrims.

Keep straight on to the **Capilla del Carmen** (sello on porch), through **Santa María de Lloriana**, and downhill to **La Bolguina** (bar). Turn right on AS-232. Proceed through the villages of **Fabarín** and **Gallegos**. Fork right onto a footpath leading down towards a ravine and steeply back uphill. Follow residential streets to AS-232, then fork left into

VENTA DEL ESCAMPLERO (7.7KM)

Bar/restaurant. Carnicería/shop with basic provisions. Albergue de Peregrinos (€5, 14 beds, kitchen, keys at Bar El Tendejón, tel 985 799 005).

Follow the road exiting town, then fork left onto a paved lane, soon forking left again onto a footpath, before returning to the highway. Turn left off the highway and follow a mix of minor roads and dirt tracks into

PREMOÑO (4.9KM)

Bar.

The chapel and **Casona de la Portalada** remain from the former pilgrim hospital, which operated until the 18th century.

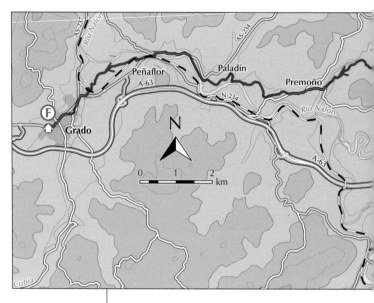

*Pilgrims headed
to Grado*

Continue through town, then fork right onto a footpath.
Follow a series of rural roads through **Paladín**, cross a bridge,
and join a dirt track. Follow this to rejoin the highway, soon
crossing the Peñaflor bridge over the Río Nalón, then turn
right onto N-634. Fork right into

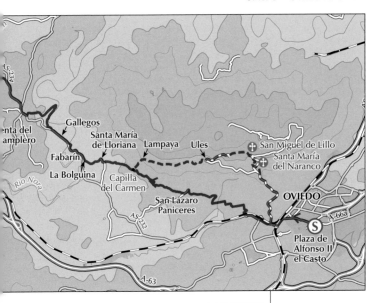

PEÑAFLOR (5.7KM)

Bar, grocery.

Romanesque bridge. As a strategically significant location, Peñaflor was the site of brutal clashes between the French and Spanish in the Peninsular War.

Make a sharp right towards and under the railroad, passing onto a gravel track. Keep straight on towards Grado. ▶ Cross the railroad, turn left, then turn right on c/ Jove y Valdés. Turn right onto N-634, cross the bridge, and join Avda Valentín Andrés. Fork left into

A long-term diversion along the road into Grado just after the Peñaflor bridge may still be in place and is wearing at the end of a long day.

GRADO (3KM)

A busy commercial town offering all facilities, with markets on Wednesday and Sunday; supermarkets are closed on Mondays. **Albergue Villa de Grado** (donativo, 16 beds, kitchen, breakfast, washing machine, @, open Mar–Oct, c/Maestra Benicia 1, tel 985 752 766), **Albergue La Quintana** (€12, 24 beds, meals available, W/D, @, c/Eulogio Díaz de Miranda 30, tel 640 377 256), **Hotel Autobar** (singles €22–24, doubles €36, Avda Flórez Estrada 29, tel 985 751 127), **Hotel Areces** (doubles €70+, triples €120, c/Alonso de Grado 20, tel 985 750 995). Buy food here if you plan to sleep in San Juan de Villapañada.

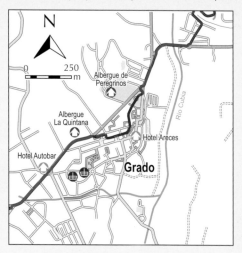

Detour to Santa María del Naranco and San Miguel de Lillo
From Oviedo's cathedral, follow the camino across N-634 and onto c/Samuel Sánchez. The route diverges from the camino at the roundabout. To reach Monte Naranco, turn right onto c/Ramiro I, which shortly becomes Avda de los Monumentos. Continue uphill for about 2km, before joining a footpath up to Naranco (staying on the road also leads to the church). From **Santa María del Naranco**, continue uphill to **San Miguel de Lillo** (Apr–Sep open Tue–Sat 0930–1300, 1530–1900, Sun–Mon 0930–1300; Oct–Mar open Tue–Sat 1000–1430, Sun–Mon 1000–1230; €3).

To rejoin the camino from San Miguel de Lillo, follow a footpath uphill, leaving the field on the church's north side. After 200 meters this joins a paved road, running alongside the Oviedo Sports Ground. After this road bends left, turn right to pass through **Ules** (bar), following signs towards El Llano, then continue straight along to **Lampaya**. Just after passing Lampaya's handful of houses, spanning about 400 meters, turn left downhill onto a dirt track. If you miss this path, continue along the paved road and turn left at the junction ahead. Follow this downhill, continue onto a paved road, and rejoin the camino just before passing **Capilla del Carmen** in Llampaxuga. This route is about 1km longer than the official camino.

STAGE 4
Grado to Salas

Start	Albergue de Peregrinos, Grado
Finish	Albergue de Peregrinos, Salas
Distance	22.8km
% unpaved	38%
Total ascent	652m
Total descent	495m
Terrain	4
Route-finding	2
Pilgrim accommodation	Santa Eulalia de Dóriga, Cornellana, Salas

Today the climb through the Cordillera Cantábrica begins in earnest. This stage opens with a steep, steady climb to Fresno, before dropping down into Cornellana, a small riverside town with an impressive monastery (now also the albergue). From there, the route gently meanders alongside open pastures and forested footpaths, to the day's destination in Salas.

▶ Proceed along the main street through Plaza Ayuntamiento and Plaza General Ponte, then continue straight on c/ Marqués Vega de Anzó. Turn right to pass through another plaza, before turning left onto Avda Flórez Estrada/N-634. Fork left just past the supermarket, then fork right, beginning a steep ascent up a mix of paved and gravel roads. Continue uphill past the turn-off for

Waymarks are limited in Grado.

SAN JUAN DE VILLAPAÑADA (3.9KM)

Albergue de Peregrinos (donativo, 22 beds, kitchen, tel 670 596 854), located 800 meters off-route. Carry food from Grado. The hospitalero, Domingo Ugarte, is friendly and helpful; he may provide a basic dinner to pilgrims without food.

A major battle occurred here in the Peninsular War for control of the village.

Turn right for Albergue Cabruñana (€5, 18 beds, kitchen, W/D, tel 985 750 068), located 1.5km off-route.

Continue uphill to **El Fresno**. ◀ Turn left downhill onto a steep gravel road. Cross A-63 onto a paved road, then briefly join the highway. Before the roundabout, turn left onto a footpath. Continue to

SANTA EULALIA DE DÓRIGA (4.2KM)

Albergue/Bar Cá Pacita (€12, 10 beds, tel 684 613 861).

This small town boasts a 12th-century Romanesque church.

To visit the town center, continue straight on after crossing the bridge. To rejoin the Camino, at the monastery turn left onto c/José María Caballero.

Follow a series of minor roads uphill. At the top, turn left downhill onto a footpath. Cross the overpass, join N-634, then cross Río Narcea. After the bridge, turn left to follow the 'official' camino along the river, proceeding 1km to the albergue. This bypasses all facilities in Cornellana. ◀

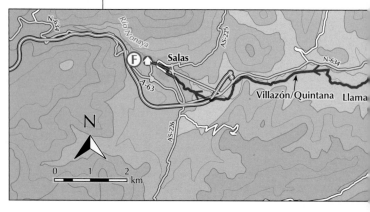

The pretty Río Narcea on the way into Cornellana

CORNELLANA (3.4KM)

Bars/restaurants, grocery stores, pharmacy. **Albergue de Peregrinos** in the old monastery (€5, 24 beds, kitchen, W/D, tel 635 485 932), **Hotel Cornellana** (singles €42, doubles €48, tel 985 588 356), **Casa el Médico** (doubles €36–72, tel 645 518 979).

The semi-ruined monastery was founded in 1024 and passed to Cluniac rule a century later. It was the major economic force in the region, until it was stripped of its holdings in 1835. Its Romanesque church still preserves its 12th-century interior, but the façade was renovated in the 17th century.

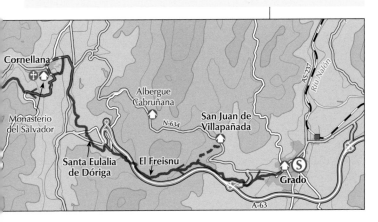

Continue past the monastery, then turn left uphill on a gravel track. Proceed along minor roads, passing through a few tiny hamlets, then fork uphill onto a shady footpath. Minor roads lead through **Llamas** and **Villazón**. Turn right under A-63. Cross a highway and join a footpath. Continue 2km into

SALAS (11.3KM)

All facilities. **Albergue de Peregrinos** (€5, 16 beds, kitchen, Plaza la Veiga 8, tel 985 832 279), **Albergue La Campa** (€10, 35 beds, kitchen, communal vegetarian meals, meditation room, @, Plaza de la Camp 7, tel 984 885 019), **Albergue El Rey Casto** (€10, 16 beds, @, Plaza Ayuntamiento 18, tel 985 830 261), **Albergue Valle del Nonaya** (€10, 20 beds, W/D, @, breakfast available, c/Arzobispo Valdés 5, tel 626 527 073), **Hotel Rural Castillo de Valdés-Salas** (singles €49–73, doubles €61–91, Plaza de la Campa, tel 985 830 173), **Hotel Soto** (singles €20–30, doubles €30–50, c/Arzobispo Valdes, tel 985 830 037).

Although Queen Urraca granted a castle here in 1120, the town wasn't founded for another 150 years. It promptly became a major stopping point on the camino. The **Valdés-Salas Palace** was the birthplace of Fernando Valdés-Salas, founder of Oviedo University, an Inquisitor General, and the Archbishop of Seville. Across the plaza from the palace is the 16th-century **Santa María la Mayor Collegiate church**, which features a square nave and pentagonal roof, and is generally acknowledged as a masterpiece of Asturian Renaissance architecture.

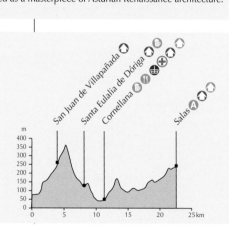

STAGE 5
Salas to Campiello

Start	Albergue de Peregrinos, Salas
Finish	Campiello
Distance	33.6km
% unpaved	69%
Total ascent	1132m
Total descent	752m
Terrain	4
Route-finding	2
Pilgrim accommodation	Bodenaya, La Espina, Tineo, Campiello

Be prepared: this stage begins with a long, steep ascent, gaining 500m in elevation as it climbs past the village of La Pereda to Bodenaya. From here, the route meanders along quiet country roads and tree-lined footpaths, but be advised that after rain the walk to Tineo can transform from pleasant stroll into a slow and muddy slog.

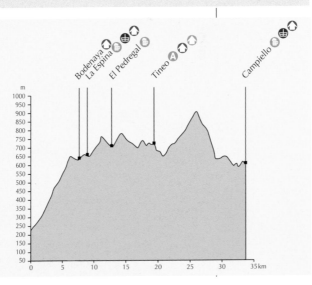

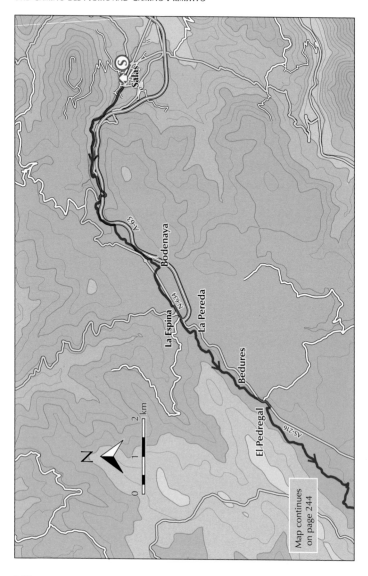

Salas

A-63

Bodenaya

N-634

La Espina

La Pereda

Bedures

El Pedregal

AS-216

N

0 1 2 km

Map continues on page 244

Follow the main street through Salas, under the arch. Fork right, proceeding as the road becomes a gravel track. Cross two bridges. Turn right onto N-634. Follow steep tracks uphill, then turn left onto a paved road. Follow a dirt road and fork right to pass under the highway. Soon fork right, passing a church. Proceed to

BODENAYA (7.6KM)

The Albergue de Peregrinos offers wonderful hospitality (donativo, 21 beds, call for availability in winter, communal meals, W/D, tel 645 888 984).

Cross N-634 and proceed on a road parallel to the highway. Turn left before the church, then right on N-634 into

LA ESPINA (1.2KM)

Bar, grocery. Two albergues: El Cruce (donativo, 12 beds, W/D, tel 639 365 210) and El Texu (€10, 24 beds, communal meals, kitchen, W/D, @, tel 669 016 667), Vista La Espina (doubles €20–25, tel 985 837 172), Pensión El Dakar (doubles €21–24, tel 985 837 062).

Another long-important pilgrim stop, with a legendary 13th-century hospital and *malatería* (hospice for terminally ill) founded by the Inquisitor General, Fernando Valdés-Salas, and funded by Santiago's archbishop.

As you leave town, fork right onto a dirt track. The route to Tineo is well marked, following minor roads through a series of small villages. Pass through **La Pereda** and **Bedures**, descend to AS-216, and arrive in **El Pedregal** (bar) after 4.1km.

Turn right uphill onto a minor road. Follow dirt roads for 5.6km. Turn right onto a paved road at the edge of Tineo. ▶ Keep straight on the main road downhill into the center of

To reach Tineo's Albergue de Peregrinos, watch for waymarks descending left on a footpath.

TINEO (11.1KM)

All facilities. Albergue de Peregrinos Mather Christi de Tineo (€5, 32 beds +6 mattresses, W/D, tel 985 800 232), Albergue Palacio de Merás (€12, 54 beds, meals available, W/D, tel 985 900 111), Pensión La Posada (doubles €30, triples €60, Avda González Mayo 25, tel 985 800 410), Pensión Bar Tineo (singles €25,

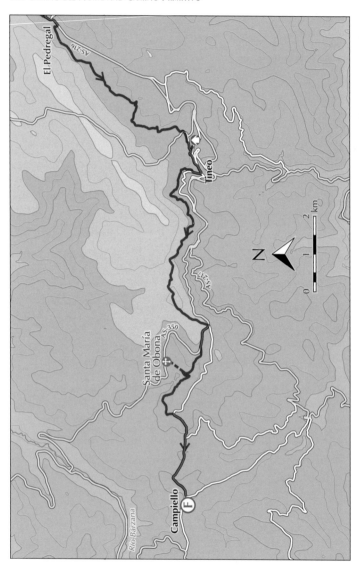

244

doubles €30, Avda González Mayo 28, tel 985 800 710), Hostal Don Miguel (doubles €40–50, Avda de Oviedo 6, tel 985 800 325).

Founded by Rome, Tineo experienced its peak in the late medieval period, during which a castle, Franciscan monastery, and pilgrim hospital were all built, none of which survives. King Alfonso IX made Tineo a compulsory pilgrimage stop in 1222. The **Iglesia de San Pedro**, formerly part of the Franciscan monastery, still preserves its Romanesque tower. The highlight is the Merás Chapel, built in 1613, which includes double doors made out of single pieces of oak. Other well-preserved buildings in Tineo include the 16th-century **Palacio de Merás**, another excellent example of Asturian Renaissance architecture, and the **Palacio de los García de Tineo**, originally a Gothic structure but overhauled in the 18th century. Today, Tineo is known as a great trout-fishing area.

The route through Tineo is well marked. Leaving the center, proceed 1.5km and continue uphill when the road becomes a gravel track. Pass the house of 'El Último de Filipinas'; the track becomes a footpath leading uphill with views of Tineo behind you. Follow a series of enjoyable tracks and minor roads uphill, crossing a paved road at the top. Wind along a road with great views on your right, eventually heading back downhill. Turn right at AS-350, then fork left onto a footpath downhill through a forest, proceeding to the fork with Santa María de Obona.

The house of 'El Último de Filipinas'

Detour to Santa María de Obona

The detour (1km round-trip) to Santa María de Obona is marked to the right. Founded in the eighth century, the monastery experienced its peak during the 13th and 14th centuries when a royal privilege ordered all pilgrims to visit. The monastery was badly damaged during the *desamortización* (privatization of church property) in 1835, but the church remains in use today.

Turn left to continue on the camino. After emerging from the forested footpath, pass along the edge of a farm. Bear left through the grass and onto a paved road. Turn right on TI-3 and keep straight on to

CAMPIELLO (13.7KM)

Bar/groceries. Albergue Casa Ricardo (€10, 26 beds, doubles €35, kitchen, W/D, @, tel 985 801 776). Albergue Casa Herminia (€10, €23 for bed+breakfast+dinner, 18 beds, meals available, W/D, @, tel 985 800 011). This quiet town has, in recent years, become the site of Herminia's growing empire, built largely around providing service to pilgrims. Both albergues offer some private rooms, pilgrim menus, and an excellent starting point for those planning to walk the Hospitales route.

STAGE 6
Campiello to Berducedo

Start	Campiello
Finish	Albergue de Peregrinos, Berducedo
Distance	27.2km
% unpaved	85%
Total ascent	1014m
Total descent	707m
Terrain	5
Route-finding	2
Pilgrim accommodation	Borres, Berducedo, Pola de Allande, Peñaseita

The camino splits today, presenting pilgrims with options through the Hospitales track or Pola de Allande. The Hospitales route is recommended: it climbs into the mountains, passing the ancient ruins of three pilgrim hospitals, while expansive mountain vistas unfold in all directions. While this is one of the most demanding walks on any camino, made more so by the lack of resources, it rewards pilgrims with its strikingly beautiful scenery. The route through Pola provides opportunities to restock or break the journey in half, while still offering impressive views. Regardless of the route, today involves a significant ascent and ranks among the pilgrimage's most strenuous stages; it also has the potential to be one of the most memorable.

Be warned that fog settles thickly in this area overnight and can restrict visibility in the morning. Although waymarking is excellent on the Hospitales route, pilgrims are strongly advised to walk through Pola if the weather is bad.

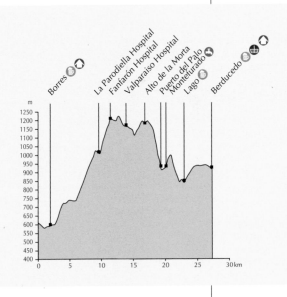

Follow TI-3 through **El Fresno**. Fork left onto a smaller road, then right onto a dirt track. Keep straight on to

Fanfarón Hospital

BORRES (2.7KM)

Bar (open at 0600). **Albergue de Peregrinos** (€5, 18 beds, keys from bar, historically quite dirty, tel 663 785 266), **Samblismo Albergue** (6 beds, reservations required, meals available, tel 623 190 006).

Pass a fountain on your left and ascend a gravel track. In 500 meters, the camino splits. The route via Pola de Allande is outlined at the bottom of this stage. To continue on the recommended Hospitales route, fork right and head into the hills. Pass through a cattle fence and find a fountain straight ahead – this is your last chance to refill for 16.5km! Follow footpaths another 2.7km to the ruined **La Parodiella Hospital**, 2.2km to **Fanfarón Hospital**, and 1.6km to **Valparaiso Hospital**.

The Hospitales and Pola de Allande routes rejoin at Puerto del Palo.

Cross the highway at **Alto de La Morta**, then continue ascending to **Puerto del Palo** (1146m). ◀ The descent begins immediately, down a steep rocky hill, cutting a straight line through the zigzagging AS-14, into

MONTEFURADO (17KM)

The chapel remains from an earlier pilgrim hospital and features a carving of an apostle.

Follow the footpath through Montefurado, skirting a rock wall around a house. After reaching a shell positioned before a tree, climb over the rock wall and join a footpath. Continue on a paved road, soon passing a church on your left. Turn left atop a steep hill, following AS-14 into **Lago** (bar).

Cross AS-14 and fork right uphill onto a footpath. After 1km, rejoin AS-14. Fork left onto a dirt track, marked with red/white stripes. Follow this to the albergue in

Pilgrims headed toward Pola de Allande

BERDUCEDO (7.5KM)

Bar/grocery, restaurants. **Albergue de Peregrinos** (€5, 12 beds, kitchen, keys from Bar El Cafetín, tel 985 923 325), **Albergue Camino Primitivo** (€12, 18 beds, meals available, tel 985 906 670), **Albergue-Pensión Casa Marqués** (€10, 16 beds, private rooms €20–40, kitchen, meals available, W/D, tel 985 909 820), **Camín Antiguo** (€15, 10 beds, doubles €60, kitchen, meals available, W/D, tel 696 929 164).

A pleasant hill town with a lot of livestock, a 14th-century church, and the last chance to buy food before Grandas. The former pilgrim hospital is now the doctor's house.

Pola de Allande variant

Keep straight on from **Borres**, proceeding to **La Mortera** (bar) and then joining the highway before **Porciles** (grocery). Fork left off AS-219, but rejoin it soon after, for the final ascent to **Alto de Lavadoira**. It's all downhill to Pola, following 3km of dirt roads and highways.

POLA DE ALLANDE (9.6KM)

All facilities. **Albergue de Peregrinos** (€6, 24 beds, kitchen, Avda de América 46, tel 663 324 783), **Hotel La Nueva Allandesa** (singles €25+, doubles €45+, c/Donato Fernández 3, tel 985 807 027), **Hotel Lozano** (doubles €40, Avda de Galicia 5, tel 985 807 102).

The route from Pola to Montefurado involves a challenging climb (roughly 600m gained) and abrupt descent. Leave Pola on AS-14, eventually forking left onto a footpath that will later join a minor road. Continue on a mix of footpaths and minor roads, past the turn-off for

PEÑASEITA (3KM)

Bar. Albergue de Peregrinos (€5, 12 beds, keys from Bar Viñas, tel 985 807 116).

The ascent soon intensifies. Follow footpaths uphill, cross AS-14, and continue climbing to **Puerto del Palo** (1146m), where the routes reunite.

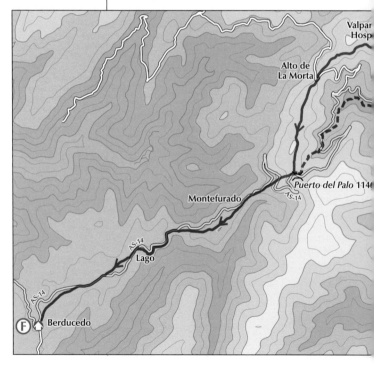

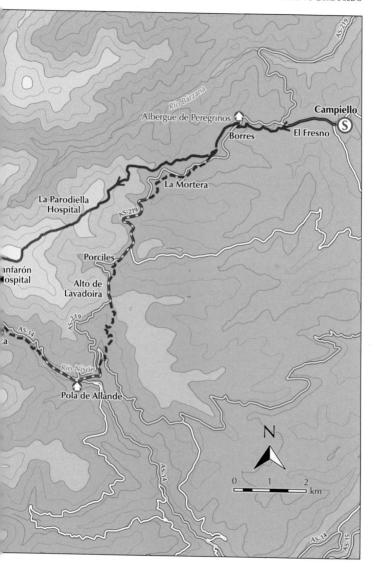

STAGE 7
Berducedo to Grandas de Salime

Start	Albergue de Peregrinos, Berducedo
Finish	Albergue de Peregrinos, Grandas de Salime
Distance	20.7km
% unpaved	46%
Total ascent	874m
Total descent	1228m
Terrain	5
Route-finding	1
Pilgrim accommodation	La Mesa, Vistalegre, Grandas de Salime

Following yesterday's difficult stage, a shorter walk is certainly in order. Be advised, however, that this walk – dropping 800m in 6km – has the potential to devour tired knees. Take your time and enjoy the stunning 360-degree views from the windmill-lined ridge above La Mesa. The dammed Río Navia below shines like an over-sized sapphire, surrounded by rugged hillside. The final climb to Grandas de Salime proceeds largely along the highway, but the paved ascent comes almost as a relief after the extended downhill.

Pass the church in Berducedo, joining a footpath after passing through town. After 1km, turn left onto a paved downhill into

LA MESA (4.6KM)

Bar/restaurant. **Albergue de Peregrinos** (€5, 16 beds, kitchen, tel 985 979 013, tel 690 764 343). **Albergue Miguelín** (€12, 20 beds, private rooms €35, breakfast €3, W/D, @, tel 985 914 353). Those staying here should buy food in Berducedo, although grocery and produce food trucks stop here on Tuesdays and Fridays around 1600. Fill your water before leaving; it may be your last chance to refill until Grandas.

This small, peaceful village has a 17th-century church dedicated to Saint María Magdalena.

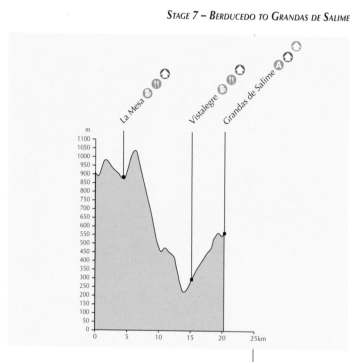

Follow a paved road uphill, towards the windmills. Fork right onto a gravel track, proceed through **Buspol** passing Capilla de Santa María and enjoying the great views of the reservoir below, and continue onto a footpath. A long, fairly steep, 6km descent follows, dropping all the way to the water below. ▸ At the bottom, turn left onto AS-14 and cross the dam. Once on the other side, the route climbs past

Following forest fires a long variant to the north is marked just before the steep forest descent, but the direct descent route is clear.

VISTALEGRE (10.6KM)

Bar/restaurant/**Albergue-Hotel Las Grandas** (€10, 18 beds, €35 singles, €45 doubles, meals available, @, tel 985 627 230).

The construction of the dam in 1954 flooded old Salime; its abandoned buildings line the hillside.

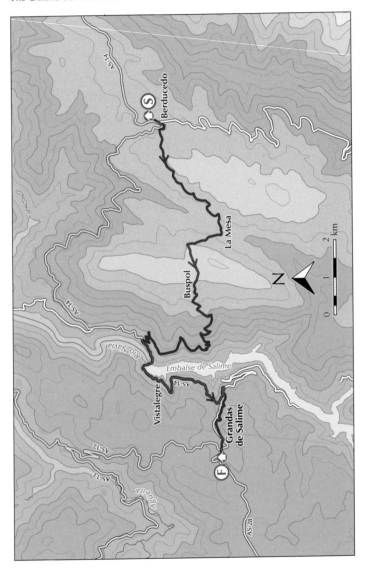

Embalse de Salime

Keep straight on the highway uphill. Eventually, fork left onto a footpath, leading up through the trees. Emerge on the road into ▶

Turn right in front of the church for the albergue.

GRANDAS DE SALIME (5.5KM)

All facilities. **Albergue de Peregrinos El Salvador** (€6, 28 beds + 22 mattresses, kitchen, W/D, @, tel 626 464 183, tel 696 221 565), **Albergue Casa Sánchez** (€12, 16 beds, kitchen, W/D, c/El Salvador, tel 626 665 118), **Hotel La Barra** (singles €40–45, doubles €50–55, Avda de la Costa 4, tel 985 627 196), **Pensión Arreigada** (c/Pedro de Pedre 9, tel 985 627 017), **Hostal Bar Occidente** (c/Antonio Machado, tel 659 123 467).

Established in the 12th century following a donation by King Fernando II, Grandas later enjoyed success thanks to gold mining. The **Collegiata de El Salvador**, built near the town's founding, has a huge porch and preserves its original Romanesque facade. The **Ethnographic Museum**, located in the former rector's house, provides an excellent introduction to rural Asturian life.

STAGE 8
Grandas de Salime to A Fonsagrada

Start	Albergue de Peregrinos, Grandas de Salime
Finish	Albergue de Peregrinos, A Fonsagrada
Distance	25.7km
% unpaved	69%
Total ascent	829m
Total descent	443m
Terrain	3
Route-finding	1
Pilgrim accommodation	Castro, A Fonsagrada

Another ascent to hilltop windmills awaits today. It's an excellent climb from Peñafuente to Alto del Acebo, providing more sweeping panoramas and rewarding walking. The route also leads into Galicia, the final region of your walk. The second half of this stage is more tedious, often proceeding along the highway, with few opportunities to refuel. Fonsagrada provides pilgrims the chance to enjoy Galician cuisine, from Pulpo a Feira (octopus) to Caldo Gallego (hearty vegetable soup).

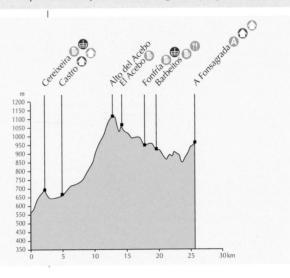

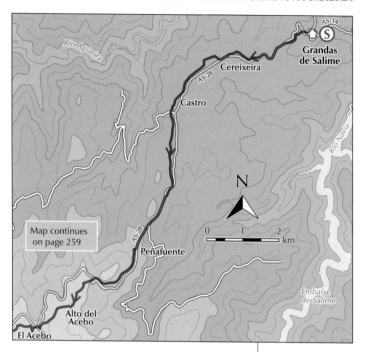

Map continues
on page 259

Continue straight through town, generally bearing uphill and
away from Grandas. Fork right onto a dirt track, which soon
becomes a footpath. From here, the route continues primarily on dirt tracks and footpaths, briefly joining AS-28 from
time to time, before heading back onto a track. AS-28 leads
through **Cereixeira** (bar, grocery). Follow another series of
minor, mostly dirt roads into

CASTRO (5KM)

Bar/Albergue Juvenil (€11, 16 beds, meals available, W/D, @, tel 985 924 197,
tel 664 732 541), **Hotel Rural Chao San Martín** (singles €30, doubles €50, tel
985 627 267).

The **Chao de San Martín**, a well-preserved prehistoric settlement (founded 800bc),
was recently excavated.

Keep straight on a dirt track, before joining AS-28, proceeding to the **Peñafuente** turn-off on the right. Follow a footpath uphill. Cross the highway and continue the steep ascent to the windmills, offering spectacular views of the valley below, reaching **Alto del Acebo** (1110m) before descending into Galicia.

EL ACEBO (8.9KM)

Bar.

Located on the Asturias–Galicia border.

In Asturias, the direction of the route was indicated by following the lines of the scallop shell as they converged. In Galicia, it is the opposite: turn in the direction that the lines diverge. Throughout Galicia, cement waymarks also indicate the distance remaining to Santiago. Neither region's marking is wholly consistent on this point.

◀ Turn left onto the gravel track behind the bar. Follow this to **Cabreira**, crossing and re-crossing LU-106/LU-701. Continue parallel to the highway, through **Fonfría** (bar/grocery). Proceed along the gravel track to **Barbeitos** (Bar Catro Ventos – open 1000). Cross the highway, follow a dirt road through **Silvela**, then head back over the highway, onto a footpath. Continue 2km. Join and cross LU-701, then continue on a mix of tracks, footpaths and minor roads to

A FONSAGRADA (11.8KM)

All facilities. **Albergue de Peregrinos** (€6, 42 beds, W/D, c/San Roque 4), **Albergue-Pensión Cantábrico** (€10, 34 beds, private rooms €30+, kitchen, @, c/Rúa Ron 5, tel 669 747 560), **Albergue Os Chaos** (€10, 22 beds, kitchen, W/D, @, c/Marmoiral 26, tel 660 011 716), **Pensión Casa Manolo** (singles €30, doubles €40, c/Burón 35, tel 982 340 408). Internet above Casa Cultural.

According to legend, Saint James was attended in this village by a poor widow and, struck by her poverty, turned the village fountain's water into milk – it thus became the *fons sacrata* ('sacred fountain'). Before ever becoming a place of Christian significance, however, the village was frequented by pagans and subsequently held a fourth-century Roman station.

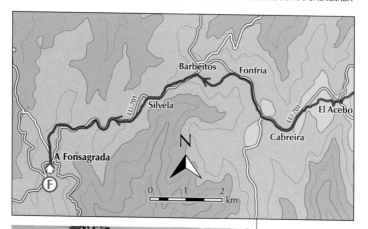

Capilla de Santa Bárbara, near Silvela

259

STAGE 9

A Fonsagrada to Castroverde

Start	Albergue de Peregrinos, A Fonsagrada
Finish	Albergue de Peregrinos, Castroverde
Distance	32.4km
% unpaved	62%
Total ascent	882m
Total descent	1253m
Terrain	5
Route-finding	2
Pilgrim accommodation	Cádavo Baleira, Castroverde

Today's walk follows footpaths and rural roads – including a few surprisingly steep sections – through some wonderful examples of rural Galician mountain villages. Montouto is a special highlight: the aged village seems to have been carved in whole out of the mountainside. The route offers plenty of stops along the way, including a pilgrim-friendly bar just before Paradavella.

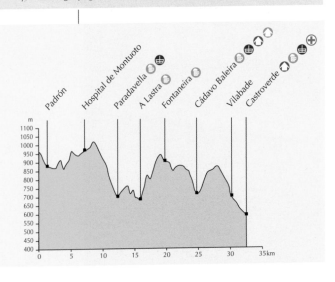

Keep the church on your left and proceed uphill. Bear left towards LU-106. Cross the highway onto a side-street headed downhill, following small roads through

PADRÓN (1.5KM)

Governed by the Knights of Saint John until 1874, Padrón has a small 18th-century church.

Follow a series of dirt roads and tracks as they cross back and forth over LU-530. ▶ Continue along minor roads to **Vilardongo**. Fork left downhill, then fork right onto a gravel track. Continue to

HOSPITAL DE MONTOUTO (6KM)

The former pilgrim hospital, founded in 1360 by Pedro I 'El Cruel', remained open until the early 20th century.

Some 2km past Padrón, 300 meters off the camino, is Albergue-Pensión O Piñeiral (€10, 44 beds, private rooms, W/D, meals available, located on LU-530, tel 982 340 350).

Capilla de Hospital de Montouto

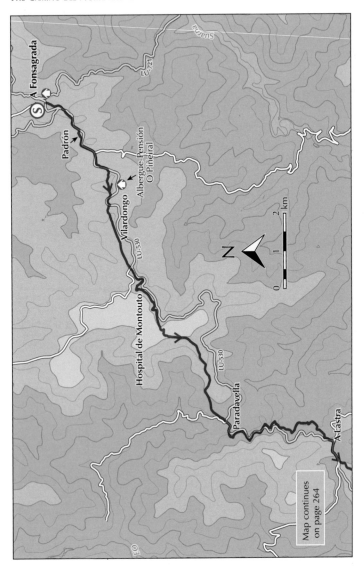

A Fonsagrada

Padrón

Albergue-Pensión
O Piñeiral

Vilardongo

LU-530

Hospital de Montouto

LU-530

Paradavella

A Lastra

Map continues
on page 264

Join a footpath and begin a steep 3.2km descent. Emerge from the woods at Bar Meson. Proceed along LU-530 into

PARADAVELLA (4.9KM)

Bars, grocery.

The Knights of Saint John of Portomarín once owned the town. A traditional Gallegan *palloza* (circular stone building with a thatched roof) is on display.

Fork right onto a footpath, proceeding uphill and then back down to LU-530. Cross to the footpath and do the reverse: wind downhill and then climb steeply back to the highway in

A LASTRA (4.8KM)

Bars.

This town was also formerly owned by the Knights of Saint John.

Fork left onto a gravel track. Keep straight on for 2km, then rejoin the LU-530 and proceed 300 meters into

FONTANEIRA (2.5KM)

Bar.

The parish church has a Santiago Matamoros.

Continue along the highway. Fork right downhill onto a gravel track into

CÁDAVO BALEIRA (4.6KM)

Bars, restaurants, grocery. **Albergue de Peregrinos** (€6, 20 beds, tel 636 020 292), **Albergue San Mateo** (€10, 40 beds, private rooms €20+, kitchen, W/D, tel 616 529 514), **Albergue-Pensión Porta Santa** (€10, 8 beds, private rooms €35+, kitchen, tel 679 828 540), **Pensión Eligio** (singles €20, doubles €35, tel 982 354 009), **Hotel Moneda** (singles €25, doubles €40, tel 982 354 001).

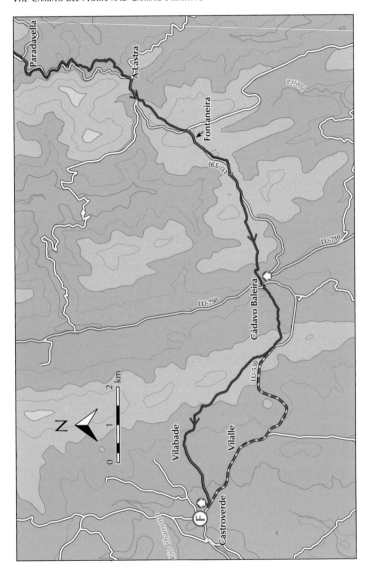

Like Fonsagrada, Cádavo Baleira features a popular legend, stating that King Alfonso II 'The Chaste' battled a Muslim army here in defense of the pilgrimage road. Excavations in the area have found extensive amounts of armor, and many swords and tombs.

Take the main road downhill, then fork left. After 1km, the route splits. ▶ We recommend turning right onto a gravel road, following the old route for 5.6km into

VILABADE (6.2KM)

Vilabade was established as a Franciscan community for pilgrims in the 15th century. **Iglesia de Santa María**, built in 1457 and restored in the 17th century, is a national historic-artistic monument. A Gothic master-piece, it features a ribbed vault and a baroque altarpiece dominated by an impressive Santiago Matamoros. Next door is the **Casa Grande de Vilabade**, a 17th-century *pazo* (manor house) built for Viceroy Escobar.

The 'official camino' route proceeds along minor roads to Vilalle and follows LU-530 to Castroverde: it is 800 meters shorter but skips the magnificent Iglesia de Santa María in Vilabade.

Continue straight through Vilabade. Turn right on LU-530. Just before Castroverde, fork left onto a dirt road skirting the town before entering

CASTROVERDE (1.9KM)

Bars, supermarket, pharmacy. **Albergue de Peregrinos** (€6, 34 beds, kitchen, tel 699 832 747), **Pensión Cortés** (doubles €38, Rúa da Feira 48, tel 982 312 166).

First mentioned in AD897, this became a major religious center in the late Middle Ages thanks to the growth of neighboring Vilabade. A pilgrim's hospital existed in the 13th century. One tower survives from the old Lemos castle.

STAGE 10

Castroverde to Lugo

Start	Albergue de Peregrinos, Castroverde
Finish	Albergue de Peregrinos, Lugo
Distance	22.3km
% unpaved	48%
Total ascent	336m
Total descent	455m
Terrain	2
Route-finding	2
Pilgrim accommodation	Vilar de Cas, Lugo

Lugo, the day's destination, promises some of the greatest sights of the trip. The massive Roman walls surrounding the historic center are nearly two millennia old and are among the most impressive works of architecture on the Primitivo. Although this stage is short, there are no provisions along the route – stock up before leaving Castroverde.

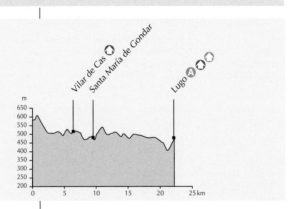

Pass the church and fountain as you leave Castroverde. Follow a series of minor roads 4.2km to Souto de Torres, 2.7km to **Vilar de Cas** (Albergue A Pociña de Muñiz – €14, 16 beds, private rooms available, kitchen, W/D, tel 616 237 776), and continue to

SANTA MARÍA DE GONDAR (9.4KM)

Take great care – legend holds that anyone who drinks from the Fontiña de Valiñas will fall in love.

The fountain in Castroverde

Keep straight on, eventually turning right to join LU-530. After 1.3km, turn right onto a minor road. Continue along a series of rural roads through **Bascuas** and **A Viña**. Cross A-6 and proceed towards Lugo. At the edge of the city, cross through an underpass, ascend a flight of stairs, and proceed uphill towards the city walls. Enter the Puerta de San Pedro. Turn right for the albergue in

LUGO (12.9KM)

All facilities. Albergue de Peregrinos (€6, 42 beds, kitchen, c/Nóreas 1, tel 618 425 578), Albergue Casa da Chanca (€15, 13 beds, meals available, W/D, Rúa da Chanca 51, tel 648 574 300). Many other options include: Shiku Hostel (€16, doubles €30, triples €41, Rúa das Noreas 2, 982 229 935), Hostel Cross (€16, Rúa da Cruz 14, tel 604 026 605), Pensión San Roque (doubles €32–44, pilgrim discount, breakfast, @, Praza Comandante Manso 11, tel 982 222 700), Hotel España (singles €23–32, doubles €36–44, Rua Vilalba 2, tel 982 231 540). Crediciál available in the cathedral.

Originally a Celtic holding (*lug* is Celtic for 'sun god' or 'sacred forest'), the city is most famous for its Roman years, thanks to its massive walls. However, despite those prominent defenses, the Romans lost Lugo in the fifth century, beginning a period of significant turnover for the settlement. Suevi rule yielded to the Visigoths in 585, only for Lugo to be passed once more to the Moors in the eighth century.

Visitors can ascend the **city walls** and walk around the old town, enjoying excellent views. Declared a UNESCO World Heritage Site in 2000, these are the world's largest surviving Roman walls – 2km long, 8.5m high, and featuring 85 rounded towers.

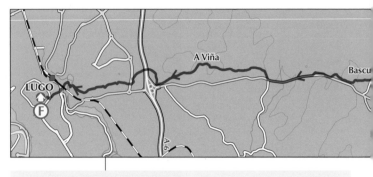

Other than the walls, Lugo's most impressive sight is the **Cathedral of Santa María**. Although construction began in 1129, the building combines Romanesque, Gothic, baroque, rococo, and neo-classical styles. Indeed, a close inspection of the interior and exterior offers a fine overview of the history of religious architecture. For Romanesque, head to the cathedral's transept and nave. Moving through the nave, the Gothic transition is obvious, particularly in the pointed groin vaulting; this style is also reflected in the main chapel, portico, and ambulatory. The cloister is purely baroque, while the apse behind the main altar, comprised of five alcoves containing extravagantly ornate chapels, blends baroque and rococo styles.

Outside, only the northern façade preserves its Romanesque origins, as seen in the striking Last Supper capitals and the Christ in Majesty. Look to the roof for Gothic flying buttresses, best seen from the city walls. Finally, the western facade exemplifies the neo-classical style, inspired by Santiago's cathedral. Lugo's patron saint, San Froilán, is featured here with his wolf. As the story goes, the saint was traveling with his mule when a wolf attacked and devoured it. The saint angrily lectured the wolf until it repented and took up the mule's load. Lugo's many

The tower of the Cathedral of Santa María in Lugo

other interesting sights demand an extra day if your schedule allows the time. Other Roman remains include the second-century **baths** (still open, as a deluxe spa), a **Roman bridge** (modified over the years; you cross this out of Lugo), and the **House of Mosaics** (c/Doctor Castro 20–22). Next to the cathedral is the **Praza Santa María**, where the 18th-century **Bishop's Palace**, a baroque structure built by Gil Taboada, is located. The **Convento de San Francisco**, which includes a Gothic cloister, now functions as a provincial museum.

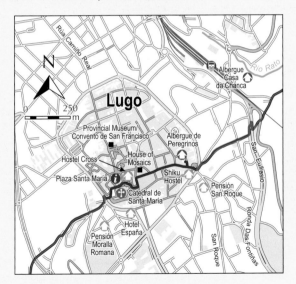

STAGE 11
Lugo to As Seixas

Start	Albergue de Peregrinos, Lugo
Finish	Albergue de Peregrinos, As Seixas
Distance	32.7km
% unpaved	12%
Total ascent	662m
Total descent	533m
Terrain	2
Route-finding	1
Pilgrim accommodation	San Román, Ferreira, As Seixas

The final 100km to Santiago begins with a long day following peaceful country roads through generally flat, wooded terrain. There are no large towns between Lugo and As Seixas, although there are a few stopping points, including a possible detour to Santa Eulalia de Bóveda, which houses a third-century Roman crypt, and the opportunity to buy provisions in San Román.

Small bronze shells in the sidewalk mark the camino out of Lugo.

Alternatively, fork right to take the route to Friol (see Primitivo–Norte Link via Friol).

Turn right to stop at the bar (100 meters off-route).

◄ Follow Rúa San Pedro through Plaza Mayor and past the cathedral. Continue straight through Puerta de Santiago, following Rúa de Santiago as it slopes downhill. Fork right onto Calzada de Ponte and descend beneath an overpass. Cross the Río Miño, then turn right onto Rúa Fermín Rivera. Fork left, heading away from the river to stay on the Primitivo. ◄ Continue through a highway underpass, heading uphill to join LU-P-2901.

You'll follow this road for much of the day, passing through **Burgo do San Vicente** (bar, fountain). ◄ Continue straight, eventually forking right to follow a shady footpath for a nice stretch before rejoining the highway.

Detour to Santa Eulalia de Bóveda
To visit **Santa Eulalia de Bóveda** (open Tue-Fri 0830–1430, Sat 1000–1400) fork right at the signpost marked for Santa Eulalia de Bóveda, onto LU-P-2903, about 2km after Burgo. To return to the camino afterwards, turn left to follow the small road through Bóveda, leading south on a minor road. Turn right at the fist intersection, then fork left to stay on

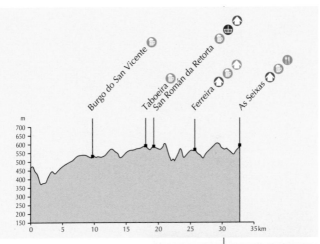

the minor road. Continue through Vilanova, Corvazal and Vigo to rejoin the Primitivo. This detour is 6.2km, adding 3km to the stage.

Proceed through **Hospital**, **San Pedro de Abaixo**, **Taboeira** (bar) and **Crecente** (bar, closed Mon). Keep straight to follow the alternative route, or turn right into the center of

Camino waymark and sign for bar

SAN ROMÁN DA RETORTA (18.7KM)

Bar/grocery. Albergue de Peregrinos (€6, 12 beds, kitchen, tel 628 173 456). Albergue O Cándido (€8, 21 beds, kitchen, tel 693 063 146, tel 982 214 081).

Another small town with Roman ties: see the Roman milestone opposite the bar. The **Iglesia de Santa Cruz da Retorta** is a 12th-century Romanesque church. Despite extensive renovation, the original floors have been preserved in the apse and nave, as have the original windows and the Trinitarian Christogram carved above the doorway.

Two waymarked routes leave San Román. The 'official' route follows the highway out of San Román, rejoining the Roman Road in Ferreira. The recommended route, 1.5km

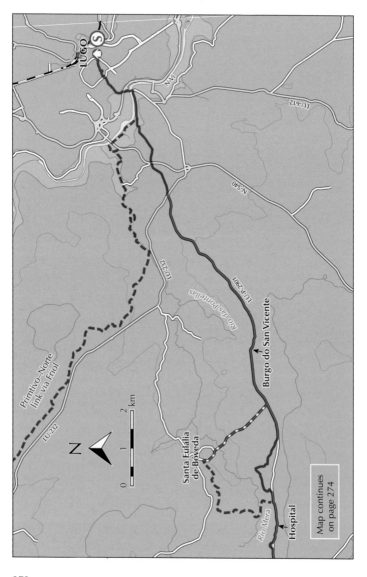

Map continues
on page 274

Horreo in San Román

shorter, follows the old Roman road. This route passes in front of the bar/grocery and the albergue. From there, it continues on a gravel track and minor roads, through a series of small villages. Follow the route through **Grela**, **Vilacarpide**, and **Pacio**. Continue along minor roads and across a Roman bridge to

FERREIRA (8KM)

Albergue A Nave de Ferreira (€12, doubles €40, meals available, W/D, @, open May–Sep, tel 616 161 594, located on Roman route near entrance to Ferreira), Albergue Ponte Ferreira (€11, 22 beds, open May–mid Dec, meals available, W/D, @, tel 982 036 949, located 200 meters after Roman Bridge), Albergue Cruz Ferreira (€10, 22 beds, meals available, W/D, tel 982 178 908), Casa Rural da Ponte (doubles €40–50, meals, W/D, tel 982 183 077).

More evidence here of the area's past, with the Roman bridge.

Continue past the casa rural and albergues, eventually joining a forested dirt track. Proceed along minor roads through **Bouzachás**, **San Xurxo**, and **Montecelo**. Join a footpath with a sign for As Seixas/Melide, leading through **Merlán** and then onward into

AS SEIXAS (6KM)

Bar/Restaurant. Albergue de Peregrinos (€6, 34 beds, kitchen, tel 609 669 057). A food truck stops here most nights. Casa Goriños (€10, 6 beds, private rooms €45, W/D, tel 665 022 637).

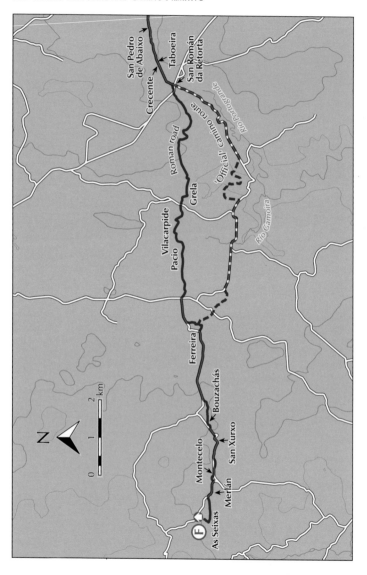

STAGE 12

As Seixas to Arzúa

Start	Albergue de Peregrinos, As Seixas
Finish	Albergue de Peregrinos, Arzúa
Distance	28.9km
% unpaved	33%
Total ascent	480m
Total descent	680m
Terrain	2
Route-finding	2
Pilgrim accommodation	Melide, Boente, Ribadiso do Baixo, Arzúa

Enjoy Galicia at its finest! Well-trodden dirt paths pass through aromatic eucalyptus groves, yielding every few kilometers to small stone villages, solemn witnesses to the generations of pilgrims preceding you. Today you join the Camino Francés. Be prepared for some major changes – the number of pilgrims will increase dramatically, there are albergues and provisions in nearly every village, and all route-finding difficulties become a thing of the past. Pause in Melide long enough to sample the regional speciality, octopus, in the town that cooks it best. Sleep in Ribadiso do Baixo, a traditional albergue resurrected from ruin to care for pilgrims once more, or continue on to Arzúa, where accommodation is as plentiful as it is varied.

Return to the dirt track and pass the Casa Rural Camiño (doubles €65–80, pilgrim discount, meals available, tel 982 036 946). Turn right uphill through a hamlet, then left onto a dirt road. Follow a series of rural roads to **O Hospital das Seixas**, **Arnade** and **Vilouriz**. Fork left onto a gravel track. Cross a bridge, keeping right to join the road ahead. Follow scallop shells through **Vilamor** (bar). Turn left at the T-junction. Keep straight on for 5km, eventually turning left onto DP-4604. Turn left towards the church in

MELIDE (14.8KM)

All facilities. **Albergue de Peregrinos** (€6, 156 beds, kitchen, W/D, Rúa San Antonio, tel 660 396 822). Many private albergues priced in the €10/bed range,

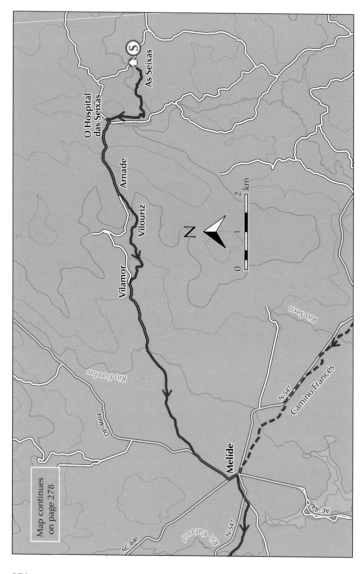

Map continues on page 278

276

including O Palpador (tel 679 837 969), O Cruceiro (tel 616 764 896), Pereiro (tel 981 506 314) and San Antón (tel 698 153 672). Hotel Xaneiro (singles €35, doubles €45, triples €60, Avda de la Habana 43, tel 981 506 140), Pensión Berenguela (singles €30, doubles €40, Rúa de San Roque 2, tel 981 505 417).

The Iglesia de San Pedro, previously the Franciscan convent of Sancti Spiritus, contains a number of tombs from the Ulloa family, one of the dominant clans in the 15th century, about which the great Galician novel *Los Pazos de Ulloa* was written. Octopus is a town gastronomic speciality and Pulperia Ezequiel is famous for it.

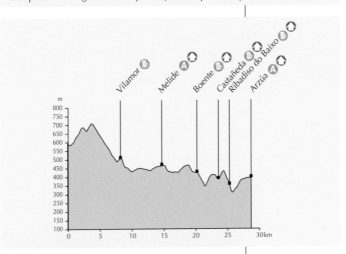

The camino leaving As Seixas

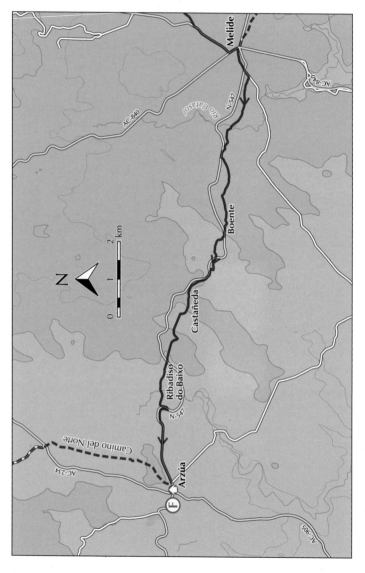

▶ Proceed uphill past the cemetery and descend along a footpath. Cross N-547 and continue on a series of minor roads and tracks, leading into

The Primitivo joins the Francés in Melide; many more pilgrims and pilgrim facilities will accompany you onward to Santiago.

BOENTE (5.7KM)

Bar. **Albergue El Alemán** (€12, 40 beds, meals available, W/D, @, tel 981 501 984), **Albergue Boente** (€10–12, 40 beds, doubles €40, meals available, W/D, @, tel 981 501 974), **Os Albergues** (€11, 30 beds, meals available, W/D, @, tel 629 146 826).

The **Iglesia de Santiago** dates from the 12th century, although little remains of the original. It is very welcoming to pilgrims, with a sello available.

Follow the highway through Boente, then turn right at Iglesia de Santiago. Proceed 2km along a dirt track to **Castañeda** (bar), passing tiny **Albergue Santiago** (€11, 4 beds, double €35, W/D, @, tel 981 501 711) soon after. Continue along minor roads before crossing the Río Iso into

RIBADISO DO BAIXO (5.2KM)

Bars/restaurants. **Albergue de Peregrinos** (€6, 70 beds, kitchen, W/D, tel 660 396 823) in a beautiful location along the river, **Albergue Milpés** (€10, 24 beds, meals available, W/D, @, tel 981 500 425), **Albergue Los Caminantes** (€10, 56 beds, private rooms, kitchen, W/D, @, tel 647 020 600), **Pensión Rústica Casa Vaamonde** (doubles €59, triples €77, tel 981 500 703).

Follow the road out of Ribadiso, cross the highway, and then turn right through a small neighborhood. Rejoin N-547 and keep straight on into

ARZÚA (3.2KM)

See the information in the Camino del Norte, Stage 31.

For the route from Arzúa to Santiago de Compostela, see the Camino del Norte, Stage 32.

PRIMITIVO–NORTE LINK VIA OVIEDO
Oviedo to Avilés

Start	Plaza de Alfonso II el Casto, Oviedo
Finish	Albergue de Peregrinos, Avilés
Distance	29km
% unpaved	17%
Total ascent	370m
Total descent	593m
Terrain	2
Route-finding	3
Pilgrim accommodation	Avilés

From Stage 18 of the Camino del Norte it is possible to follow the Primitivo to Oviedo (Stages 1 and 2) and then use this link to return to the Norte at Avilés (Stage 20/21) without backtracking. While the route from Oviedo to Avilés is not the 'traditional' way, it provides the opportunity to visit Oviedo, a pilgrimage site in its own right, before returning to the coast. Although this is not the most pleasant of walks – you've only just passed the outskirts of Oviedo before joining the highway into Avilés – it does follow some quiet country roads and may be a more enjoyable route into Avilés than the walk on the Camino del Norte from Gijón (Stage 20). In many ways, the choice comes down to which city you would prefer to visit: coastal Gijón or Oviedo and its famous cathedral.

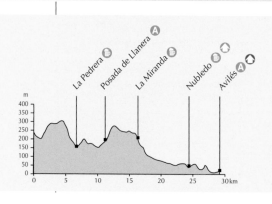

Waymarking and signage for the route to Avilés

▶ By the cathedral in Plaza de Alfonso II, a bronze marker directs pilgrims either left onto the Primitivo or right for the Camino de la Costa (Norte). Follow the waymarks for the coast, heading right onto c/Águila to c/Gascona. Continue across General Elorza onto Avda de Pumarín. Fork left onto Avda Pando, continuing under the highway and railroad tracks, then turn right onto a minor road uphill. Follow this through a few small hamlets. ▶ Follow the minor road, which eventually becomes a footpath leading through the forest. Turn right past some houses onto another minor road. This meanders through the countryside, eventually crossing the railroad into La Pedrera (bar). Cross the Río Nora and follow a series of minor roads, eventually crossing AS-17 into

For a map of Oviedo, see Stage 2, Camino Primitivo.

The route overlaps here with a local walking trail – keep an eye out for any conflicting waymarks.

POSADA DE LLANERA (11.0KM)

All facilities.

Continue straight through Posada on c/Carrión, then fork right on Agustín González to leave town. Follow a series of rural roads and dirt tracks before crossing through an intersection, near **Asador la Miranda**. Follow rural roads through **La Miranda**, cross the railroad, and then turn right onto AS-17. Follow the highway through **Cancienes** and onto

NUBLEDO (12.8KM)

Bar/restaurant. **Pensión La Estación** (singles €16, doubles €30, La Estación 2, tel 985 505 567).

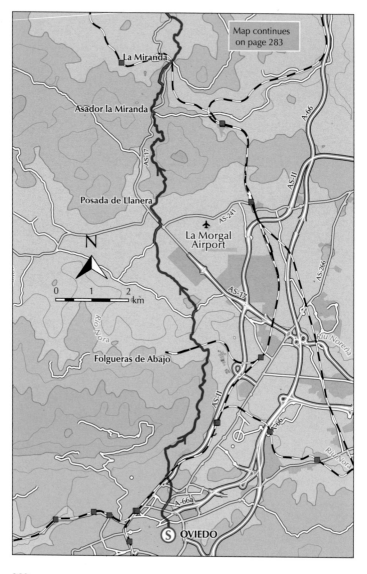

Map continues
on page 283

La Miranda

Asador la Miranda

AS-17

Posada de Llanera

La Morgal
Airport

AS-241

AS-17

N

0   1   2
km

Rio Nora

AS-11

Folgueras de Abajo

A-66

A-11

AS-266

Riu Noreña

Riu Nora

A-66a

S OVIEDO

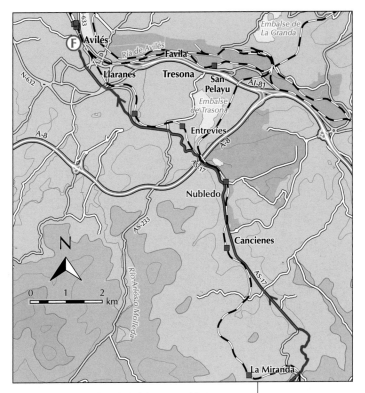

Follow AS-17, then fork left onto c/del Carmen on the outskirts of the city. Turn left on the highway and proceed through the roundabout. Keep straight on c/Gutiérrez Herreo, soon arriving at the albergue on your left in

AVILÉS (5.2KM)

All facilities. **Albergue de Peregrinos** (€6, 56 beds, kitchen, credenciáles, W/D, c/Magdalena 1, tel 984 703 117), **Pensión La Fruta** (doubles €40, c/La Fruta 19, tel 985 512 288), **Hotel Don Pedro** (singles €50–70, doubles €60–80, triples €70–90, open all year, @, c/La Fruta 22, tel 985 512 288), **Hotel El Magistral** (doubles €43+, c/Llano Ponte 4, tel 985 561 100), **Hostal Puente Azul** (singles €25, doubles €35–45, open all year, @, c/Acero 5, tel 985 550 177).

A prominent naval town in the Middle Ages, with an economy built around ship-building and trade with France. Pedro Menéndez de Avilés, the founder of Saint Augustine, Florida (the first permanent European settlement in the US), was born here. Like Gijón, Avilés has become an industrial center, but its preserved pedestrian center feels more relaxed. Architecture buffs can anticipate a full range, from the 12th-century Romanesque **Iglesia de los Padres Franciscanos** to the stunning **Óscar Niemeyer International Cultural Center**. The **Plaza de España** is home to the monumental *ayuntamiento* (town hall) and Palacio de Llano Ponte, while the expansive **Parque de Ferrera** is just left of c/Rivero. The 17th-century **Fuente de los Caños de San Francisco**, located just southwest of the Plaza de España, is a masterpiece of civil engineering.

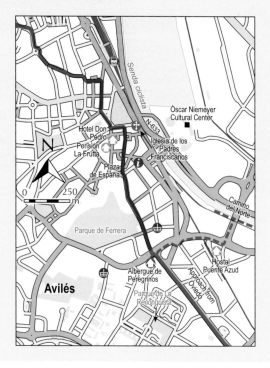

PRIMITIVO–NORTE LINK VIA FRIOL

Lugo to Sobrado dos Monxes

Start	Albergue de Peregrinos, Lugo
Finish	Albergue de Peregrinos, Sobrado dos Monxes
Distance	51.2km
% unpaved	65%
Total ascent	679m
Total descent	634m
Terrain	1
Route-finding	4
Pilgrim accommodation	No albergues: Casa Benigno in Friol offers pilgrim discounts on rooms

From Lugo, it is possible to follow an alternative route to join the Camino del Norte at the magnificent monastery in Sobrado dos Monxes (at the end of Stage 30). This is mostly off-road, following dirt tracks through the damp, shady forests so common in Galicia. The bustling town of Friol, halfway between Lugo and Sobrado, provides an ideal overnight location on this two-day walk. From Friol, the route continues along rural paths and roads to the town of Meson, where it joins the Norte. This route is a good option for those looking to spend more time off-road and in near solitude before heading into Santiago, or for those eager to visit the monastery in Sobrado, which is one of the architectural gems along the Norte.

The route is waymarked with green arrows, although these aren't quite as plentiful or as bright as camino waymarkings have been – be sure to watch carefully. Keep in mind that this route is particularly rural; there are no provisions or towns between Lugo and Friol, so bring ample food and water.

Follow the Primitivo from Lugo (Stage 11) outside of the city walls and across the Río Miño. Turn right onto Rúa Fermín Rivera. The route to Friol diverges at the next fork: those headed to Friol should turn right, following green arrows. This continues through a wonderful forested stretch through Monte Segade along the river, passing a particularly picturesque old mill, eventually heading out of the woods onto a rural road. Follow a series of rural roads, dirt tracks and

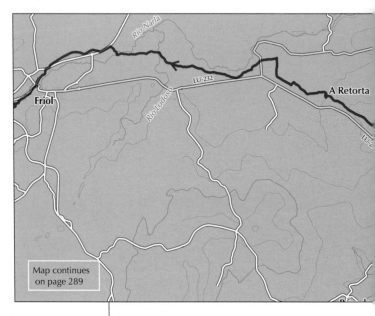

Map continues
on page 289

footpaths, passing through tiny hamlets, including **Veral** (9km), **Marcoi** (3km), and **A Retorta** (4km). Eventually, the route joins a larger paved road, leading into Plaza Andón Cebreiro in

FRIOL (25.3KM)

All facilities. Casa Benigno (singles €15–18, doubles €20–30, Rúa Ramón y Cajal 15, tel 639 150 450, tel 982 375 028, reservations recommended).

From Plaza Andón Cebreiro, head out of town through the riverside park, following a track along the Río Narla. After leaving the park, the route continues along minor roads and tracks, passing farms and tiny hamlets. Pass through Ordoñez (5.3km), Xía (500 meters), and Fonteseca (500 meters), then continue a long stretch before reaching AC-934. Turn left on the highway and join the Camino del Norte in **O Mesón**, 19.3km from Friol.

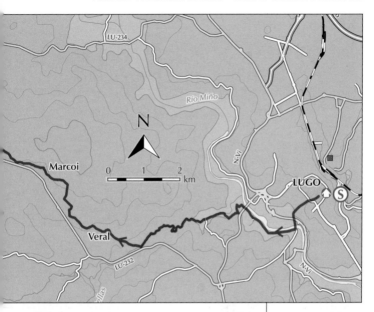

The route through Monte Segade

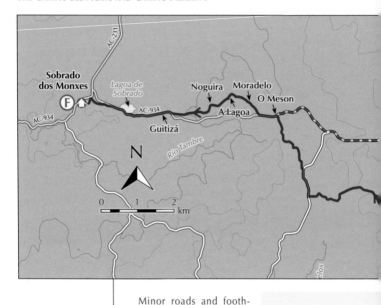

See the Camino del Norte, Stage 30, for information on Sobrado dos Monxes.

Minor roads and footpaths lead through three villages: **Moradelo**, **A Lagoa**, and **Noguira**. Join AC-934 and keep straight on through **Guitizá**. Fork right onto a gravel track downhill, skirting the lake below. Rejoin the highway and proceed across the bridge. Continue into **Sobrado dos Monxes** (5.5km). ◄

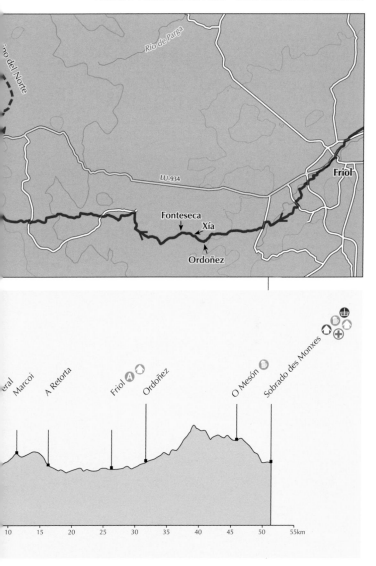

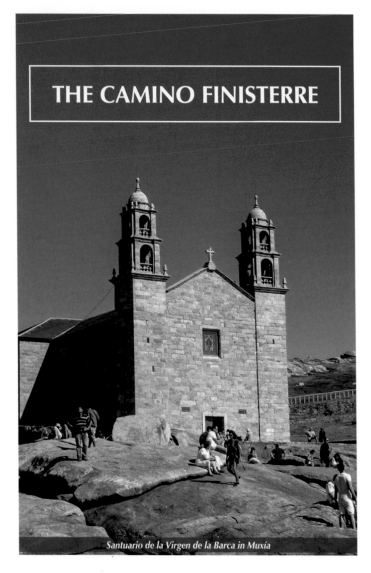

THE CAMINO FINISTERRE

Santuario de la Virgen de la Barca in Muxía

INTRODUCTION

For many modern pilgrims, the walk does not end in Santiago de Compostela. Instead, they are drawn still farther west, as far as the land will permit. They walk to Finisterre, the 'end of the world.'

During Roman times, Finisterre was believed to be the westernmost point in Europe – and therefore the end of the world. (It turns out that Portugal's Cabo da Roca is farther west, and there is more to the world beyond Europe.) While there is no firm evidence about when the pilgrimage to Finisterre began, its perceived geographic position accorded it a certain status that would have carried special meaning for a pagan population. The Christian trek thus ends on a pagan track. Many of today's pilgrims tap into their own primal instincts, burning their clothes at the lighthouse while watching the sunset. We do not recommend this; wildfires have been started in the process.

The pilgrimage to Finisterre can be completed comfortably in three days, but the emergence of new private albergues over the last few years makes it easy to take a more leisurely pace. As was the case on the camino, pilgrims should get sellos every day (ideally two per day); upon arrival in Finisterre, it is possible to get a certificate (the Fisterrana), similar to the Compostela. The route is very well marked, the only potential complication being that it is marked in both directions allowing pilgrims to make the return trip. And, while Finisterre may be the 'end of the world', it doesn't have to be the end of your pilgrimage, as an additional walk to Muxía and another traditional pilgrim shrine is possible and increasingly popular. Located north of Finisterre, this can be reached via waymarked routes from Finisterre and Hospital.

STAGE 1

Santiago de Compostela to Negreira

Start	Praza do Obradoiro, Santiago de Compostela
Finish	Albergue El Carmen, Negreira
Distance	21km
% unpaved	30%
Total ascent	501m
Total descent	592m

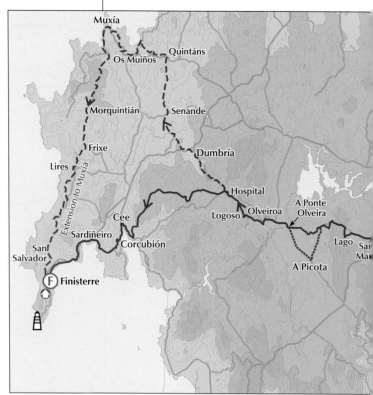

Terrain	4
Route-finding	1
Pilgrim accommodation	Castelo, Negreira

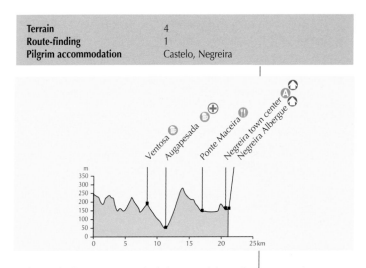

With your back to Santiago cathedral, proceed down the steps out of the back-right corner of the **Praza do Obradoiro**. Keep straight on through several intersections to arrive in the Carballeira de San Lourenzo, a small park. Turn right through the park and then left down a minor cement road. Proceed through modest **Piñeiro**, the tiny village of Villestro and cross the Río Roxos, leading into

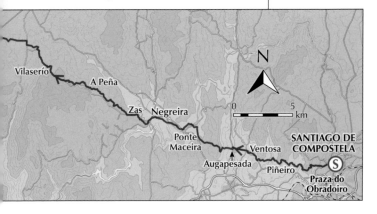

VENTOSA (8.9KM)

Bar, with excellent food options.

Turn here for Albergue Casa Riamonte (€12, 8 beds, W/D, tel 981 890 356, located in Castelo 500 meters off-route).

Follow a mix of minor roads and AC-453 through Lombao. ◀ As you approach a T-junction, turn left past a medieval bridge into

AUGAPESADA (2.8KM)

Bar with small grocery, pharmacy.

Proceed along a mix of dirt tracks and paved roads, including a surprisingly sharp ascent. Pass through Carballo and Trasmonte (bar), continuing to

PONTE MACEIRA (5.2KM)

Bar/restaurant.

This may be the prettiest town on the whole camino. The medieval bridge over the Río Tambre overlooks boulders on one side and a fortress-like pazo on the other. The river is dammed, and a rope swing on the northwest side has tempted even the most determined of walkers into a lengthy break.

Cross the bridge and turn left. Follow a series of well-marked minor roads, winding back and forth across AC-544. Continue through Barca, soon passing Albergue Anjana (€12, 18 beds, W/D, tel 607 387 229) on the way into

NEGREIRA (4.1KM)

This busy little town with all facilities presents your best opportunity to stock up before reaching the coast. Albergue de Peregrinos on the way out of town (€6, 20 beds, kitchen, @, tel 664 081 498) and four private albergues: Lua (€12, 40 beds, kitchen, W/D, @, Avda de Santiago 22, tel 698 128 883), San José (€12, 50 beds, kitchen, W/D, @, Rúa de Castelao 20, tel 881 976 934), El Carmen (€12, 24 beds, meals, W/D, @, c/del Carmen, tel 981 881 652), Alecrin (€12, 42 beds, open Apr–Nov, kitchen, W/D, @, Avda Santiago 52, tel 981 818 286). Hostal La Mezquita (singles €30, doubles €50, c/del Carmen 2, tel 636 129 691).

STAGE 2

Negreira to Olveiroa

Start	Albergue El Carmen, Negreira
Finish	Albergue de Peregrinos, Olveiroa
Distance	34.1km
% unpaved	37%
Total ascent	601m
Total descent	492m
Terrain	2
Route-finding	1
Pilgrim accommodation	A Peña, Vilaserío, Santa Mariña, Lago, A Ponte Olveira, Olveiroa

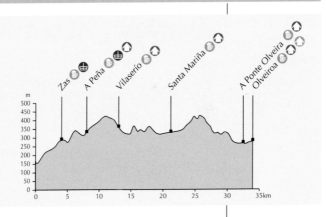

Follow the arrows back to the camino, soon ascending a tree-covered footpath. Re-emerge on AC-5603 and proceed into

ZAS (3.3KM)

Bar with small grocery along left side of highway (poorly marked).

Fork right off the highway. A combination of footpaths and dirt tracks follows, leading through Rapote and onward to

A PEÑA (5.1KM)

Bars, grocery, Albergue Alto da Pena (€12, 20 beds, meals, W/D, tel 609 853 486).

Rejoin the highway before diverging once again onto dirt tracks. Follow AC-5603 to

VILASERÍO (4.6KM)

Bar. Albergue de Peregrinos on the road out of town (€6, sleeping pads on floor, tel 648 792 029), Albergue Casa Vella (€12, 12 beds, singles €25+, doubles €35+, kitchen, meals available, W, tel 981 893 516), Albergue O Rueiro (€12, open Mar–Oct, 30 beds, W/D, tel 981 893 561).

Follow the highway out of town, then turn right to pass through Cornado. Continue on a series of dirt tracks and minor roads into Maroñas, before joining AC-400 into

SANTA MARIÑA (8.1KM)

Bars. Albergue Santa Mariña (€10, 21 beds, meals available, W/D, tel 981 852 897), Albergue Casa Pepa (€12, 18 beds, meals available, W/D, tel 981 852 881).

Continue through the small towns of Gueima, Vilar de Castro, and **Lago** (Albergue Monto Oro – €12, 28 beds, open Mar–Nov, W/D, @, tel 682 586 157).

A Picota variant

Those seeking more facilities today should consider this route. About 1km on from Lago, at a minor intersection with a bus shelter and signs for Casa Jurjo and Abeleiroas, ignore the waymarks and keep straight on. Follow the road for 3km, then turn right at the T-junction into the center of A Picota, which offers all facilities, including Albergue Picota (€15, 6 beds, doubles €35, W/D, tel 981 852 019) and the pilgrim-friendly Casa Jurjo (singles €30–35, doubles €45–60, pilgrim discounts, tel 981 852 015). At the main intersection in town, turn right on AC-3404, rejoining the official route in Mallón and continuing into A Ponte Olveira. This detour is 6.8km, making it 3km longer than the official route.

Staying primarily on minor roads, pass the church of **San Cristovo de Corzón** and continue onto AC-3404 in **Mallón**. Cross the Río Xallas to arrive in

A PONTE OLVEIRA (11.2KM)

Bar/restaurant. **Albergue-Pensión Ponte Olveira** (€12 beds, 20 beds, doubles €30, open Easter–Oct, kitchen, W/D, @, tel 603 450 145).

Continue on AC-3404. Fork left off the highway into

OLVEIROA (1.8KM)

Bars/restaurants. **Albergue de Peregrinos** (€6, 34 beds, kitchen, tel 981 744 001), **Albergue Hórreo** (€12, 53 beds, kitchen, W/D, @, tel 981 741 673), **Albergue O Peregrino** (€12, 12 beds, W/D, meals available, tel 981 741 682), **Casa Loncho** (doubles €40, triples €60, tel 981 741 673), **Casa Rural As Pias** (singles €40, doubles €50–60, tel 981 741 520).

The camino has transformed no town more over the last decade than Olveiroa. When the authors first visited it in 2004, it was covered in a thick layer of cow manure, had one bar offering little food, and was in a general state of disrepair. Today, flowerbeds line the camino, new bars and accommodations seem to pop up daily, and traditional buildings are being restored.

STAGE 3
Olveiroa to Finisterre

Start	Albergue de Peregrinos, Olveiroa
Finish	Albergue de Peregrinos, Finisterre
Distance	32.2km
% unpaved	66%
Total ascent	468m
Total descent	728m
Terrain	3
Route-finding	2
Pilgrim accommodation	Logoso, Hospital, Cee, Corcubión, Finisterre

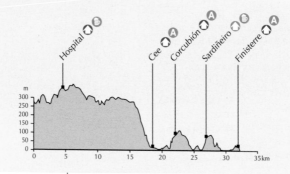

Continue straight through town, soon forking left off-road. Follow the route as it dips and climbs through **Logoso** (Albergue O Logoso – €12, 22 beds, singles €35, kitchen, W/D, tel 659 505 399). Continue into

HOSPITAL (4.9KM)

Bar offering excellent bocadillos and the last opportunity for food or water until the coast. Refill water here. Albergue O Casteliño (€12, 18 beds, private room, meals available, W/D, tel 615 997 169).

For details of the Muxía option, see Extension to Muxía, below.

The camino splits 600 meters after the bar at a highway roundabout. Pilgrims continuing to Finisterre turn left, while those heading for Muxía should turn right. ◀

Follow the road, then fork right onto a gravel track. From here to Cee the route is entirely off-road, completely rural, and offers sweeping views. Along the way, pass by 15th-century Santuario de Nosa Señora das Neves. There is a sacred fountain here, and a local pilgrimage to the site every year. In another 3km, arrive at Ermita de San Pedro Mártir, which has a sacred fountain of its own. The descent to Cee begins soon after, with views of the coast, including Cabo Finisterre, unfolding beneath.

Head downhill, reaching the *cruceiro* (crucifix) next to the Igrexa de Nosa Señora da Xunqueira in the center of

CEE (14.1KM)

Modern beach town with all facilities and many private albergues, including O Bordón (€12, 24 beds, kitchen, tel 981 746 574), Casa da Fonte (€11, 42 beds, Rúa de Arriba 36, tel 699 242 711), Moreira (€12, 22 beds, open late-Apr–early-Nov, kitchen, W/D, c/Rosalía de Castro, tel 620 891 547) and Tequerón (€12–15, 8 beds, W/D, @, Rúa de Arriba 31, tel 666 119 594). Hotel Insua (singles €45–55, doubles €50–65, Avda Finisterre 82, tel 981 747 575), Hotel La Marina (singles €35–45, doubles €50–65, Avda Fernando Blanco 26, tel 981 747 381).

Proceed through the center of town, eventually forking right uphill to reach

CORCUBIÓN (2.4KM)

All facilities. Albergue de Peregrinos San Roque on outskirts of town (donativo, 16 beds, communal meals, tel 679 460 942), Albergue Camiño de Fisterra (€10, Avda Fisterra 220, tel 981 745 040). Many hotels, including: Casa da Balea (singles €40+, doubles €50+, c/Rafael Juan 44, tel 981 746 645), Casa Bernarda (singles €35+, doubles €70+, Plaza Párroco Francisco Sánchez 3, tel 981 747 157).

Proceed left uphill out of the plaza. At the 13th-century Iglesia San Marcos, turn right upstairs and then curve right, proceeding along a footpath between high walls. Climb past the Albergue de Peregrinos. At the Encrucijada de San Roque, veer right onto a footpath, before returning to the highway in Amarela. Follow the route on a series of small roads and tracks through Estorde (bars, grocery in campsite, Hostal Playa de Estorde – singles €40–50, doubles €60–80, tel 981 745 585). Keep straight on AC-445 into

SARDIÑEIRO (4.7KM)

Bars, restaurants. Hotel Merendero (singles €20, doubles €35, tel 981 743 535), Pensión Playa de Sardiñero (doubles €40, triples €60, tel 981 743 741).

From here, the route winds around and occasionally joins AC-445, before eventually forking left onto the Corredoira de Don Camilo and descending to the Praia de Langosteira. Once there, you can follow the paved walkway or remove your shoes and splash along the beach. At the beach's end, return to AC-445. Fork left on Avda de A Coruña and proceed into

FINISTERRE (6.1KM)

All facilities. **Albergue de Peregrinos** (€6, 36 beds, kitchen, W/D, c/Real 2, tel 981 740 781). Many private albergues, including **Finistellae** (€12, 20 beds, kitchen, W/D, @, c/Manuel Lago Pais 7, tel 637 821 296), **Sol e da Lúa** (€11, 18 beds, private rooms, kitchen, W/D, @, c/Atalaya 7, tel 881 108 710), **Cabo da Vila** (€12, 28 beds, private rooms, kitchen, W/D, @, Avda da Coruña 13, tel 607 735 474) and **Paz** (€12–15, 30 beds, W/D, @, c/Victor Cardalda 11, tel 981 740 332). **Hostal Mariquito** (singles €25–30, doubles €36–48, c/Santa Catalina 44, tel 981 740 044), **Hotel A Langosteira** (singles €32–42, doubles €40–52, Avda de Coruña 61, tel 981 740 543), **Hotel Áncora** (singles €28+, doubles €35+, c/Alcalde Fernández 43, tel 981 740 791). The certificate commemorating your pilgrimage to Finisterre, the Fisterrana, is available from the municipal Albergue de Peregrinos.

Buses returning to Santiago depart from the stop situated around the corner from the municipal albergue. The service is run by Monbus, with eight departures on weekdays (the first leaves at 0820, the last at 1900), six on Saturdays, and five on Sundays/holidays. The earliest departure on weekends is 0945. The trip takes up to three hours and costs €9.85. Schedules can change, so double-check with Monbus in advance: www.monbus.es.

Although you have arrived in the town of Finisterre, the **lighthouse** at the 'end of the world' remains 3.3km away, following AC-4408. Heading there after an early dinner is recommended, as this gives you a few hours of daylight to climb around the point and enjoy the views before watching the sunset. Bring a flashlight for the walk home. Most albergues allow pilgrims to return late, but double-check in advance. It is now possible to sleep next to the lighthouse in the Hotel O Semáforo (doubles €99–150, tel 981 110 210).

Extension to Muxía

Many pilgrims, not ready to go home, add Muxía to their itinerary – either before or after they visit Finisterre. Medieval pilgrims are documented as having made the trek to Muxía to visit the Santuario de la Virgen de la Barca, although the current structure dates to 1719. Located on the coast north of Finisterre, Muxía can be reached via waymarked routes from both Olveiroa and Finisterre.

Those visiting Muxía before Finisterre will fork right when the camino splits shortly after **Hospital** (see Camino Finisterre, Stage 3), 6km after Olveiroa. From there, the route covers 25.5km. The best place for supplies along the way is **Dumbría**, 4.6km from the fork (bars, grocery store, and Albergue de Peregrinos – €6, 26 beds, kitchen, tel 981 744 001). Bars are also available in **Senande** (5.5km), **Quintáns** (5.2km), and **Os Muiños** (5.6km), with several others sprinkled over the remaining 4.5km to **Muxía**.

The route between Finisterre and Muxía spans 27km of rugged Galician countryside. Plan ahead. The only facilities available on this route are in **Lires**, which is nearly halfway between the two towns (two bars and several places to stay: Casa Raúl – doubles €30–58, tel 981 748 156, and Albergue As Eiras– €12, 22 beds, W/D, tel 981 748 180). It is critical to get your credenciál stamped in Lires if you hope to either obtain a certificate or stay in the municipal albergues.

The 'end of the world' at Finisterre

Muxía has all facilities, including an Albergue de Peregrinos (€6, 32 beds, kitchen, c/Enfesto 22, tel 610 264 325) and many private albergues including: Albergue@ Muxia (€11, 40 beds, kitchen, W/D, @, c/Enfesto 12, tel 651 627 768), Bela Muxia (€12, 52 beds, private rooms, kitchen, W/D, @, Rúa Encarnación 30, tel 687 798 222) and da Costa (€10, 10 beds, kitchen, W/D, Avda Doctor Toba 33, tel 676 363 820). As was true in Finisterre, there is a certificate given to those who walk this route, available from the municipal albergue. There are two direct buses per day from Muxía to Santiago. For more information on the route, including detailed turn-by-turn directions, visit the Confraternity of Saint James website (www.csj.org. uk), where an online guide is available.

APPENDIX A
Useful sources of information

Updated information on albergues

Eroski/Consumer Camino de Santiago:
The best resource online for up-to-date
albergue information, on all of the
major caminos.
caminodesantiago.consumer.es

Gronze: Another excellent site is
www.gronze.com.

Transport

For additional information see 'Getting
there and back' in the Introduction.

Bus

Movelia: www.movelia.es

ALSA: www.alsa.es

Vibasa: www.vibasa.com

(Basque Country) Chronoplus:
www.chronoplus.eu

Ekialdebus: www.ekialdebus.net

Bizkaibus: www.bizkaia.net

Lurraldebus: www.lurraldebus.eus

Pesa Bus: www.pesa.net

(Galicia) Empresa Freire:
www.empresafreire.com

Arriva: www.arriva.es

Castromil: www.monbus.es

ASICASA: www.autoscalpita.es

Train

Renfe: www.renfe.com

EuskoTren: www.euskotren.es

SNCF: www.sncf.com/en

Air

RyanAir: www.ryanair.com

EasyJet: www.easyjet.com

Vueling: www.vueling.com

Iberia: www.iberia.com

TAP Portugal: www.flytap.com

Air Berlin: www.airberlin.com

Baggage transport

Spain's mail carrier Correos offers an
easy-to-use website to book your bag
transfer (on most stages of either route):
www.elcaminoconcorreos.com, tel 683
440 022, paqmochila@correos.com.

On the Camino del Norte

Le P'tit Bag: tel 635 730 852, g.car.
trans@gmail.com

On the Camino Primitivo

Taxi Camino: tel 619 156 730,
trastinos@gmail.com (taxi and bag
transfer)

Credenciál

Before departure, you can obtain the
credenciál from camino-related groups
including:

Confraternity of Saint James (CSJ):
www.csj.org.uk

American Pilgrims: www.
americanpilgrims.com

Canadian Company of Pilgrims:
www.santiago.ca

Once you arrive in Spain, the credenciál can be obtained from albergues in Irún, Santander, San Sebastián, Avilés, and Oviedo, in the cathedrals in Oviedo and Lugo, and may be available at the tourist center in Villaviciosa.

APPENDIX B
English–Spanish–Euskera glossary

English	Spanish	Euskera
altarpiece	retablo	erretaula
bakery	panadería	okindegia
bathroom	baño	komona
beach	playa	hondartza
beware of dog	cuidado con el perro	kontuz zakurrarekin
bill (in a restaurant)	cuenta	kontua
blister	ampolla	baba
bridge	puente	zubia
building	edificio	eraikuntza
bull ring	plaza de toros	zezen-plaza
bus station	estación de autobuses	autobus geltokia
butcher's shop	carnicería	harategi
central plaza	plaza mayor	plaza nagusia
chapel	capilla	kapera
church	iglesia	eliza
city	ciudad	hiria
close the gate	cierren la puerta	itxi atea
closed	cerrado	itxita
clothes washing place	lavadero	garbitokia
corn crib/granary	hórreo	garai
corner	esquina	kantoi, izkin
crucifix	cruceiro	kalbario
dam	embalse	urtegi
detour	desvío	desbideratze

English	Spanish	Euskera
doctor	médico, doctor	mediku
donation	donativo	dohaintza
door, gate	puerta	atea
far	lejos	urruti, urrun
food	comida	janari
fountain	fuente	iturri
good morning	buenos días	egun on
goodbye	adiós	agur
guesthouse	casa de huéspedes	ostatu
help	ayuda, socorro	lagundu
here	aquí	hemen
hermitage	ermita	ermita
highway	carretera	errepide
hill	colina	gailur, tontor, gain
historic center	casco antiguo	alde zaharra
hospital	hospital	ospitalea
hotel	hotel, hostal	hotela
how much is it?	cuanto cuesta?	zenbat balio du?
hunting preserve	coto de caza	ehiza lekua
inn	fonda, hospedaje	ostatu
kiosk	estanco, tabac	estanko, tabako denda
left	izquierda	ezkerra
manor house	pazo	jauretxe
mill	molino	errota
monastery	monasterio	monasterioa, zenobio
near	cerca	hurbil
neighborhood	barrio	auzo
no	no	ez
open	abierto	zabalik
pain	dolor	mina
path	camino, senda	bidea
pelota court	frontón	pilotalekua

English	Spanish	Euskera
petrol station	gasolinera	gasolindegia
pilgrim	peregrino	erromes
pilgrim hostel	albergue de peregrinos	erromes aterpetxea
plateau	meseta	goi-lautada
please	por favor	mesedez
post office	correos	posta
prehistoric fort	castro	historiaurreko gotorlekua
restaurant	restaurante	jatetxea
right	derecha	eskuina
roadside cross	cruce de carretera	errepide gurutzea
Saint James	Santiago	Done Kakue
sports center	polideportivo	kiroldegia
stamp	sello	zigilu
stepping stones	peldaños	koska, maila
straight	recto, directamente	zuzen
stream	arroyo	erreka
street	calle	kalea
supermarket	supermercado	supermerkatua
telephone	teléfono	telefonoa
time	hora	ordua
thank you	gracias	eskerik asko
tourist office	turismo	turismo bulego
town	pueblo	herria
town hall	ayuntamiento	udaletxea
valley	valle	haran, bailara, ibar
viewpoint	mirador	begiratokia
water (drinkable)	agua potable	edateko ura
waymark	señal	seinalea
where	donde	non
yes	sí	bai
youth hostel	albergue juveníl	gazte-aterpetxe

APPENDIX C

Suggestions for further reading

Although an overwhelming amount of literature has been produced about the Camino Francés, very little is available in English on the other caminos. Many of the websites and guides below are in Spanish; all other books are in English.

Friends of the Camino de Santiago websites

Amigos del Camino de Santiago de Guipúzcoa: Provides up-to-date information on the first leg of the Camino del Norte, from Irún to Markina-Xemein. www.caminosnorte.org

Asociación Astur-Leonesa de Amigos: Has route information on the Camino Primitivo and runs Oviedo's albergue. www.caminosantiagoastur.com

Asociación Galega de Amigos: Includes route descriptions and albergue information for all of the Caminos de Santiago through Galicia. www.amigosdelcamino.com

The Confraternity of Saint James: Based in London, this continues to be the pre-eminent source for English-language information on the Caminos de Santiago. www.csj.org.uk

Other recommended guides

Guia del Camino de Santiago en tu Mochila–Camino Norte, Madrid: Anaya, 2017. A recently updated Spanish-Language guidebook to both the Camino del Norte and the Camino Primitivo.

El Cuaderno del Peregrino: Camino Norte de Santiago, Madrid: Anaya, 2010. A very clever concept: a moleskine-style compact journal with route maps interspersed.

CSJ Guides. Available from the Confraternity of Saint James, individual guides to the Camino del Norte and Camino Primitivo. Be warned that although these are often very useful, the route descriptions are sometimes outdated.

Books on pilgrimage

Susan Alcorn, *Healing Miles: Gifts from the Caminos Norte and Primitivo,* Oakland: Shepard Canyon, 2017. A compelling narrative to one pilgrim's experience walking the Camino del Norte and Primitivo.

Phil Cousineau, *The Art of Pilgrimage,* San Francisco: Canari Press, 2012. A multi-faceted look at pilgrimage and the pilgrim experience.

Nancy Louise Frey, *Pilgrim Stories: On and Off the Road to Santiago*, Berkeley: University of California Press, 1988. An anthropologist's study of the modern pilgrim's experience.

Cees Nooteboom, *Roads to Santiago: A Modern-Day Pilgrimage Through Spain*, New York: Harcourt Brace, 1997. Although this is not written by a walker, and it does not follow the pilgrimage road explicitly, it serves to nicely place Santiago within the larger context of Spanish history.

Landon Roussel, *On the Primitive Way*, Louisiana: Communitas Press, 2015. An account of two brothers on the Camino Primitivo.

Jonathan Sumption, *The Age of Pilgrimage: The Medieval Journey to God*, Mahweh: HiddenSpring, 2004. A detailed survey of the pilgrimage boom in the medieval Christian world.

DOWNLOAD THE ROUTES
IN GPX FORMAT

All the routes in this guide are available for download from:

www.cicerone.co.uk/1014/GPX

as GPX files. You should be able to load them into most formats of mobile device, whether GPS or smartphone.

When you go to this link, you will be asked for your email address and where you purchased the guide, and have the option to subscribe to the Cicerone e-newsletter.

www.cicerone.co.uk

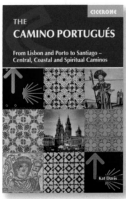

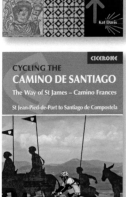
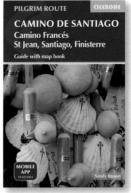

SELECTION OF CICERONE GUIDES

ALPS CROSS-BORDER ROUTES

100 Hut Walks in the Alps
Across the Eastern Alps: E5
Alpine Ski Mountaineering Vol 1 – Western Alps
Alpine Ski Mountaineering Vol 2 – Central and Eastern Alps
Chamonix to Zermatt
The Karnischer Hohenweg
The Tour of the Bernina
Tour of Mont Blanc
Tour of Monte Rosa
Tour of the Matterhorn
Trail Running – Chamonix and the Mont Blanc region
Trekking in the Alps
Trekking in the Silvretta and Rätikon Alps
Trekking Munich to Venice
Walking in the Alps

PYRENEES AND FRANCE/SPAIN CROSS-BORDER ROUTES

The GR10 Trail
The GR11 Trail
The Pyrenean Haute Route
The Pyrenees
The Way of St James – Spain
Walks and Climbs in the Pyrenees

AUSTRIA

Innsbruck Mountain Adventures
The Adlerweg
Trekking in Austria's Hohe Tauern
Trekking in the Stubai Alps
Trekking in the Zillertal Alps
Walking in Austria

SWITZERLAND

Cycle Touring in Switzerland
Switzerland's Jura Crest Trail
The Swiss Alpine Pass Route – Via Alpina Route 1
The Swiss Alps
Tour of the Jungfrau Region
Walking in the Bernese Oberland
Walking in the Valais

FRANCE AND BELGIUM

Chamonix Mountain Adventures
Cycle Touring in France
Cycling London to Paris
Cycling the Canal de la Garonne
Cycling the Canal du Midi
Écrins National Park
Mont Blanc Walks
Mountain Adventures in the Maurienne
The GR20 Corsica
The GR5 Trail
The GR5 Trail – Vosges and Jura
The Grand Traverse of the Massif Central
The Loire Cycle Route
The Moselle Cycle Route
The River Rhone Cycle Route
The Robert Louis Stevenson Trail
The Way of St James – Le Puy to the Pyrenees
Tour of the Oisans: The GR54
Tour of the Queyras
Vanoise Ski Touring
Via Ferratas of the French Alps
Walking in Corsica
Walking in Provence – East
Walking in Provence – West
Walking in the Auvergne
Walking in the Briançonnais
Walking in the Cevennes
Walking in the Dordogne
Walking in the Haute Savoie: North
Walking in the Haute Savoie: South
Walks in the Cathar Region
The GR5 Trail – Benelux and Lorraine
Walking in the Ardennes

GERMANY

Hiking and Cycling in the Black Forest
The Danube Cycleway Vol 1
The Rhine Cycle Route
The Westweg
Walking in the Bavarian Alps

ICELAND AND GREENLAND

Trekking in Greenland – The Arctic Circle Trail
Walking and Trekking in Iceland

IRELAND

The Irish Coast to Coast Walk
The Mountains of Ireland
The Wild Atlantic Way and Western Ireland

ITALY

Italy's Sibillini National Park
Shorter Walks in the Dolomites
Ski Touring and Snowshoeing in the Dolomites
The Way of St Francis
Through the Italian Alps
Trekking in the Apennines
Trekking in the Dolomites
Via Ferratas of the Italian Dolomites: Vol 1
Via Ferratas of the Italian Dolomites: Vol 2
Walking and Trekking in the Gran Paradiso
Walking in Abruzzo
Walking in Italy's Stelvio National Park
Walking in Sardinia
Walking in Sicily
Walking in the Dolomites
Walking in Tuscany
Walking in Umbria
Walking Lake Garda and Iseo
Walking on the Amalfi Coast
Walking the Italian Lakes
Walks and Treks in the Maritime Alps

For full information on all our
guides, books and eBooks,
visit our website:
www.cicerone.co.uk

Walking – Trekking – Mountaineering – Climbing – Cycling

Over 40 years, Cicerone have built up an outstanding collection of over 300 guides, inspiring all sorts of amazing adventures.

 Every guide comes from extensive exploration and research by our expert authors, all with a passion for their subjects. They are frequently praised, endorsed and used by clubs, instructors and outdoor organisations.

All our titles can now be bought as **e-books**, **ePubs** and **Kindle** files and we also have an online magazine – **Cicerone Extra** – with features to help cyclists, climbers, walkers and trekkers choose their next adventure, at home or abroad.

Our website shows any **new information** we've had in since a book was published. Please do let us know if you find anything has changed, so that we can publish the latest details. On our **website** you'll also find great ideas and lots of detailed information about what's inside every guide and you can buy **individual routes** from many of them online.

It's easy to keep in touch with what's going on at Cicerone by getting our monthly **free e-newsletter**, which is full of offers, competitions, up-to-date information and topical articles. You can subscribe on our home page and also follow us on **Facebook** and **Twitter** or dip into our **blog**.

Cicerone – the very best guides for exploring the world.

CICERONE

Juniper House, Murley Moss, Oxenholme Road, Kendal, Cumbria LA9 7RL
Tel: 015395 62069 info@cicerone.co.uk
www.cicerone.co.uk